Sitecore Cookbook for Developers

Over 70 incredibly effective and practical recipes to get you up and running with Sitecore development

Yogesh Patel

BIRMINGHAM - MUMBAI

Sitecore Cookbook for Developers

First published: April 2016

Production reference: 1260416

Published by Packt Publishing Ltd.
Livery Place
35 Livery Street
Birmingham B3 2PB, UK.

ISBN 978-1-78439-652-7

www.packtpub.com

Credits

Author

Yogesh Patel

Reviewer

Pavel Nezhencev

Commissioning Editor

Amarabha Banerjee

Acquisition Editor

Reshma Raman

Content Development Editor

Pooja Mhapsekar

Technical Editor

Manthan Raja

Copy Editor

Tasneem Fatehi

Project Coordinator

Judie Jose

Proofreader

Safis Editing

Indexer

Mariammal Chettiyar

Graphics

Disha Haria

Abhinash Sahu

Production Coordinator

Arvindkumar Gupta

Cover Work

Arvindkumar Gupta

About the Author

Yogesh Patel has been programming since the year 2000, and has been working in the IT industry for over ten years on a variety of technologies. He was mainly involved in Sitecore or .NET-based development in the Indian offices of US and UK-based organizations. He has worked at Investis Ltd as a technical architect and has lead a Sitecore development team. Yogesh has held a number of positions and has a lot of responsibilities, having worked at Investis since 2009. He has been recognized as a Most Valuable Professional (MVP) by Sitecore for 2014, 2015, and 2016.

As a developer, Yogesh enjoys learning new programming techniques, practices, and tactics. He has worked on .NET since 2005 and Sitecore since 2009. He has also spent plenty of time developing in C, VC++, MATLAB, VB6, ASP, Java, PHP, AppleScript, SQL, and MySQL, but his current focus is on .NET—especially Sitecore. His blog can be found at `http://sitecoreblog.patelyogesh.in`. You can find Yogesh on Twitter at `@patelyogesh_in`, as well as LinkedIn (`yspatel`) and Facebook (`patelyogesh.in`).

Avni, my beloved wife and my parents, I thank you for your love, support, and encouragement, without which I would have been unable to carry on this endeavor. I'd particularly like to thank Pavel Nezhencev for reviewing this book. I'd also like to thank my colleagues at Investis, Muktesh Mehta and Siddhi Kabra, for supporting me throughout the project.

About the Reviewer

Pavel Nezhencev is an experienced .NET/JS web developer working in the Denmark department of Creuna, which specializes in creating web platforms for businesses of any scale. Pavel has a bachelor's degree in software engineering from Kharkiv National University of Radio Electronics, Ukraine. He worked for five years with Sitecore and Episerver systems and successfully launched several solutions on these platforms.

www.PacktPub.com

eBooks, discount offers, and more

Did you know that Packt offers eBook versions of every book published, with PDF and ePub files available? You can upgrade to the eBook version at www.PacktPub.com and as a print book customer, you are entitled to a discount on the eBook copy. Get in touch with us at customercare@packtpub.com for more details.

At www.PacktPub.com, you can also read a collection of free technical articles, sign up for a range of free newsletters and receive exclusive discounts and offers on Packt books and eBooks.

https://www2.packtpub.com/books/subscription/packtlib

Do you need instant solutions to your IT questions? PacktLib is Packt's online digital book library. Here, you can search, access, and read Packt's entire library of books.

Why subscribe?

- ▶ Fully searchable across every book published by Packt
- ▶ Copy and paste, print, and bookmark content
- ▶ On demand and accessible via a web browser

Instant updates on new Packt books

Get notified! Find out when new books are published by following @PacktEnterprise on Twitter or the *Packt Enterprise* Facebook page.

Table of Contents

Preface

Sitecore Experience Platform (XP), which is more than a content management system (CMS), is global leader in experience management. It continues to be very popular due to its robust framework, continuous innovations, and ease of implementations compared to other CMS available. Developers love Sitecore for its flexibility, scalability, and power. It has great out-of-the-box capabilities, but one of its great strengths is the ease of extending these capabilities.

Sitecore Cookbook for Developers is intended to provide a surprising amount of recipes to use out-of-the-box core capabilities and customize them. It also focuses on helping developers that are new to Sitecore to achieve maximum productivity and satisfaction with minimum efforts. It also includes tips, tricks, and best practices for working with the platform.

What this book covers

Chapter 1, Basic Presentation Components, focuses on creating information architecture and presenting it using out-of-the-box components and different Model-View-Controller (MVC) renderings. It also shows how effectively you can utilize out-of-the-box components to provide greater ease and flexibility for future enhancements.

Chapter 2, Extending Presentation Components, gives examples for extending out-of-the-box components to develop multilingual and multidevice websites, integrate the content with external systems, and provide easier content management for content owners.

Chapter 3, Customizing the User Interface Framework, demonstrates you how to create new interfaces or extend existing interfaces, using different framework components. It also provides some recipes to please content authors.

Chapter 4, Leveraging the Sitecore Backend, gets you completely involved in Sitecore backend architecture. This chapter gives you a brief tour of different the features to extend the core engine using pipelines, processors, events, handlers, hooks, jobs, schedulers, and so on.

Chapter 5, Making Content Management More Efficient, shows you different tricks and techniques to manage the content in a better way and provide better usability with the use of backend and frontend frameworks and different functionalities such as dictionary, validations, rule engine, Rich Text Editor, Item Web API, and so on.

Chapter 6, Working with Media, explores different techniques while working with Sitecore media items such as securing them, serving them through content delivery network (CDN), and utilizing them for responsive web designs.

Chapter 7, Workflow and Publishing, shows how you can extend the workflow and publishing architecture to achieve scheduled publishing and unpublishing, using web deploy while publishing and customizing pipeline and events.

Chapter 8, Security, explains how to create different user profiles and give custom permissions to it. It also explains how to achieve single sign-on (SSO) securely and allow extranet access in a secure way.

Chapter 9, Sitecore Search, describes different techniques for accessing data from indexing. It explains how to implement different search techniques, which modern search engines use such as tagging, autosuggest, boosting search results, finding more like this, and did you mean.

Chapter 10, Experience Personalization and Analytics Using xDB, explains how to provide the best user experience using different techniques of real-time personalization, it is the heart of marketing programs. It also briefs features for engaging users. This chapter will also provide good recipes to use and extend Experience Database (xDB) and generate different analytics reports.

Chapter 11, Securing, Scaling, Optimizing, and Troubleshooting, focuses on different techniques for making the Sitecore environment more secure. It also explains techniques to troubleshoot slowness, create clustered environments to get better performance, high availability, and scalability. It also briefs some techniques to troubleshoot.

Appendix A, Getting Started with Sitecore, contains information to help you in Sitecore installation, and create a project for your Sitecore solution using Microsoft Visual Studio.

Appendix B, Tools and Resources for Sitecore Developers, provides information on tools and resources available for Sitecore developers to install, and maximize their productivity and expertise by using it.

What you need for this book

The minimum requirements for this book would be Sitecore 8 or later, .NET Framework 4.5 or later, ASP.NET MVC 5.1 or later, MS SQL 2008 R2 or later, and IIS 7.5 or later. You can refer to Sitecore Compatibility Table at `https://goo.gl/4kkCHe` for more details.

It is recommended that you use a plain Sitecore setup to implement the recipes of this book in order to avoid unnecessary conflicts with existing implementations.

To download and install Sitecore and create a project, you can refer to *Appendix A*, *Getting Started with Sitecore*, which you will find at the end of this book.

Who this book is for

If you are a Sitecore developer or programmer who wants to expand your Sitecore development skills, this book is ideal for you. As this book targets readers of various experience levels, you should be able to find recipes of beginner, intermediate, and advanced nature. You will need working knowledge of ASP.NET WebForms or MVC, as well as HTML, and a basic knowledge of Sitecore installation.

Sections

In this book, you will find several headings that appear frequently (Getting ready, How to do it, How it works, There's more, and See also).

To give clear instructions on how to complete a recipe, we use these sections as follows:

Getting ready

This section tells you what to expect in the recipe, and describes how to set up any software or any preliminary settings required for the recipe.

How to do it...

This section contains the steps required to follow the recipe.

How it works...

This section usually consists of a detailed explanation of what happened in the previous section.

There's more...

This section consists of additional information about the recipe in order to make the reader more knowledgeable about the recipe.

See also

This section provides helpful links to other useful information for the recipe.

Conventions

In this book, you will find a number of text styles that distinguish between different kinds of information. Here are some examples of these styles and an explanation of their meaning.

Code words in text, database table names, folder names, filenames, file extensions, pathnames, dummy URLs, user input, and Twitter handles are shown as follows: "Make sure that you have added a reference of `Sitecore.Kernel.dll` and `Sitecore.Mvc.dll` files to the `SitecoreCookbook` project."

A block of code is set as follows:

```
<div id="header"> <a href="/">
  @Html.Sitecore().Field("Logo",
    Sitecore.Context.Database.GetItem(
    "/sitecore/Content/Global/Configurations"))
</a> </div>
```

When we wish to draw your attention to a particular part of a code block, the relevant lines or items are set in bold:

```
<div id="sidemenu">
  @Html.Sitecore().Rendering(
    "{2383A57F-21FF-4A77-9E2A-C467F0CEDA57}")
</div>
```

New terms and **important words** are shown in bold. Words that you see on the screen, for example, in menus or dialog boxes, appear in the text like this: "From the ribbon, select **Standard Values** in the **Builder Options** tab."

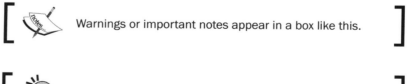

> Warnings or important notes appear in a box like this.

> Tips and tricks appear like this.

Reader feedback

Feedback from our readers is always welcome. Let us know what you think about this book—what you liked or disliked. Reader feedback is important for us as it helps us develop titles that you will really get the most out of.

To send us general feedback, simply e-mail feedback@packtpub.com, and mention the book's title in the subject of your message.

If there is a topic that you have expertise in and you are interested in either writing or contributing to a book, see our author guide at www.packtpub.com/authors.

Customer support

Now that you are the proud owner of a Packt book, we have a number of things to help you to get the most from your purchase.

Downloading the example code

You can download the example code files for this book from your account at http://www.packtpub.com. If you purchased this book elsewhere, you can visit http://www.packtpub.com/support and register to have the files e-mailed directly to you.

You can download the code files by following these steps:

1. Log in or register to our website using your e-mail address and password.
2. Hover the mouse pointer on the **SUPPORT** tab at the top.
3. Click on **Code Downloads & Errata**.
4. Enter the name of the book in the **Search** box.
5. Select the book for which you're looking to download the code files.
6. Choose from the drop-down menu where you purchased this book from.
7. Click on **Code Download**.

You can also download the code files by clicking on the **Code Files** button on the book's webpage at the Packt Publishing website. This page can be accessed by entering the book's name in the **Search** box. Please note that you need to be logged in to your Packt account.

Once the file is downloaded, please make sure that you unzip or extract the folder using the latest version of:

- WinRAR / 7-Zip for Windows
- Zipeg / iZip / UnRarX for Mac
- 7-Zip / PeaZip for Linux

Downloading the color images of this book

We also provide you with a PDF file that has color images of the screenshots/diagrams used in this book. The color images will help you better understand the changes in the output. You can download this file from https://www.packtpub.com/sites/default/files/downloads/SitecoreCookbookForDevelopers_ColorImages.pdf.

Errata

Although we have taken every care to ensure the accuracy of our content, mistakes do happen. If you find a mistake in one of our books—maybe a mistake in the text or the code—we would be grateful if you could report this to us. By doing so, you can save other readers from frustration and help us improve subsequent versions of this book. If you find any errata, please report them by visiting http://www.packtpub.com/submit-errata, selecting your book, clicking on the **Errata Submission Form** link, and entering the details of your errata. Once your errata are verified, your submission will be accepted and the errata will be uploaded to our website or added to any list of existing errata under the Errata section of that title.

To view the previously submitted errata, go to https://www.packtpub.com/books/Content/support and enter the name of the book in the search field. The required information will appear under the **Errata** section.

Piracy

Piracy of copyrighted material on the Internet is an ongoing problem across all media. At Packt, we take the protection of our copyright and licenses very seriously. If you come across any illegal copies of our works in any form on the Internet, please provide us with the location address or website name immediately so that we can pursue a remedy.

Please contact us at copyright@packtpub.com with a link to the suspected pirated material.

We appreciate your help in protecting our authors and our ability to bring you valuable content.

Questions

If you have a problem with any aspect of this book, you can contact us at questions@packtpub.com, and we will do our best to address the problem.

1
Basic Presentation Components

In this chapter, we will see how to build pages in Sitecore with the help of different rendering techniques using different Sitecore presentation components. You will learn the following recipes:

- Creating a simple content page using template and layout
- Creating a sidebar menu using view rendering and RenderingModel
- Creating breadcrumb using the view and custom model
- Creating carousel using view and controller renderings
- Placing renderings dynamically using placeholders
- Empowering the Experience Editor using placeholder settings
- Restricting or swapping rendering controls on placeholders

Introduction

If you are reading this book, you already know that Sitecore **XP** (**Experience Platform**) is not only an enterprise-level **content management system** (**CMS**) but also a web framework or web platform. Sitecore has robust and in-depth APIs to offer maximum flexibility to developers to implement custom solutions. It has many features designed to support enterprise-level requirements.

Sitecore provides extensive out-of-the-box components such as layout, device, placeholder, and some rendering controls, which play important role in designing and editing interfaces. We can also develop custom rendering components using **Extensible Stylesheet Language Transformations** (**XSLT**), ASP.NET **Web Forms**, and **Model-View-Controller** (**MVC**) frameworks to render content to the pages. All these frameworks currently exist in Sitecore, but MVC is now becoming widely used in Sitecore solutions and also provides better options compared to Web Forms and XSLT. Hence, we will prepare all the recipes using the MVC framework.

This chapter first serves recipes to create rendering components using model, view, and controller, and then explains how we can integrate them with Sitecore's out-of-the-box components. Looking into the depth of presentation components, you will learn extending these components in the next chapter.

For this chapter, it's required that you create a Visual Studio solution. You can refer to *Appendix A, Getting Started with Sitecore*, which explains how you can set up Sitecore solutions. Make sure that you have added a reference of `Sitecore.Kernel.dll` and `Sitecore.Mvc.dll` files to the `SitecoreCookbook` project.

Creating a simple content page using template and layout

As a developer, you will first have to understand the architecture of how a web page works. To create web pages, you first need to create a data structure using data templates, based on which you can create content items. Layout is used to place content with some presentation logic on it. In this recipe, we will take a quick look at creating a simple content page showing the title, body, logo, and other details.

How to do it...

We will first create and define a data template for the `Home` item (that is, home page):

1. Log in to Sitecore. Open the **Content Editor** from **Launch Pad**. You will find a default `/sitecore/Content/Home` item with the `Title` and `Text` fields. Delete this item as we will create our own custom template for the `Home` item.

2. In the `/sitecore/Templates` item, create a new **Template Folder** item, `Cookbook`. In this, create a `Site Root` template, leaving the base template set to the default `Standard template`, as shown in the following image:

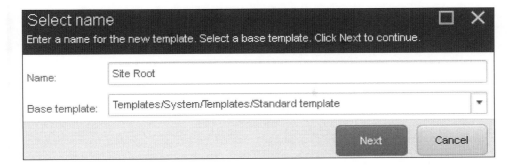

3. In template builder, create different fields, `Title` and `Body`, as shown in the following image, and save the details:

4. We will now create a content page using this data template. Create a new content item, `Home`, in the `/sitecore/Content` path using the `Site Root` template that we created and fill in the appropriate information in these fields:

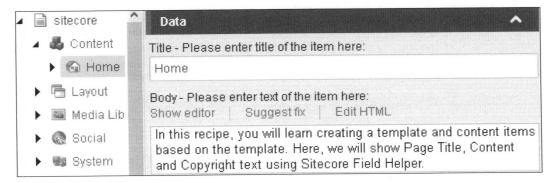

5. To show common details of websites, such as logo, copyright text, and some other information, create another `Site Configuration` template with fields such as `Company Name`, `Logo`, `Copyright Text`, and so on.

6. The `Site Configuration` item will be a non-visual item, so it should be created outside the `Home` item. Create a folder item `Global` in `/sitecore/Content`, and in this, create a content item, `Configurations`, using the preceding template, and fill in the appropriate details.

7. We will now create a layout from Visual Studio. From the `SitecoreCookbook` project, create an MVC `main.cshtml` view in the `/Views` folder to render field values from the previously created items. For this, put the following code in the view file inside the `<html/body>` tag:

```
<div id="header"> <a href="/">
   @Html.Sitecore().Field("Logo",
     Sitecore.Context.Database.GetItem(
     "/sitecore/Content/Global/Configurations"))
</a> </div>

<div id="contentarea">
   <h1>@Html.Sitecore().Field("Title")</h1>
   @Html.Sitecore().Field("Body")
</div>

<div id="footer">
   @Html.Sitecore().Field("Copyright Text",
     Sitecore.Context.Database.GetItem(
     "/sitecore/Content/Global/Configurations"))
</div>
```

8. We will now register this view file as a layout in Sitecore. In the `/sitecore/layout/Layouts` item, create a layout folder, `Cookbook`. In this, create a layout named `Main Layout`. Set the path field of this layout to `/Views/main.cshtml`.

9. Now we will assign the layout to the content items. Select the `Site Root` data template. From the ribbon, select **Standard Values** in the **Builder Options** tab. This will create the `__Standard Values` item for the template.

10. Select the __Standard Values item. From the ribbon, select the **Details** button in the **Layout** group from the **Presentation** tab. It will open a **Layout Details** dialog. For a **Default** layout, click on the **Edit** button, which will open the **Device Editor** dialog. Here, in the **Layout** section, select **Main Layout** and select **OK**. See the following image, which represents both the dialogs:

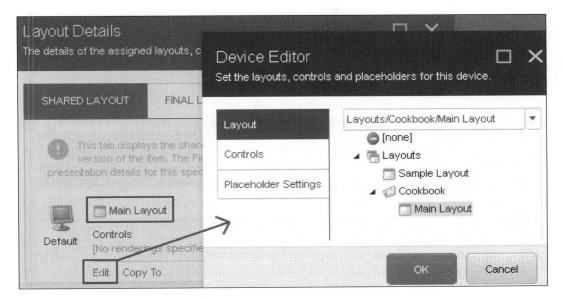

Instead of standard values, you can also assign a layout directly to the Home item. However, it's a recommended practice to apply presentation components to a template's standard values so that all items created from the template will inherit the field values from standard values.

11. From the Content Editor, select the Home item. From the ribbon, click on the **Preview** button in the **Publish** group from the **Publish** tab. This will open your home page in preview mode, as shown in the following image, where you will find Logo, Title, Body, and Copyright Text.

You can get the layout and style sheet files from the code bundle provided with this book to make it work, as shown in the following image:

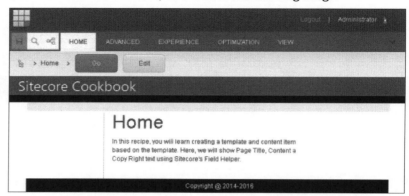

Downloading the example code

You can download the example code files for this book from your account at `http://www.packtpub.com`. If you purchased this book elsewhere, you can visit `http://www.packtpub.com/support` and register to have the files e-mailed directly to you.

You can download the code files by following these steps:

- Log in or register to our website using your e-mail address and password.
- Hover the mouse pointer on the **SUPPORT** tab at the top.
- Click on **Code Downloads & Errata**.
- Enter the name of the book in the **Search** box.
- Select the book for which you're looking to download the code files.
- Choose from the drop-down menu where you purchased this book from.
- Click on **Code Download**.

You can also download the code files by clicking on the **Code Files** button on the book's webpage at the Packt Publishing website. This page can be accessed by entering the book's name in the **Search** box. Please note that you need to be logged in to your Packt account.

Once the file is downloaded, please make sure that you unzip or extract the folder using the latest version of:

- WinRAR / 7-Zip for Windows
- Zipeg / iZip / UnRarX for Mac
- 7-Zip / PeaZip for Linux

How it works...

Sitecore layouts are reusable ASP.NET Web Forms (`.aspx`) or MVC views (`.cshtml`) that you register with Sitecore. ASP.NET uses Web Forms or views to serve HTTP requests. Here, on requesting the `Home` item, Sitecore first reads the item and renders the physical file of the layout associated with the item.

In the view file, we used the Sitecore field helper, `@Html.Sitecore().Field(<field name>)`, to render the `Title` and `Body` field values from the context item (in our case, `Home`). This helper method can also render a field of items other than the context item, which we used in order to render the `Logo` and `Copyright Text` fields of the `Configurations` item, `@Html.Sitecore().Field(<field name>, Sitecore.Context.Database.GetItem(<ItemId or path of item>))`.

Here, the `Sitecore.Context.Database.GetItem()` method provides the `Sitecore.Data.Items.Item` object, which has a collection of all the field values associated with the item.

> To learn more APIs, download Sitecore *Presentation Component API Cookbook* (`https://goo.gl/fu99Vh`). It provides APIs from Sitecore 6.4 or later with examples of Web Forms or Web controls, but they are still valid for Sitecore 8 or later with MVC as well.

Apart from the Content Editor, Sitecore also provides another tool, **Experience Editor**, to view pages in editing mode. From the ribbon, click on the Experience Editor button in the **Publish** tab to open an item in the **Experience Editor**. You can open it from Launch Pad as well. Here, you can change field values (for example, **Body** in the following image) rendered on the layout or view:

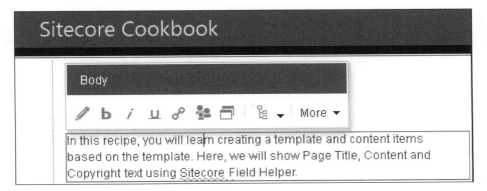

To disable content editing for an item field, you can pass additional parameters to the field helper, as shown in the following code:

```
@Html.Sitecore().Field("<field name>", new {DisableWebEdit=true})
```

You can also customize its rendering behavior by extending the Sitecore helper class. You can learn this from `https://goo.gl/ZHruKe` and `http://goo.gl/Kx8MQl`.

Creating a sidebar menu using view rendering and RenderingModel

In the previous recipe, you learned rendering simple field values in the layout itself. In this recipe, we will create a sidebar menu control using **view rendering** and **RenderingModel** and place them statically on layouts.

Getting ready

For this recipe, we will use the same layout file created in the previous recipe.

How to do it...

We will first create a template with some common fields required on all the content items of the site:

1. Create one `Common Fields` data template with the **Title**, **Body**, **Show in Menu**, **Image**, and **Icon** fields. From its standard values, set **Title** as $name and tick the **Show in Menu** checkbox field. Also, from **Layout Details**, assign **Main Layout** to it, which we created in the previous recipe:

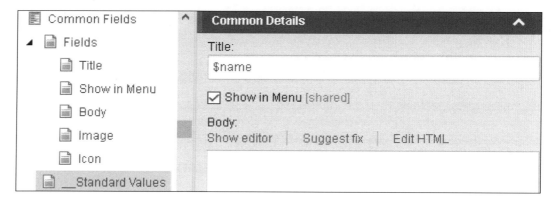

We will first create different subitems inside the Home item so that we can have enough items to render menu control properly. Here, $name entered in the **Title** field is a **standard value token** so that the name of the item will be stored in the **Title** field for newly created items. You can learn more about standard value tokens at http://goo.gl/qUE85h.

2. Create a few templates, for example, Product Section, Product Category, Product, and others. From their base template field, select the Common Fields template so that these fields, along with layout details, can get inherited to all these templates.

3. Create content items under the Home item, following the /Home/<Product Section>/<Product Category>/<Product> hierarchy, and fill in their **Title**, **Body**, and other fields' values. For example, refer to the following image:

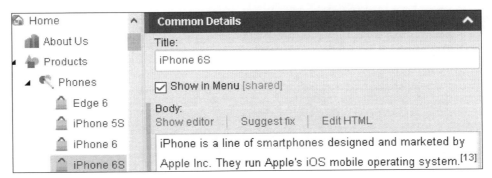

4. Now, we will create a menu control to show all items created on the same hierarchical level of the context item. From Visual Studio, create a SideMenu.cshtml view in the /Views/Navigation folder and write the following code in it:

```
@model RenderingModel
<ol class="sidemenu">
  @foreach (var item in
    Model.Item.Parent.Children.ToArray())
  {
    if (@item["Show in Menu"] == "1")
    {
      <li>
        <a href=
          "@Sitecore.Links.LinkManager.GetItemUrl(@item)">
          @item["Title"]
        </a>
      </li>
    }
  }
</ol>
```

5. Now we will register this view in Sitecore. Select `/sitecore/layout/Renderings/`, and create the `Cookbook` folder. In this, create a view rendering `Side Menu` and enter the view file path in the **Path** field, as shown in the following image:

 It's good practice to assign an icon to each rendering, which will increase usability for content editors while working from the **Experience Editor**.

6. In `Main Layout` or `main.cshtml` that we created in the previous recipe, place the following code in the appropriate place to render the menu on the page. Remember to update the item ID of the `Side Menu` rendering in this code:

```
<div id="sidemenu">
  @Html.Sitecore().Rendering(
    "{2383A57F-21FF-4A77-9E2A-C467F0CEDA57}")
</div>
```

7. Now, preview any product item; you will find that all the items at the same hierarchical levels will be displayed, as shown in the following image:

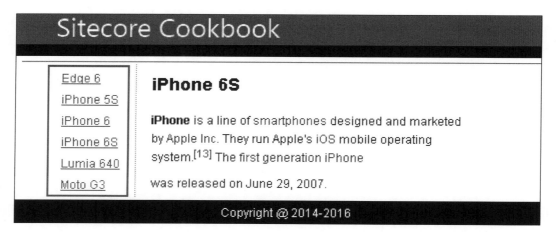

In the same way, you can also create top menu rendering. You can find its `TopMenu.cshtml` and `SiteHelper.cs` code files from the code bundle provided with this book.

How it works...

Sometimes, we get a requirement to hide an item from the menu, which requires having a common field such as **Show in Menu** or **Hide from Menu** in all items under Home. So, here we created the Common Fields template with the most common fields and inherited it in other data templates rather than duplicating these fields in all templates.

 Use Template inheritance to reuse content definitions, which makes a developer's life easier while doing further changes in it. Read best practices for template inheritance at http://goo.gl/1ePTtF.

We generated a simple menu using a view rendering. A view accepts a view model, which can be defined in the @model directive to determine the type of the model. If you don't specify the directive, Sitecore by default passes its default model, Sitecore.Mvc.Presentation. RenderingModel, which passes the context item to the view. You can also pass custom models to views, which you will learn in the next recipe.

In step 6, we bound the view statically (hardcoded on layout), which is also called **static binding**, and Sitecore provides two approaches for this:

```
@Html.Sitecore().Rendering("{2383A57F-21FF-4A77-9E2A-C467F0CEDA57}")
@Html.Sitecore().ViewRendering("<view file relative path>")
```

In the first approach, Sitecore itself finds the view definition from the view rendering registered in step 5. In the second approach, we can directly write the path of the view file.

There's more...

Here, we rendered the Side Menu view from its parent view Main Layout. Nested views can be very useful in reusing view renderings. For example, if you need to render a list of child items in different places, for example, news, events, products, and so on with the same interface, then you can achieve all this using a single view rendering!

Creating breadcrumb using the view and custom model

In the previous recipe, you learned creating a simple menu using a view with the default RenderingModel. In this recipe, we will create breadcrumb using a view and custom **model**.

Getting ready

For this recipe, we will use the same layout and items created in the previous recipes.

How to do it...

We will first create two classes: a simple `BreadcrumbItem` and `BreadcrumbList`. Here, `BreadcrumbList` will contain a list of `BreadcrumbItem` objects.

1. In the `SitecoreCookbook` project, create a `BreadcrumbItem` class in the `Models` folder. This class will contain properties useful to render breadcrumb items. We inherited this class from `Sitecore.Data.Items.CustomItem` to implement custom items:

```
public class BreadcrumbItem : CustomItem
{
  public BreadcrumbItem(Item item)
    : base(item) {Assert.IsNotNull(item, "item");}

  public string Title
  {get { return InnerItem["Title"]; }}

  public bool IsActive
  {get { return Sitecore.Context.Item.ID == InnerItem.ID;}}

  public string Url
  {get { return LinkManager.GetItemUrl(InnerItem); }}
}
```

2. In the `SitecoreCookbook` project, create a rendering `BreadcrumbList` model class in the `Models` folder, which will make a list of all the breadcrumb items. Make sure that it inherits the `Sitecore.Mvc.Presentation.RenderingModel` class so that Sitecore will automatically invoke its `Initialize()` method when the view is invoked:

```
public class BreadcrumbItemList : RenderingModel
{
  public List<BreadcrumbItem> Breadcrumbs { get; set; }
  public override void Initialize(Rendering rendering)
  {
    Breadcrumbs = new List<BreadcrumbItem>();
    List<Item> items = GetBreadcrumbItems();
    foreach (Item item in items)
    {
      Breadcrumbs.Add(new BreadcrumbItem(item));
    }
    Breadcrumbs.Add(new
      BreadcrumbItem(Sitecore.Context.Item));
  }
}
```

3. Create the `GetBreadcrumbItems()` method to collect a list of breadcrumb items as follows:

```
private List<Sitecore.Data.Items.Item> GetBreadcrumbItems()
{
  string homePath = Sitecore.Context.Site.StartPath;
  Item homeItem =
    Sitecore.Context.Database.GetItem(homePath);
  List<Item> items =
    Sitecore.Context.Item.Axes.GetAncestors()
    .SkipWhile(item => item.ID != homeItem.ID)
    .ToList();
  return items;
}
```

4. We will now register this model in Sitecore. From the **Content Editor**, select the `/sitecore/layout/Models` item. Create a `Cookbook` folder, and create a `BreadcrumbItemList` model in it. Set the **Model Type** field value to the fully qualified type name of this class, as shown in the following image:

5. Now we will create a view to render breadcrumb items. In the `SitecoreCookbook` project, create a `Breadcrumb.cshtml` view in the `/Views/Navigation` folder. Set the created `BreadcrumbItemList` model in the `@model` directive. Place the view content as follows:

```
@model SitecoreCookbook.Models.BreadcrumbItemList
<ol class="breadcrumb">
  @foreach (var item in Model.Breadcrumbs) {
    <li>
      @if (@item.IsActive)
        { @item.Title }
      else {
        <a href="@item.Url">
          @item.Title
        </a>
      }
    </li>
  }
</ol>
```

6. Register this view in Sitecore, and remember to assign the registered model to this view. So, when the view is invoked, Sitecore will initialize the mentioned model to collect the breadcrumb item list and pass it to the view:

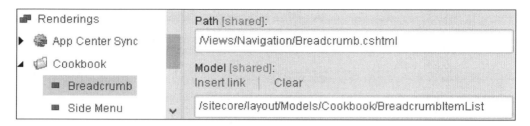

7. In the same way as the previous recipe, place this `breadcrumb` view rendering in `Main Layout` so that it will get applied to all the items having this layout. Use the following code for this, and update the item ID of the view rendering in the code:

```
<div id="breadcrumb">
  @Html.Sitecore().Rendering(
    "{764C9697-EA31-4409-8208-0CAECBD76500}")
</div>
```

8. Now, preview an item; you will find the breadcrumb on the site, as shown in the following image:

How it works...

Here, we built breadcrumb using a custom `RenderingModel`. For this, we should either inherit the `Sitecore.Mvc.Presentation.RenderingModel` class or implement the `Sitecore.Mvc.Presentation.IRenderingModel` interface.

The Sitecore MVC framework gives a nice feature of invoking a model to pass data to the view without creating a **controller**. For this, in step 6, we mapped the model to our view rendering. In the next recipe, you will learn how to use **controller rendering** with the view.

See also

If you are interested in knowing how **Web control** and **sublayout** works, you can find a working sample of breadcrumb and `Side Menu` from the code bundle provided with this book. As an alternative, you can also learn basic Web Forms components from `https://goo.gl/nlX3Cp`.

Creating carousel using view and controller renderings

In the previous recipe, you learned how to use a custom model to pass data to the view using `RenderingModel`. In this recipe, we will create carousel using controller rendering and view rendering.

How to do it...

We will first create a template to generate carousel slides:

1. Create a `Carousel Slide` template, as shown in the following image. Set the **Source** property of the `Image` field so that a user can pick carousel images directly from the source media folder. Do the same for the `Link Item` field.

2. Create some carousel slide content items with appropriate field values.

3. We want to show some selected carousel slides on our Home page, so we will add the tree list type carousel slides field to the Site Root template so that we can select multiple carousel slide items, as shown in the following image:

4. We will now create a CustomItem class to represent carousel slide properties in the same way as the previous recipe. In the SitecoreCookbook project, create a CarouselSlide class in the Models folder and inherit it from the CustomItem class. Add Title, Image, and Url properties to it:

```
public class CarouselSlide: CustomItem
{
    public CarouselSlide(Item item)
        : base(item) { }

    public string Title{
        get { return InnerItem["Title"]; }
    }

    public HtmlString Image {
        get {
            return new HtmlString(FieldRenderer.Render(InnerItem,
                "Image"));
        }
    }

    public string Url {
        get {
            Item linkItem = Sitecore.Context.Database.GetItem(
                InnerItem["Link Item"]);
            if (linkItem != null)
                return LinkManager.GetItemUrl(linkItem);
            return "";
        }
    }
}
```

5. Now we will create a `Controller` class, which will create a list of `CarouselSlide` objects. In the `SitecoreCookbook` project, create a `NavigationController` controller in the `Controllers` folder. Create the `ActionResult` or `ViewResult` `Carousel()` method that will return a list of carousel items to the view:

```
public class NavigationController : Controller
{
  public ActionResult Carousel()
  {
    List<CarouselSlide> slides = new List<CarouselSlide>();

    MultilistField multilistField =
      Sitecore.Context.Item.Fields["Carousel Slides"];
    if (multilistField != null) {
      Item[] carouselItems = multilistField.GetItems();
      foreach (Item item in carouselItems) {
        slides.Add(new CarouselSlide(item));
      }
    }
    return PartialView(slides);
  }
}
```

6. Now we will register this controller and action method in Sitecore. Select the `/sitecore/layout/Renderings/Cookbook` item. Create a `Carousel` controller rendering and set the **Controller** and **Controller Action** fields, as shown in the following image:

7. Now we will create a view to render the carousel slides. In the `SitecoreCookbook` project, create a `Carousel.cshtml` view file in the `/Views/Navigation` folder:

```
@model IEnumerable<SitecoreCookbook.Models.CarouselSlide>
<div class="carousel-inner" role="listbox">
  @foreach (var item in Model) {
    <div>
      <a href="@item.Url" title="@item["Title"]">
        @item.Image
      </a>
    </div>
  }
</div>
```

8. In the `Main Layout` file, place this rendering using the following code. Remember to update the item ID of this controller rendering in the code.

    ```
    @Html.Sitecore().Rendering("{62104CCC-D747-4671-BB3B-
    CFF041F42A5A}")
    ```

9. Preview the content item; it will show carousel images on the page. Making the carousel work fully, as shown in the following image, you may need to change HTML in the view and append style sheets, which you can get from the code bundle provided with this book:

How it works...

We can render item fields using the field helper, but there is no item field available to render item URL. So, we need some custom properties to items, and that is possible by implementing custom items. A custom item is an item that has special properties and functionality that match the functionality and semantics of the item that it is associated with. Here in step 4, we created the `CarouselSlide` class by inheriting from the `CustomItem` class and also created different custom properties such as `Url`, `Title`, and `Image`.

Here, we also used the `HtmlString` (or `MvcHtmlString`) return type to get image, unlike `Title`, which has the `string` type. It's because we want to render HTML without encoding it what view engine does for string.

In step 4, we used the `FieldRenderer.Render(<item>, <fieldName>)` method to render the HTML image tag. We can also use `item.Fields[].Value` or `item["<field>"]` to get field value, but it will return raw value of the image field as shown in the following code:

```
<image mediaid=\"{E0A48978-2D1A-4431-8FED-BEDE851B3FD6}\" />
```

In step 5 and 6, we created the `NavigationController` class with the `Carousel()` action method and registered them in Sitecore. The `Carousel()` method prepares a list of `CarouselSlide` objects and pass it to the `Carousel` partial view, which we created in step 7.

In step 8, we placed the `NavigationController` rendering to the layout, so when it's invoked, it returns a `ViewResult` with list of `CarouselSlide` objects as a model and the partial view will get rendered accordingly.

If you have noticed, we registered the controller only and bound to the item and done nothing with the view. It's because, MVC finds the view itself from `/Views/{Controller}/{Action}.cshtml`.

See also

Sitecore also provides some other renderings such as **item rendering**, **method rendering**, and **url rendering**, which we will not cover in this book as they are easy to understand, rarely get used, and serve for very specific requirements. You can learn these renderings from the following links:

- `http://goo.gl/SSPD2R`
- `http://goo.gl/Bphz2P`
- `http://goo.gl/Zx4Cy7`

Placing renderings dynamically using placeholders

In the previous recipes, you learned placing components on a layout or view statically. You can empower the dynamic placement of components using a placeholder, which comes with lots of benefits that you will learn in this recipe.

How to do it...

We will first replace statically placed renderings with placeholders in `Main Layout`:

1. We will first decide places where we can put content dynamically or we need placeholders, for example, breadcrumb, side menu, and main content area.

2. From `Main Layout`, remove the existing renderings from these places and add placeholders, `breadcrumb`, `left-column`, and `main-content` as follows:

```
<div class="container">
  <div id="breadcrumb">
    @Html.Sitecore().Placeholder("breadcrumb")
  </div>
  <div id="sidemenu">
    @Html.Sitecore().Placeholder("left-column")
  </div>
  <div id="contentarea">
```

```
      <article>
        @Html.Sitecore().Placeholder("main-content")
      </article>
    </div>
  </div>
```

3. We already have `breadcrumb` and `Side Menu` view renderings; we will create a simple view rendering to show the `Title`, `Body`, and other fields in the main content area. In the `SitecoreCookbook` project, create a `TitleAndBody.cshtml` view file in the `/Views/Content/` folder with the following content, and register this rendering:

```
<h1>@Html.Sitecore().Field("Title")</h1>
<div> @Html.Sitecore().Field("Body") </div>
```

4. Now, we will place **Breadcrumb**, **Side Menu**, and **Title and Body** renderings in `breadcrumb`, `left-column`, and `main-content` placeholders accordingly. From the **Content Editor**, select **Standard Values** of the `Site Root` template. From the ribbon, click on the **Details** button in the **Layout** group from the **Presentation** tab to open the **Layout Details** dialog. Click on the **Edit** button to open the **Device Details** dialog and select the **Controls** section. It will show an empty list, but once you add renderings on placeholders, they will be displayed, as shown in the following image:

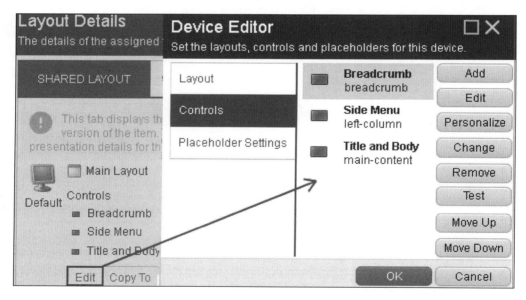

5. To add renderings, click on the **Add** button from the **Device Editor** dialog. It will open the **Select a Rendering** dialog, where you can add renderings to particular placeholders, as shown in the following image:

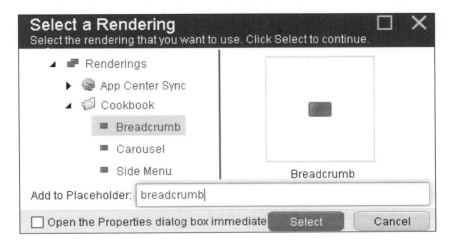

6. Repeat steps 4 and 5 for all template standard values, where you want to add renderings. Now, preview different pages to see the power of placeholders; you will find the renderings are displayed on the pages!

 We could also have used the benefit of inheriting presentation details from base templates. In Sitecore 8 onward, if you don't find your renderings inherited, you can get a bug fix for it from `https://goo.gl/OSMNkR`.

How it works...

A placeholder is a Sitecore component used within a layout, view, or sublayout, which allows the dynamic placement of components in it. It does not have any user interface, the same as the ASP.NET placeholder control. In Sitecore MVC, a placeholder can be created using the `@Html.Sitecore().Placeholder("<placeholder name>")` helper class. In Web Forms, you can use `<sc:Placeholder runat="server" />`.

It allows users to have design flexibility and minimize the number of layouts and renderings. For example, in this recipe, we can convert our layout from a two-column (side menu and content area) to a three-column layout, simply by adding a two-column view in the `main-content` placeholder. Thus, you can create any type of dynamic design just using a single layout.

When you have multiple components in a single placeholder, their order is managed by **layout engine**, considering the order they are added to the layout details. Their order can be changed using the **Move Up** and **Move Down** buttons in the **Device Editor** dialog, shown in step 4. You can remove or replace any control by clicking on the **Remove** or **Change** button.

If you apply layout details to an individual item, it will override layout details defined in standard values of the data template associated with the item. To revert them to standard values, use the **Reset** button in the **Presentation** tab and **Layout** group from the **Content Editor** ribbon.

See also

You can also implement dynamic placeholders (`https://goo.gl/6NIF3z`).

 It's also possible to use nested placeholders. When you use a view inside a view, you can set the placeholder key as `/<outer placeholder key>/<inner placeholder key>` to place renderings to the inner placeholder.

Empowering the Experience Editor using placeholder settings

Being a content owner, the Experience Editor provides a simpler user interface to change the page design. In this recipe, we will take a look at how to add components from the **Experience Editor** using **Placeholder Settings**.

Getting ready

In the previous recipe, we placed different components on different placeholders, for example, the **Title and Body** rendering on the `main-content` placeholder. We will place `Carousel` or any other rendering on the same placeholder from the **Experience Editor**.

How to do it...

As we want to place components on the `main-content` placeholder of the `Home` page from the **Experience Editor**, we will first create a placeholder setting for it:

1. From the **Content Editor**, select the `/sitecore/layout/Placeholder Settings` item. Create a placeholder setting `main content` item in it. In its **Placeholder Key** field, enter the name of the placeholder that we defined in the `Main Layout`, for example, `main-content`.

2. Now open the Home page in the **Experience Editor**. Find the **Title and Body** rendering that is placed on the main-content placeholder, as shown in the following image. From the floating toolbar visible there, click on **Go to parent component** to reach its parent component, which is the main-content placeholder in our case. Now, you will find two **Add here** buttons in the main-content placeholder to place components before and after the **Title and Body** rendering:

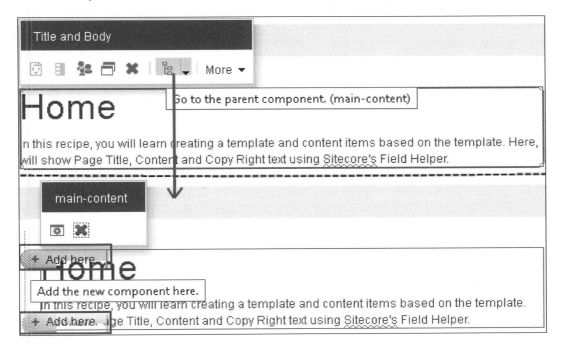

 As an alternative to this step, you can also find all the placeholder settings on the page directly. For this, from the **Experience Editor** ribbon, in the **Home** tab, in the **New** group, click on the **Component** button.

3. Clicking on this button will open a **Select a Rendering** dialog, from which you can select a component to add to that place. Select the **Carousel** rendering to place it before the **Title and Body** rendering, save the changes, and see how your page has been changed!

How it works...

There are two types of placeholder settings: **global placeholder settings** and **data template specific placeholder settings**.

In the preceding steps, we used the global placeholder setting as we specified a placeholder key in the placeholder setting. So, whenever Sitecore finds the `main-content` placeholder in any component of the requested page, it will allow us to manage components on that placeholder. In our case, it will be shown on all the pages of the website. So ideally, it's good practice to use the global placeholder setting for placeholders of the main layout of the site.

We can also set placeholder settings on the data template level. For example, we want to restrict the `main-content` placeholder setting only for `Site Root` or other selected templates. For this, we should follow these steps:

1. In the placeholder setting that we created, don't specify the **Placeholder Key** field (leave it blank) so that we can override it on the template level.

2. Select the standard values of the `Site Root` template. Open its **Layout Details**, and select the **Select the Placeholder Settings** tab in the **Device Details** dialog. Click on the **Add** button, which will open the **Placeholder Setting** dialog. Here, select the created placeholder setting, **main content**, and set the `main-content` placeholder name, as shown in the following image, and save the settings:

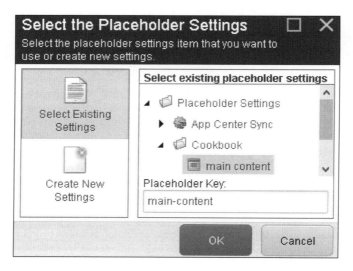

Now you will be wondering how Sitecore adds the components directly to **Layout Details** of the page. Open the **Layout Details** of Home item; you will find that the Carousel rendering we added from the **Experience Editor** got stored to **FINAL LAYOUT**, where **SHARED LAYOUT** is still the same as before, as shown in the following image. This is because of the **Versioned Layouts** feature we got from Sitecore 8. Read more about it at https://goo.gl/FXxHkP:

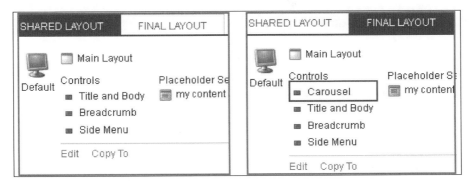

You can also remove any components by clicking on the **Remove component.** button found on the floating toolbar of the component, as shown in the following image:

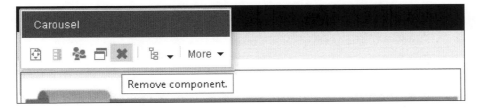

Learn more about the Experience Editor at https://goo.gl/1ZFIpX.

Restricting or swapping rendering controls on placeholders

While adding renderings from the Experience Editor, by default, it allows you to add all the renderings from the /sitecore/layout/Renderings folder. However, just imagine how difficult it would be for content owners to choose a logically valid and compatible rendering from the huge list.

In this recipe, you will learn how we can show a template-specific list of the allowed and placeholder-compatible renderings from the Experience Editor.

Getting ready

We have the `main-content` placeholder placed on all pages of the website. We want to restrict content authors to use **Carousel, Highlight Featured Products**, and **Highlight News** renderings only on the `Home` page. Similarly, for the **Products** landing page, we will restrict them to use **Carousel** and **Highlight Featured Products** renderings only. This recipe assumes that you have created the mentioned renderings.

How to do it...

Here, we will first override placeholder settings for the data template of the `Home` page:

1. From the **Content Editor**, select standard values of the `Site Root` template. Open the **Placeholder Setting** dialog from the **Device Editor**. Remove any placeholder settings, if any. Create a new setting.

2. Set the **Name** to `Home Content` and the **Placeholder Key** field to our `main-content` placeholder key. In the **Parent** field, select the `main content` placeholder setting that we have already created. Here, select the required renderings from the **Allowed Controls** field:

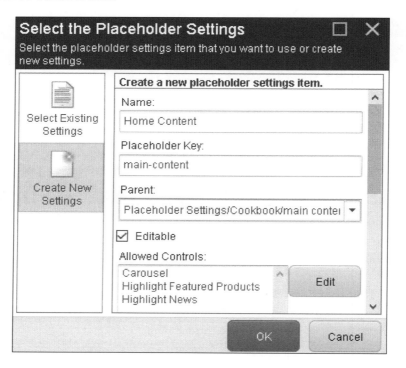

3. Open the Home page in the **Experience Editor**. Add the renderings to it; you will find that only the preceding selected renderings will be available to pick, as shown in the following image:

4. In the same way, you can apply these settings to standard values on **Product** or any other template, as per your requirement.

How it works...

Once you create this placeholder setting, you will find a new item created in the main content placeholder setting item, where you will find all the selected renderings in the **Allowed Controls** field:

You can also change placeholder settings from the **Experience Editor** by clicking on the highlighted button in the floating bar of the placeholder, as shown in the following image:

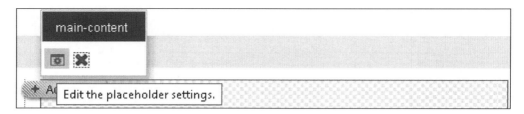

You learned how to place allowed controls on placeholders. Sitecore renderings have a **Compatible Renderings** field, as shown in the following image, where you can select compatible renderings to a particular rendering. So, while replacing any rendering from the **Experience Editor**, it will allow you to choose renderings from the selected compatible renderings only. For example, as shown in the following image, Sitecore will allow you to replace Carousel rendering with Banner rendering only. You can learn more about it at `http://goo.gl/Tk5ybI`:

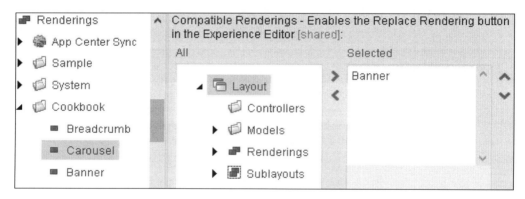

2

Extending Presentation Components

In this chapter, we will cover how to extend Sitecore presentation components to fulfil some real-life requirements. You will learn the following recipes:

- ► Altering rendering behavior using component properties
- ► Creating strongly-typed rendering parameters
- ► Achieving asynchronous operations using a custom device
- ► Creating multilingual content pages
- ► Generating RSS feeds for syndicated items
- ► Improving site performance by caching renderings
- ► Personalizing components

Introduction

In the previous chapter, you learned how to build pages with different presentation components, but presentation components are useful beyond just building pages. As a developer, you should provide an easier, error-free, and smart user interface to content authors to save time and improve accuracy by extending Sitecore presentation components.

This chapter will show you a number of tricks that will open up a whole new world of possibilities to extend Sitecore presentation components. Some recipes here will explain how we can reuse existing components with minor modifications to fulfil different requirements. Some recipes will explain working with multidevice and multilingual websites. This chapter also enlightens out-of-the-box features to serve content from external systems to Sitecore sites and vice versa. In this chapter, you will learn such presentation components extensions along with improving the performance of sites.

Altering rendering behavior using component properties

Sitecore provides you with different component properties such as data sources, rendering parameters, and so on. By default, the context item becomes data source for the component. By passing data source, we can change the behavior.

In this recipe, we will create a rendering to list products on the products' landing page. We will reuse the rendering on the home page to show a limited number of products with a different look and feel.

Getting ready

In the first chapter, we created the `Product Category` and `Product` templates having `Common Fields` as a base template, which contains fields such as the title, body, and image. Make sure that you created multiple product categories and products inside it.

How to do it...

First, we will create a model to list Sitecore items:

1. In the `SitecoreCookbook` project, create an `ItemList` model in the `Models` folder with properties as follows:

    ```
    public class ItemList : RenderingModel
    {
      public List<Item> Items { get; set; }
      public string Title { get; set; }
      public string CssClass { get; set; }
    }
    ```

2. Override the `Initialize()` method of `RenderingModel` to fetch data source and different rendering parameters—`CssClass` and `RecordsCount`—using them, we will change the styling of the component and limit the showing of the number of children accordingly:

```
public override void Initialize(Rendering rendering)
{
    int records = 0;
    int.TryParse(rendering.Parameters["RecordsCount"], out
        records);
    CssClass = rendering.Parameters["CssClass"];

    string dataSource = rendering.DataSource;
    Item sourceItem = GetDataSource(dataSource);
    Title = sourceItem["Title"];

    Items = sourceItem.GetChildren().ToList();
    if (records > 0)
        Items = Items.Take(records).ToList();
}
```

3. Create the `GetDataSource()` method to validate and assign data source provided to render:

```
private Item GetDataSource(string dataSource)
{
    Item sourceItem = null;
    if (dataSource != null) {
        Item item = Context.Database.GetItem(dataSource);
        if (item != null)
            sourceItem = item;
    }

    if (sourceItem == null)
        sourceItem = Context.Item;
    return sourceItem;
}
```

4. Now let's create an `ItemList.cshtml` view to list the children's details:

```
@model SitecoreCookbook.Models.ItemList
<div class="@Model.CssClass">
    <h4>@Model.Title</h4>
    @foreach (var row in Model.Items)
    {
        <div class="row show-grid">
            <div class="photo">
```

```
        @Html.Sitecore().Field("Image", row, new { mw=65,
          mh=65 })
      </div>
      <div class="content">
        <h6>
          <a href="@Sitecore.Links.LinkManager.GetItemUrl(
            row)">
            @Html.Sitecore().Field("Title", row)
          </a> </h6>
        <p>@Html.Sitecore().Field("Body", row)</p>
      </div>
    </div>
  } </div>
```

5. Now, register the view—Simple List and map the above created ItemList model in it. Add the view, rendering it on standard values of the Products Category template.

6. Preview a product category page, for example, /Home/Products/Phones. You will see that all the products under the **Phones** category will be displayed.

    Now, we will add this view rendering on the home page to show a limited number of products.

7. Add the view rendering to standard values of the Site Root template and preview the page. You will find that it shows a list of all the landing pages; this is because the context item is the default data source for any rendering.

8. Now, select the component from the **Experience Editor**, click on **More**, and select the **Edit component properties** menu to open the component properties dialog, as shown in the following screenshot. You can also perform the same from **Device Editor** from the **Content Editor**.

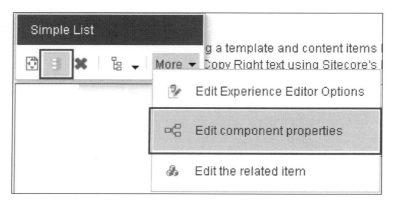

9. In the component properties dialog, assign **Data Source** and add **Additional Parameters**, as shown in the following image:

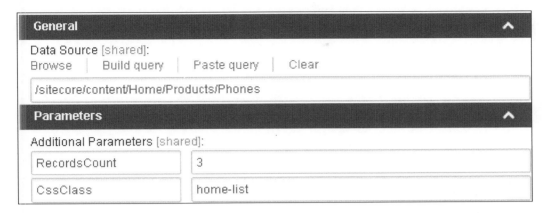

 The key of additional parameters supports only alphanumeric characters.

10. Now, preview the home page and check; you will find that only the first three products are listed instead of all the landing pages.

How it works...

You can take advantage of the reusability of components if you design it properly with additional parameters and data source. Here, apart from limiting the number of records to be shown, we also provided functionality to change the class of a stylesheet so that the rendering can have a different look and feel in different places that it gets used. You can pass any number of parameters to the components in this way.

Creating strongly typed rendering parameters

In the previous recipe, you learned using additional parameters, but these are loosely typed. So, chances are that content authors may enter invalid values such as non-numeric values for the RecordsCount parameter and a style class in CssClass that does not exist, and so on, which can lead to misbehavior of the application. Now, just imagine how happier your content authors will be if they see strongly typed parameters such as checkbox, integer, droplist, and so on.

In this recipe, we will use the Integer field for RecordsCount and a Droplist field for CssClass so that we always get valid values from the input.

Getting ready

Create a `Stylesheet Class` template and create different items outside the `Home` item, as shown in the following image. We will use the `CssClasses` folder as a source of the droplist field.

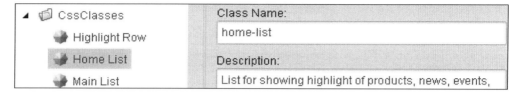

How to do it...

We will first create a template with the required input parameters as its fields:

1. Create a `List Rendering Parameters` template, set `/sitecore/templates/System/Layout/Rendering Parameters/Standard Rendering Parameters` as its base template, and create the required fields as follows:

2. Select the **Simple List** view rendering that we created in the previous recipe. In its **Parameters Template** field, select the parameter template that we just created:

3. Now, select the component from either the Experience Editor or Content Editor, and open component properties. You will find strongly typed parameters that we just created, as shown in the following image:

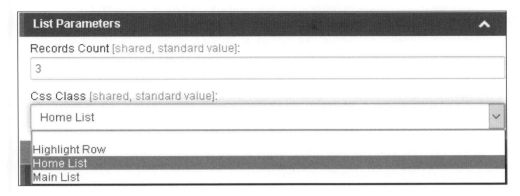

4. Remove these additional parameters from component properties. Additionally, if you have changed the parameters' names here, then make sure that you update in the `ItemList` model too.

5. Preview the page; you will see how your own parameters are working.

 You can use any Sitecore field type for strongly typed rendering parameters.

Achieving asynchronous operations using a custom device

Sitecore allows building site-supporting multiple devices so that we can have different renderings for different devices, that is, desktop, mobile, print, crawler, and so on. You can also associate a fallback device with each device. If the context item does not contain layout details for the context device, then the layout engine applies the layout details for the fallback device. Learn about setting up the device layout from `https://goo.gl/JYVSWJ`.

Apart from these uses of devices, in this recipe, we will consider a business requirement to list products on the products page. Now clicking on individual products instead of redirecting the user to that product's page, we will asynchronously pull product details using JavaScript and display on the same page to get better user experience and performance of the page. We will achieve this using a custom device.

How to do it...

We will first create a custom device and layout to load only the product content asynchronously:

1. Create a new `Async` device under `/sitecore/layout/Devices`. Set the **Query string** field value to `async=true`, as shown in the following image. It means that when requesting any URL having a query string as `async=true`, Sitecore automatically resolves an async device for this request; otherwise, it will resolve the default device:

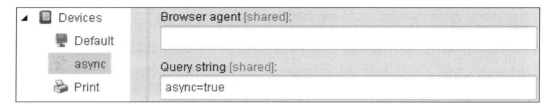

2. Create an `async.cshtml` layout in the `\Views` folder with the following code, which has one `async-content` placeholder to place content requested through an async device. Register this layout to Sitecore—`Async`:

```
<div id="asynccontent">
  @Html.Sitecore().Placeholder("async-content")
</div>
```

Now we will bind components to the async device and layout.

3. In the `Product` template standard values, we already have **Breadcrumb**, **Side Menu**, and **Title and Body** renderings with **Main Layout** on the **Default** device. We will add only the **Title and Body** with the **Async** layout on the **async** device, as shown in the following image:

4. Now, preview any product page and compare its output after adding the `async=true` query string. You will find that a regular URL (with the **Default** device) shows full details with navigation components, while the async URL shows only product details, for example, `http://sitecorecookbook/products/phones/iphone-6s` and `http://sitecorecookbook/products/phones/iphone-6s?async=true`.

   Now you can use both these URLs as per your needs. Here, we will create a view rendering to list products on the product category page.

5. Create a `ProductList.cshtml` view and write the following code. Register it in Sitecore as a `Product List` view rendering and map the `ItemList` model that we created in the previous recipe:

```
@model SitecoreCookbook.Models.ItemList
<script language="javascript">
  function LoadAsync(url) {
    $j = jQuery.noConflict();
    $j.get(url, function (data, status) {
    $j("#productcontent").html(data);  });
  }
</script>
<div class="async-list">
  @foreach (var row in Model.Items)
  {
    <a onclick="LoadAsync('@Sitecore.Links.LinkManager.
      GetItemUrl(row)?async=true')" href="javascript:">
      <div class="row">
        @Html.Sitecore().Field("Title", row, new {
          DisableWebEditing = true })
      </div>
    </a>
  }
</div>
<div id="productcontent"></div>
```

6. Add this view to the `Product Category` template standard values and preview the product category page. You will find that when clicking on any product in the list, it will fetch product details with an async device request and display the `productcontent` div element, as shown in the following image. The URL is `http://sitecorecookbook/products/phones/`.

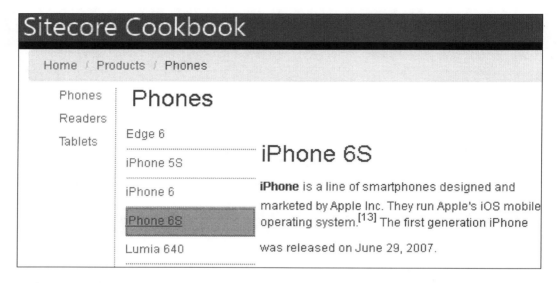

How it works...

While working in the Experience Editor, we may find that the content loaded asynchronously is editable or sometimes you may find the content with a ribbon. To disable them, you can change the page mode temporarily for that request using the following code after the device gets resolved. You can do this by customizing the `<httpRequestBegin>` pipeline, which you will learn in the *Customizing pipelines to achieve a custom 404 page* recipe in *Chapter 4, Leveraging the Sitecore Backend*.

```
Sitecore.Context.Site.SetDisplayMode(Sitecore.Sites.DisplayMode.
Normal, Sitecore.Sites.DisplayModeDuration.Temporary);
```

You learned that we can get a different output of the same page using different devices. Devices get resolved using either a query string or user agent.

Creating multilingual content pages

Till now, we created pages in the en (English) language, which is the default language in Sitecore. Sitecore supports all the languages or cultures that are supported by the .NET framework.

In this recipe, we will create content pages in multiple languages (English, Spanish, and Italian) and create a language switcher component to switch and view pages in these languages.

How to do it...

Sitecore by default contains the en (English) language. We will first create es-ES (Spanish) and it-IT (Italian) languages:

1. From the Content Editor, select the /sitecore/system/Languages item. Add a new language, **Spanish**, as shown in the following image. Similarly, create the **Italian** language as well:

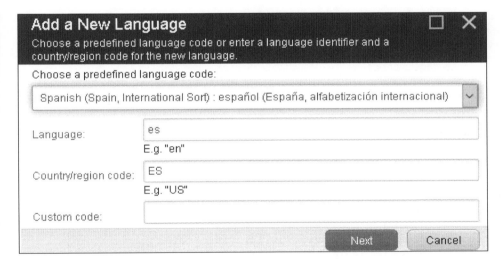

2. Now, from the Content Editor, select any content item on the right-hand side pane. You will find a language drop-down menu; clicking on this will display all the languages created in Sitecore, as shown in the following image:

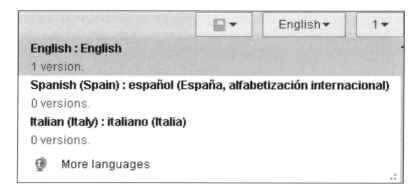

3. Select **Spanish** from this drop-down; it will navigate to the Spanish language content for that item. To create a version for the item in the Spanish language, click on the **Add a new version** button. Now enter your content in the Spanish language. You can do the same for the Italian language for all the other items.

   We will now create a language switcher component to switch to different languages from content pages of the website.

4. In the SitecoreCookbook project, Controller folder, create an action method, LanguageSwitcher(), in the NavigationController class file, as follows:

```
public ActionResult LanguageSwitcher()
{
  Dictionary<string, string> list = new Dictionary<string,
    string>();
  LanguageCollection langColl =
    LanguageManager.GetLanguages(Context.Database);

  foreach (Language language in langColl) {
    string url = GetItemUrl(Context.Item, language);
    list.Add(language.Title, url);
  }
  return View(list);
}
```

5. Create the `GetItemUrl()` method to get a language-specific item URL. We can use `UrlOptions` to get a language-specific URL, as mentioned in the following code:

```
private static string GetItemUrl(Item item, Language
   language)
{
   string url = LinkManager.GetItemUrl(item,
      new UrlOptions {
         LanguageEmbedding = LanguageEmbedding.Always,
         LanguageLocation = LanguageLocation.FilePath,
         Language = language
      } );
   return url;
}
```

6. Create a `LanguageSwitcher.cshtml` view in the `\Views\Navigation` folder to show all the languages and relevant URLs for the current item:

```
@model IDictionary<string, string>
<div id="languageswitcher">
   @foreach (var language in Model) {
      <div>
         <a href="@language.Value">@language.Key</a>
      </div>
   }
</div>
```

7. Add this controller to **Main Layout** to render the language switcher on the header. By clicking on the languages, you can switch to that language for the current content page. The following output shows a page in the Spanish language. You will find that your URL for the Spanish language will look like `http://sitecorecookbook/es-ES/products/phones/iphone-6s`, and the same for other languages:

The **Language fallback** feature is launched in Sitecore 8.1 so that if any item or field does not have content in the requested language can still serve other language content set as fallback. Sitecore supports language, template, item, and field-level fallback language. Learn more about this from `http://goo.gl/EtQVfa`.

How it works...

By default, Sitecore does not embed language in the item URL. So, we used `UrlOptions` to get a language-based URL. Instead of using `UrlOptions`, we could also have achieved URLs by doing the following setting in the `\App_Config\Sitecore.config` file: (This configuration file got introduced from Sitecore 8.1. In earlier versions, you can find it in the `Web.config` file.)

```
<linkManager defaultProvider="sitecore">
  <providers>
   <clear/>
   <add name="sitecore" type="Sitecore.Links.LinkProvider, Sitecore.Kernel"
        addAspxExtension="false" alwaysIncludeServerUrl="false"
        languageEmbedding="Always" languageLocation="filePath"
        encodeNames="true" lowercaseUrls="false" />
  </providers>
</linkManager>
```

There's more...

It's also possible to achieve language-specific unique URLs or language-specific friendly URLs, using the Display Name field of an item. `Display Name` field value can act as a language-specific item name, and will be considered while generating item URL as well. Learn more about this from `http://goo.gl/b28s2y`.

Generating RSS feeds for syndicated items

You can define any number of RSS feeds, and each feed can include any number of syndicated items. Let's check how we can prepare an RSS feed of products.

Getting ready

In the previous recipes, we have already created products under `/sitecore/Content/Home/Products/<Product Category>`. We will create an RSS feed to list down all the products that we have.

How to do it...

1. Create an `RSS` folder under `/sitecore/Content/Home`. Create an RSS feed item product using the `/sitecore/templates/System/Feeds/RSS feed` template.

2. In the field editor pane, fill in valid values in the items, title, and description link fields in the data section. Here, the feed will contain details of all the descendants of the item selected here. You can also use Sitecore query here.

   We have configured the RSS feed and now we have to make the product items available for syndication.

3. Select standard values of the product template. From the ribbon, select the **Design** button in the **Feeds** group in the **Presentation** tab. It will open the **RSS Feed Design** dialog, as shown in the following screenshot:

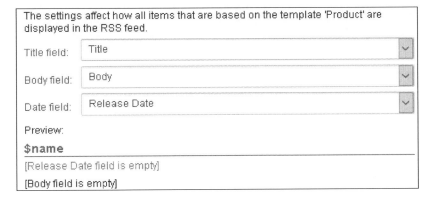

4. Select the title, body, and date fields from the drop-down and save the item. The drop-down shows fields of the product template.

5. Preview the **products** RSS feed; it will show the RSS feed as shown in the following screenshot:

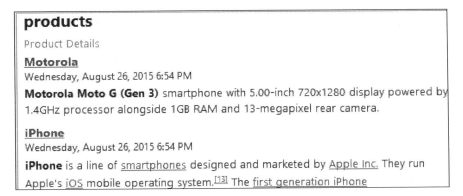

There's more...

This is the default behavior of the Sitecore RSS feed. We can also customize the feed behavior by creating a custom feed behavior. Create the custom class and register it in the feed item **Type** field, as shown in the following image. Learn customizing the RSS feed from `http://goo.gl/4OzMfc`:

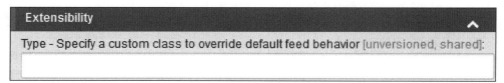

Improving site performance by caching renderings

Sitecore provides you with a feature to cache the output of presentation components to maximize performance and throughput by applying caching settings on renderings or sublayouts. It is also known as **Output Cache** or **HTML Cache**.

In this recipe, we will implement different static and dynamic output caching provided by Sitecore based on its usage.

Getting ready

In this recipe, we will consider that you have already created different components such as **Breadcrumb, Title and Body**, and **Footer** renderings. You can understand that the **Footer** will have the same output on all the pages for any device, while **Breadcrumbs** will get changed on every page. Also, chances are that we have content pages that can vary the output based on query strings or device types. We will apply caching on these renderings.

How to do it...

We will first apply caching settings to the **Breadcrumb** rendering and publish it:

1. Select the **Breadcrumb** rendering from the Content Editor. In the field editor pane, go to the **Caching** section. You will find the following options:

2. Tick the **Cacheable** and **Vary By Data** checkboxes and save the rendering item. From the ribbon, publish it in the **Publish** group in the **Publish** tab. Make sure that you have published required templates, content items, renderings, and media items.

3. Now, when you view any published page in **normal mode**, which will serve content from the web database (or from the content delivery server), Sitecore will cache the **Breadcrumb** rendering output for individual data sources (here, for every page) and will serve for all the subsequent requests from the cache itself.

4. You can apply the same settings for **Title and Body**, **Side Menu**, and other renderings as well.

5. If we apply caching to any rendering with only **Cacheable** ticked, it will create a common cache for all the pages as we have not configured it with any *varying by* criteria. Such a setting can be useful for static content of websites, which remains the same wherever used, such as the **Footer** renderings.

How it works...

Sitecore provides you with caching options that allow the rendered data to be retrieved from the cache if the data source, device, authentication status, user, rendering parameters, and/or query string parameters are the same as the previous request. Sitecore creates different caches for each variation of cache setting that we set.

The following table shows you different **Vary By** caching parameters and their uses, which will be helpful in deciding caching criteria:

Cache criteria	How it caches
Data	This will cache the output based on the data source of rendering
Device	This will cache the output for each device getting used

Cache criteria	How it caches
Login	This will create separate caching for authenticated and unauthenticated users
Param	This will cache based on additional parameters applied to rendering
QueryString	This will cache based on a unique combination of query string parameters
User	This will cache for each authenticated user separately

Each output cache consists of a list of any number of key-value pairs. Each cache key is a unique string identifying a presentation component and applies various caching variations. There is no option available such as Vary By language as each cache key automatically includes the context language.

 The whole HTML cache gets cleared on each publish. So, it's wise to avoid unnecessary publishing.

HTML cache statistics

We can also check how many renderings are cached, how frequently they are getting used, how much time they take to serve cached data, and other details using Sitecore's own tool, `stats.aspx`, as shown in the following image. You can access this tool with `http://sitecorecookbook/Sitecore/admin/stats.aspx`.

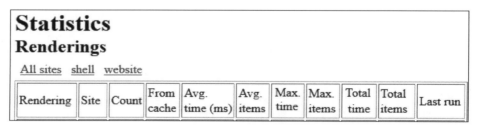

Statistics
Renderings
All sites   shell   website

Rendering	Site	Count	From cache	Avg. time (ms)	Avg. items	Max. time	Max. items	Total time	Total items	Last run

Each Sitecore site has a configurable maximum size for the output cache, which is called HTML cache. You can check the usage of caches using a cache page, as shown in the following screenshot, which you can access using `http://sitecorecookbook/Sitecore/admin/cache.aspx`:

website[filtered items]	0	0	0	10MB
website[html]	8	3.12MB	7.9KB	50MB
website[registry]	0	0	0	0

The preceding screenshot says that the **website** site has a total of eight different HTML caches generated that occupy a total of **3.12MB** and its capacity is to store **50MB**. The value **7.9KB** shows the difference between the last fetched occupied cache size and current occupied cache size.

 For high-volume websites, use the fewest caching criteria if possible to minimize memory usage. You can also increase the HTML cache size, which you will learn in the *Improving the performance of Sitecore instances* recipe in *Chapter 11, Securing, Scaling, Optimizing, and Troubleshooting*.

When to avoid caching

You should avoid using output caching for a rendering when:

▶ It has a form postback mechanism. (If caching is applied, postbacks won't work.)

▶ It pulls frequent content from external services or serves time-based content. (It will cache external content once and serve older content.)

There's more...

Here, we applied caching on renderings globally. However, it's not recommended all the time. So, we can also apply caching options to renderings on the template or item level as well. For this, select the template standard value or content item from the Content Editor, and open the **Layout Details** dialog. Select any rendering; it will open **Component Properties**, where you will find the same caching settings.

See also

You can also create custom caching parameters such as Vary By Cookie; you can learn more about this from `https://goo.gl/QANKeq`. If you are eager to learn more about different types of Sitecore caching, refer to `http://goo.gl/YHUwD2`.

Personalizing components

Sitecore components provide you with a facility to personalize placed components on a page, which is processed by Sitecore **Rule Engine**. We can do personalization based on many settings related to the field, item, security, user, system, analytics, and so on.

In this recipe, we will cover a very basic example to personalize rendering. On our website, we are showing sale or discounts on products in the form of a carousel. Now, at the end of the month or on any selected date, we want to show these carousel slides. After that, it should get hidden automatically.

Getting ready

We will personalize carousel rendering that we created in the previous chapter. If you are using Sitecore 8, you should enable analytics to enable personalization by doing the following setting in the `\App_Config\Include\Sitecore.Analytics.config` file. For older versions, personalization will be available by default.

```
<setting name="Analytics.Enabled" value="true" />
```

How to do it...

Let's see how we can create rules and change renderings conditionally:

1. From the Content Editor, select the standard values of a template, for example, **Site Root**, where we added the **Carousel** controller rendering. Open Device Editor, and select the **Carousel** rendering from the **Controls** tab. Click on the **Personalize** button found on the right-hand side, as shown in the following image:

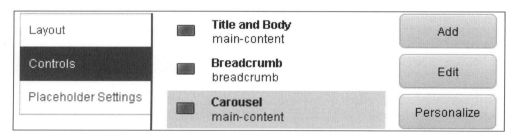

2. This will open the **Personalize the Component** dialog. Tick the **Hide Component** checkbox in the **Default** condition so that, by default, the **Carousel** rendering will be hidden on the page. Additionally, create **New Condition—Show Carousel**, as shown in the following image:

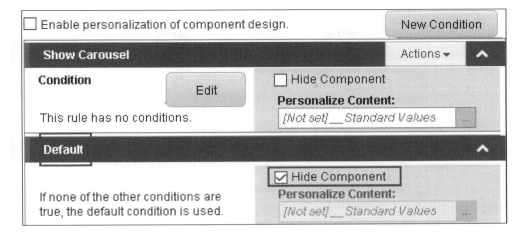

3. Click on the **Edit** button to open the **Rule Set Editor** dialog. Select conditions from the list. In our case, go to the **Date** section, and select **when the current day of the month compares to number** and **when the current month is month**:

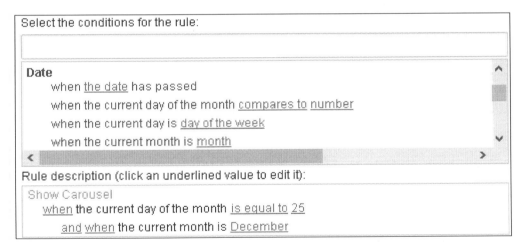

4. At the bottom of the **Rule description** section, you will find the selected rule condition. Select **compares to** and set its value to **is equal to**. Select **number** and set its value to **25**. Select **month** and set its value to **December**.

5. To test this, set today's date and month in this condition. Make sure that you publish all the modified items and view pages in **Normal mode** or **Explore mode** to check how personalization works.

How it works...

When a request is made to the Sitecore web page, the layout engine first invokes the rules engine. The rules engine applies the given rules to the item and performs the actions accordingly before the actual rendering is done. So, it regenerates the whole layout structure before the actual execution starts.

 Heavier usage of rules and personalization may affect performance.
If you have cached components, personalization on them will not work properly.

Here, we applied personalization just to show or hide renderings. We can also **Personalize Components** (replace components) or **Personalize Content** (change data source of components). To view these options, just tick the **Enable personalization of component design** checkbox, as shown in the following image:

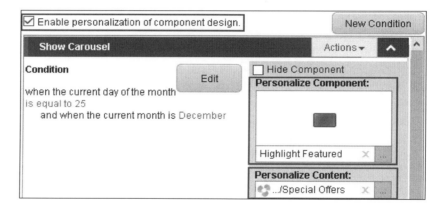

You can also personalize renderings from the Experience Editor in the floating bar of rendering:

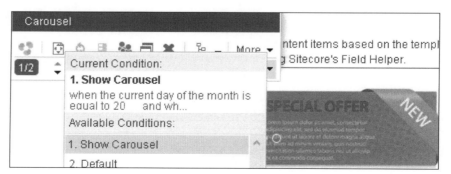

There's more...

Here, you learned a very basic example of using **Component Properties** to achieve personalization. In *Chapter 10, Experience Personalization and Analytics Using xDB*, you will learn more realistic personalization techniques.

3

Customizing the User Interface Framework

In this chapter, we will cover the following recipes:

- ► Adding a custom command to item context menu
- ► Creating a gutter to show unpublished items
- ► Creating a Sheer UI application using XAML control to list products
- ► Creating a SPEAK application to list and sort products
- ► Searching and filtering products using SPEAK
- ► Building a custom form to bind product details using SPEAK
- ► Creating a custom editor tab in the Content Editor
- ► Creating a custom experience button using the Field Editor
- ► Creating a custom rule to validate item fields
- ► Creating a custom sorting routine to sort the content tree items
- ► Creating a custom field to save the date time with time zones

Introduction

Sitecore user interface customization is a very wide topic, so this chapter focuses on covering different aspects of it to solve some real-world problems. Content management users typically update content through one of these two interfaces: the Content Editor and Experience Editor. You can extend the Sitecore user interface using commands, ribbons, context menu, gutters, custom experience buttons, custom editor tab, Web Forms, Sheer UI, or SPEAK UI. There are several ways to update content in both the interfaces.

In this chapter, you will learn how to work with all these UI components along with validating items and fields and managing a huge list of items by applying custom sorting algorithms. It also explains how we can create our custom fields and render content from them.

Adding a custom command to item context menu

The context menu is designed to increase the efficiency of content authors. The requirements may vary for content authors across different organizations.

In this recipe, we will create a menu item in the context menu of a Sitecore item that will display the number of children that the selected item contains. In the same way, you will be able to create a command button for the Content Editor and Experience Editor ribbons as well.

How to do it...

We will first create a `Command` class:

1. In the `SitecoreCookbook` project, create a `GetChildCount` class in the `Commands` folder. Inherit the class from `Sitecore.Shell.Framework.Commands.Command`.

2. Override the `Execute()` method of the `Command` class to apply a command action as follows:

```
public override void Execute(CommandContext context)
{
  if (context.Items.Length == 1)
  {
    Item currentItem = context.Items[0];
    SheerResponse.Alert(string.Format("Children count:
      {0}", currentItem.Children.Count));
  }
}
```

3. Override the `QueryState()` method of the `Command` class to show or hide the button, which means changing the state of the command based on its children count. Here, when an item does not have any children, we hide the command:

```
public override CommandState QueryState(CommandContext
  context)
{
  if (context.Items.Length == 1)
  {
    Item currentItem = context.Items[0];
    if (currentItem.Children.Count == 0)
```

```
        return CommandState.Hidden;
    }
    return base.QueryState(context);
}
```

4. Open the `\App_Config\Commands.config` file, and add the following command above the `</configuration>` node with the fully qualified name of the class created in step 1:

    ```
    <command name="item:getchildcount"
      type="SitecoreCookbook.Commands.GetChildCount,
      SitecoreCookbook" />
    ```

5. Open the Sitecore desktop mode and switch the database to `core`. Open the Content Editor and select the `/sitecore/Content/Applications/Content Editor/ Context Menus/Default` item. Create a new item, `Child Count`, in it using the `/ sitecore/templates/System/Menus/Menu item` template.

6. Enter field values in the item, as shown in the following image. Here, `item:getchildcount` is the command that we created in the `Commands.config` file in step 4:

7. Now, right-click on any item in the content tree of the Content Editor; you will get a new menu item **Count Children** in the context menu, as shown on the left-hand side of the following image. Clicking on it will show an alert box displaying the number of children that it contains:

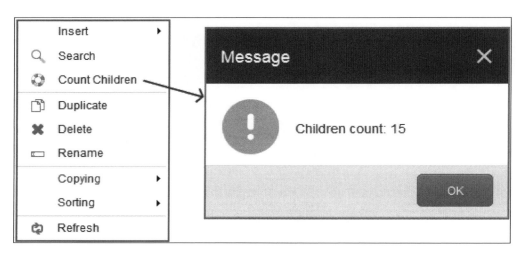

How it works...

The following image shows you how Sitecore renders the menu item in HTML. When the menu item is clicked, the scForm.postEvent() JavaScript method is called with parameters of the current event and an item:getchildcount(id=$Target) message, which passes these parameters to the Sitecore command engine:

```
<tr onclick="javascript:return
scForm.postEvent(this,event,'item:getchildcount(id=
{01FDA8E0-52EE-4A60-93B2-5A78986DE209})')">
    <td class="scMenuItemCaption">Count Children</td>
    <td class="scMenuItemHotkey">
</tr>
```

When Sitecore receives the message from the browser, it first interprets it and extracts the command name (item:getchildcount) and parameters (id={$Target}). Then, based on the commands from Commands.config, it invokes the Execute() method of the respective class where we can write our custom logic.

Here, if you see step 2, the Execute() method of Command contains a parameter of the CommandContext type, where we can get parameters passed from. We can also get multiple parameters passed from the command using context.Parameters["Parameter Name"];.

In step 3, we overrode the `QueryState()` method, which returns `CommandState` to the ribbon or context menu. `CommandState` is the state of the menu item, which we can set as `CommandState.Hidden`, `CommandState.Enabled`, or `CommandState.Disabled` to hide, enable, or disable the menu item accordingly.

There's more...

We can add a custom tab (ribbon), group (Strip), or button (Chunk) to the Content Editor ribbon under the `/sitecore/Content/Applications/Content Editor/Ribbons` item of the `core` database. The button on the ribbon will look like the following image:

To create a custom button (Chunk) on the Content Editor ribbon, create an item named `Count Children` in `/sitecore/Content/Applications/Content Editor/Ribbons/Chunks/Operations` with the `/System/Ribbon/Small Button` item template and fill in fields as follows:

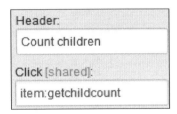

In the same way, you can find all the buttons of the Experience Editor ribbon under the `/sitecore/Content/Applications/WebEdit/Ribbons/WebEdit` item. You can add different types of buttons to the ribbon. You can find more details about this at `https://goo.gl/4nNSQu`.

See also

Sitecore provides two frameworks—Sheer UI and SPEAK—to manage user interfaces. Here, we used the Sheer UI to show an alert message. We could also use SPEAK to show an alert or open a modal dialog, which you can learn from `http://goo.gl/8rFKr5`.

Creating a gutter to show unpublished items

In the Content Editor, the left margin of the content tree is known as **gutter**. This area contains icons that can be used to display the status or type of the corresponding item and icons can be toggled on or off.

Let's create a custom gutter icon to identify unpublished items so that we will be able to know the publishing status of all expanded items very easily.

How to do it...

1. In the `SitecoreCookbook` project, create a `PublishGutter` class in the `Gutters` folder, and inherit it from the `Sitecore.Shell.Applications. ContentEditor.Gutters.GutterRenderer` class.

2. Add `enum PublishStatus` to show the publishing status as follows:

```
enum PublishStatus
{
   Published, NeverPublished, Modified
}
```

3. Add the `CheckPublishStatus()` method to know the publishing status of the current item:

```
private PublishStatus CheckPublishStatus(Item currentItem)
{
   Database webDB = Factory.GetDatabase("web");
   Item webItem = webDB.GetItem(currentItem.ID);
   if (webItem == null)
     return PublishStatus.NeverPublished;
   if (currentItem["__Revision"] != webItem["__Revision"])
     return PublishStatus.Modified;

   return PublishStatus.Published;
}
```

4. Override the `GutterIconDescriptor()` method to decide which gutter icon to show for the current item, which we will decide based on the publishing status:

```
protected override GutterIconDescriptor
   GetIconDescriptor(Item item)
{
   PublishStatus publishStatus = CheckPublishStatus(item);
   if (publishStatus != PublishStatus.Published)
   {
```

```
GutterIconDescriptor desc = new GutterIconDescriptor();
if (publishStatus == PublishStatus.NeverPublished)
{
  desc.Icon = "Core2/32x32/flag_red_h.png";
  desc.Tooltip = "Item never published!";
}
else
{
  desc.Icon = "Core2/32x32/flag_yellow.png";
  desc.Tooltip = "Item published but modified!";
}
desc.Click = string.Format("item:load(id={0})",
  item.ID);

return desc;
  }
  return null;
}
```

5. Open the Sitecore desktop and switch the database to `core`. Open the Content Editor and select the `/sitecore/Content/Applications/Content Editor/ Gutters` item. Under it, create a `Publishing Status` item using the `/Sitecore Client/Content editor/Gutter Renderer` template.

6. In the Field Editor pane, enter field values, as shown in the following image:

7. Now, open the Content Editor with the `master` database. Right-clicking on the left-hand side of the content tree will open a pop-up menu of all gutters, as shown on the left-hand side of the following image. Clicking on the **Publishing Status** gutter will show gutters with red and yellow flags, as shown on the right-hand side of the the following image:

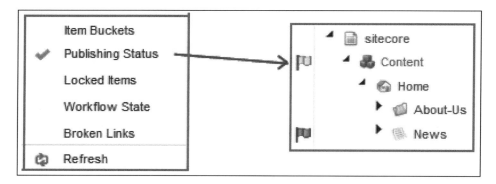

8. The preceding image shows that the **Content** item has been published but has some modifications to it (marked with a yellow flag). The **News** item was never published (marked with a red flag) and all other items have been published (no flag).

There's more...

Gutter is very helpful in showing the status (such as **Publish**, **Lock**, and **Workflow**) of multiple items on one screen while navigating to the Content Editor.

 Heavier use of gutters may take extra load so the user interaction may get slower.

Creating a Sheer UI application using XAML control to list products

Extensible Application Markup Language (**XAML**) is a declarative markup language used to create user interfaces. There are two types of XAML control frameworks available in Sitecore, **XML control** and **xamlControls**. In this recipe, we will create the Sheer UI application using XML control and, based on this, you will be able to create an application using xamlControls as well. You can get some basic information about both from `https://goo.gl/4WWeVw`.

Sitecore has built a new framework, SPEAK, which is a replacement for the XAML/Sheer UI, so we will not focus much on it. However, it's good to know how it works so that it can be helpful in customizing existing applications. Here, we will create an application to list all products as well as delete selected products. You will learn how to use different controls, invoke methods, handle messages, and create events in XML control.

How to do it...

We will first create an XML layout for the Sheer UI application:

1. Create an XML file named `ProductList.xml` in the `\sitecore\shell\Applications\Cookbook\` folder, and place the following contents in it:

```xml
<?xml version="1.0" encoding="utf-8" ?>
<control xmlns:def="Definition"
  xmlns="http://schemas.sitecore.net/
  Visual-Studio-Intellisense">
  <ProductListing>
    <FormDialog Icon="People/16x16/clock_run.png"
      Header="Product List" Text="View all the products">
      <CodeBeside Type="SitecoreCookbook.XAML.
        ProductListPage,SitecoreCookbook"/>
      <Stylesheet Src="/sitecore/shell/Applications/Content
        Manager/Dialogs/Properties/Properties.css" />

      <GridPanel ID="Viewer" Height="315" class="scBackground"
        vAlign="top" Width="100%" Cellpadding="5">
      </GridPanel>
    </FormDialog>
  </ProductListing>
</control>
```

2. Now, find the `<GridPanel>` node in the preceding code, and place `ListView` to list products as follows:

```xml
<Border align="center">
  <Scrollbox ID="Summary" Width="100%" Height="300"
    Style="padding:14px 4px 0px 4px; border-width:1px;
    border-style:solid">
    <Listview ID="ProductList" View="Details" Width="100%"
      Background="white" MultiSelect="true">
      <ListviewHeader>
        <ListviewHeaderItem Name="Title" Header="Title" />
        <ListviewHeaderItem Name="Price" Header="Price" />
        <ListviewHeaderItem Name="Id" Header="Item Id" />
      </ListviewHeader>
    </Listview>
  </Scrollbox>
</Border>
```

3. Now, we will place two button controls (to delete the selected product) in the `<GridPanel>` node. One button will get invoked by a method named `DeleteProducts` and the other by a message named `product:delete`:

```
<Border align="left">
  <Button Header="Delete with method" Click="DeleteProducts" />
  <Button Header="Delete with message" Click="product:delete" />
</Border>
```

4. Now we will do the coding part to list products. In the `SitecoreCookbook` project, create a `ProductListPage` class in the `XAML` folder, and inherit it from `Sitecore.Web.UI.Pages.DialogForm`:

```
public class ProductListPage : DialogForm
{
  protected GridPanel Viewer;
  protected Button btnDelete;
  protected Listview ProductList;
}
```

5. Create a `LoadProducts()` method in the class to list all products and add them to the current page as an object of `ListViewItem`:

```
private void LoadProducts()
{
  string ProductsPath =
    "/sitecore/Content/Home/Products/Phones";
  Item products =
    Factory.GetDatabase("master").GetItem(ProductsPath);
  foreach (Item product in products.Children)
  {
    ListviewItem productItem = new ListviewItem();
    Context.ClientPage.AddControl(ProductList,
      productItem);
    productItem.ID = Control.GetUniqueID("I");
    productItem.Header = product["Title"];
    productItem.ColumnValues["Id"] = product.ID.ToString();
    productItem.ColumnValues["Title"] = product["Title"];
    productItem.ColumnValues["Price"] = product["Price"];
  }
}
```

6. Now, override the `OnLoad()` event of the `DialogForm` class to invoke the preceding `LoadProducts()` method. Here, `ClientPage.IsEvent` works the same as Webform's `Page.IsPostBack`. So, products will be loaded on the first request of the dialog:

```
protected override void OnLoad(EventArgs e)
{
  base.OnLoad(e);
  if (!Context.ClientPage.IsEvent) {
    LoadProducts();
    this.OK.Visible = false;
    this.Cancel.Value = "Close";
  }
}
```

7. Build the project and open our XAML application using the following URL:

```
http://sitecorecookbook/sitecore/shell/default.
aspx?xmlcontrol=ProductListing
```

You can find a list of products, as shown in the following image:

Product List
View all the products

	Title	Price	Item Id
	Edge 6	680	{AF47693B-F60A-4C65-91FC-F04D2E966F5F}
	iPhone 5S	470	{E19394B4-7897-4332-B981-FA327C6C2827}
	iPhone 6	570	{D7C22E6B-CE00-4A6C-816D-4D29343252D2}
	iPhone 6S	670	{EFEC7449-480A-45EE-8541-5E56D7CB0F65}

Delete with method   Delete with message

XAML provides different types of events that we can achieve using invoking methods or passing messages to the event. Here, we will use both approaches to delete selected products.

8. If you check, as per the code that we placed in the XML file in step 3, the first button is expecting the `DeleteProducts()` method, which is defined in the button's `Click` property. Here, we will define this method to delete selected products:

```
protected void DeleteProducts()
{
  if (ProductList.SelectedItems.Length > 0) {
    foreach (ListviewItem productItem in
      ProductList.SelectedItems) {
```

```
      Item product =
        Factory.GetDatabase("master").GetItem(new
        ID(productItem.ColumnValues["Id"].ToString()));
      product.Recycle();
    }

    ProductList.Controls.Clear();
    LoadProducts();
    ProductList.Refresh();

    SheerResponse.Alert("Selected products are deleted!");
  }
  else
    SheerResponse.Alert("No product selected!");
}
```

9. The second button is expecting the application to handle the `product:delete` message on its click, which is again defined in the `Click` property of the button. We can handle this message by overriding the `HandleMessage()` method as follows:

```
public override void HandleMessage(Message message)
{
  if (message.Name == "product:delete")
    DeleteProducts();
}
```

10. Run this application again and select one or more products. Click on any button to delete the product.

How it works...

We created a XAML dialog using an XML file. In the XML, we defined a `<ProductListing>` tag after the `<control>` tag, which describes the name of the control. The control name is the identity of the execution of this application and should be unique across the Sitecore solution. While building the solution, the XML file also gets compiled, and while accessing the XAML application, it finds the XML file where the requested control name is defined.

We can create multiple controls like this, but Sitecore recommends creating one control per XML file. Sitecore stores its controls in two locations: `/sitecore/shell/Applications` and `/sitecore/shell/Controls`. If you want to override any existing Sitecore control, you can place the overridden XML file in the `/sitecore/shell/override` folder to separate it from Sitecore's original copy. If you want to place your custom XML file outside of these directories, you have to register it in `<controlSources>` in the `\App_Config\Sitecore.config` file as follows:

```
<source mode="on" namespace="SitecoreCookbook.XAML"
    folder="/SitecoreCookbook" deep="true"/>
```

In the XML file, the `Type` attribute in `<CodeBeside>` expects assembly details, which means where the server-side code will get executed.

Steps 7 and 8 show you how to invoke a method and pass a message to delete selected products. Both the method and message can be used in any event of buttons or controls, like we used it in button's `Click` event:

```
<Button Header="Delete with method" Click="Delete Products" />
<Button Header="Pass with message" Click="product:delete" />
```

There's more...

You learned how to invoke a method and pass a message to respond to user interaction. We can use events such as `Button.OnClick += new EventHandler(BesideButton_ OnClick);` in the same way.

Instead of the `HandleMessage()` method, we can also handle a message with a custom method by just adding the `HandleMessageAttribute` attribute to this method, passing a relevant message to its constructor such as the following:

```
[HandleMessage("product:delete")]
public void DeleteProductMethod(Message message){}
```

State management is also possible in XAML to persist some values. We can achieve this using the `ServerSettings` property in the `ClientPage` class. We can use `Context. ClientPage.ServerProperties["PersistentValue"]` to persist information.

xamlControls

The xamlControls needs the `<xamlControls>` node unlike the XML controls, which use the `<controls>` node. It also needs a file extension, such as `.xaml.xml`, unlike `.xml` for XML controls.

In XML controls, we create a control name such as `<ProductListing>`, while in xamlControls, we have to use `<SitecoreCookbook.XAML.ProductListing>` as a control name.

XML controls can be viewed at the following URL:

`http://sitecorecookbook/sitecore/shell/default. aspx?xmlcontrol=<ControlName>`

xamlControls can be viewed at the following URL:

`http://sitecorecookbook/sitecore/shell/~/xaml/<ControlName>.aspx`

The structure of xamlControls is slightly different from XML controls, as follows:

```
<xamlControls xmlns:x="http://www.sitecore.net/xaml">
  <SitecoreCookbook.XAML.ProductsListing
    x:inherits="SitecoreCookbook.XAML.ProductListPage,
    SitecoreCookbook">
  </SitecoreCookbook.XAML.SitecoreSitesList>
</xamlControls>
```

We can also create a wizard using XAML controls such as a template creation wizard. You can read more about this at `https://goo.gl/pL1npo`.

Creating a SPEAK application to list and sort products

The traditional Sitecore applications were designed for developers and content authors. **Sitecore Process Enablement & Accelerator Kit** (**SPEAK**) UI is a third-generation framework introduced in Sitecore 7.2. There are many SPEAK applications in Sitecore such as dashboard pages, list pages, task pages, and others.

In this recipe, we are going to create a SPEAK application that will be helpful to content authors to see all products on one page and allow them to sort products based on different fields. The SPEAK 2.0 framework was released with Sitecore 8.1 but, as it is not stable and changes are expected in it, we will cover these SPEAK recipes in the 1.1 framework itself.

Getting ready

Creating or editing SPEAK applications is not supported in the Content Editor, so we will use the **Sitecore Rocks** plugin from Visual Studio to prepare this recipe. You can download this plugin from `https://goo.gl/hHK6S9`.

To list products, we will use the `Products` template that we have created in the previous recipes, which should have the `Title`, `Company`, `Price`, and `Release Date` fields.

How to do it...

We will first create a SPEAK application item:

1. Open Sitecore Rocks in Visual Studio and create a connection to the relevant website. Expand the `core` database. Under the `/sitecore/client/Your Apps` item, create a base folder, `Cookbook`, where we will create application pages.

2. In side the `Cookbook` folder, add a new `ProductListing` item using the `/sitecore/client/Business Component Library/`**`version 1`**`/Templates/Branches/Applications/`**`ListPage`** template (for Sitecore 8.1) and the `/sitecore/client/Business Component Library/Templates/Branches/Applications/`**`ListPage`** template for earlier versions. So, the item will get a preconfigured layout and rendering details from the standard values of the template.

   Select the `ProductListing` item and press *Ctrl + U* (or right-click on it in the context menu, and select **Tasks** and **Design Layout**). This will open the layout presentation details, as shown in the following image:

Layout:				
/sitecore/client/Speak/Layouts/Layouts/Speak-Layout			Browse...	Clear

Renderings and Place Holders: Filter ✕

Id	Rendering	Placeholder	Data Source
	PageCode	Page.Code	
	List	Page.Body	
	GlobalHeader	GlobalHeader	
GlobalLogo	GlobalLogo	GlobalHeader.StartButton	
NavigationToggler	NavigationPanelToggleBu	GlobalHeader.NavigationToggler	

3. View this created application in the browser with `http://sitecorecookbook/sitecore/client/Your%20Apps/Cookbook/ProductListing`, and you will find a blank page created with some basic components.

4. We will now create column definitions to show different fields of products. Create a `ProductColumns` folder under the `ProductListing/PageSettings` item. Under this folder item, create `ColumnField` items named `Company`, `Product`, and `Price`. Set relevant values in **HeaderText**, **DataField**, and **SortField**, and tick the **Sortable** field for all these items:

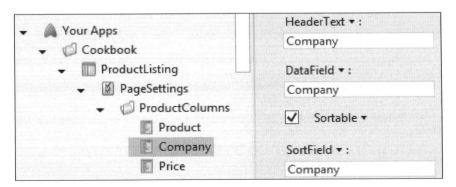

5. For the **Product** item, we will set a customized output so that we will not need to set **DataField**. Instead of this, we will use the **HTMLTemplate** field and assign a hyperlink by showing the **Title** field and passing the item ID in the query string. Clicking on this will open a new page to edit product details, which we will cover later in this chapter. In the **HTMLTemplate** field, we can get an item's field values using {{FIELDNAME}}, for example {{Title}}. However, you can't find item ID from item fields, so you must have an additional field ItemId in the **Product** template with standard values as $id so that every created product item will get its item ID assigned in the ItemId field, so we can use it in the HTML template as follows:

 Remember to add renderings of SPEAK version 1.1 only as we created SPEAK 1.1 application.

6. We will now add and configure ListControl in the presentation details. Select the **ProductListing** item, and open its layout in the **Design** mode. Add ListControl (the /sitecore/client/Business Component Library/Version 1/ Layouts/Renderings/Lists and Grids/ListControl template) to the ApplicationContent.Main placeholder and set its **ID** as ListProducts.

7. Set its datasource as the ProductColumns item folder, which we created in step 4. This means that ListControl will show the columns that we created under the ProductColumns folder.

8. Preview the application in the browser, and you will see an empty grid, as shown in the following image. This is because we have not provided a data source yet (products list) to ListControl:

9. We will now configure datasource of ProductList to show product details. Add a SearchDataSource rendering to the Page.Body placeholder. Set its **ID** as ProductDataSource, **Database** field value as $context_contentdatabase, **Language** as en, and **RootItemId** as the root item of the Products page of the master database (/sitecore/Content/Home/Products).

However, this Products section contains products as well as product categories, so all these items will be fetched in this data source. However, we want to show only the products' list. So, we will make a filter here.

10. In the `ProductListing/PageSettings` item, add a `SearchConfig` item using the `SearchConfig` template. Set its **Template** field value to the item ID of the **Product** template of the master database, as shown in the following image. This means that this will filter items that have the **Product** template:

11. Now, select the **SearchDataSource** rendering. In its **SearchConfigItemId** field, set the value as the item ID of the `SearchConfig` item that we created before. This will filter the data source by the **Product** template.

12. Select the **ListProducts** rendering, and set its **Items** field to `{Binding ProductDataSource.Items}`. This will bind the items of **ProductDataSource**.

13. Preview the application in the browser, and you will see a list of products, as shown in the following image:

Product Listing

Product	Company ▲	Price ▲
Edge 6	Samsung	749
iPhone 6	Apple	730

14. We will now apply sorting to the columns of the list. Set the **ProductDataSource** rendering's **Sorting** field to `{Binding ListProducts.Sorting}` so that sorting on any column of `ListControl` will bind the **ProductDataSource** again, based on the sorting applied.

15. Preview the page, and you will find that the sorting is working through the columns.

How it works...

You can see that we achieved the listing of products without using a physical layout file, unlike the XAML controls, and this is simpler and quicker. SPEAK applications are stored in `core` database, under `/sitecore/client`. By default, there is a folder called `Your Apps` where you can create your own applications. We created `Cookbook` folder inside it, where we created our custom application.

In step 4, we created three columns in the `ProductColumns` folder and set them as the datasource of `ListControl` so that `ListControl` will know that it should build columns based on the `ColumnField` items.

Here, we used the **SearchDataSource** component to retrieve Sitecore items from the defined root item and the `SearchConfig` item to filter items from the data source. If you check the **View Source** page, you will find that the datasource attributes are reflected there, which we defined in step 9. So, you will not see any product details in the **Page Source** as it is fetched later asynchronously using another request once the page is loaded:

```
<script data-sc-id="ProductDataSource" data-sc-fields="[]"
    data-sc-root-id="{28C65C97-5520-4C27-BB49-36AC3E1B8EF3}"
    data-sc-showHiddenItems="false"
    data-sc-language="en" data-sc-database="master"
    type="text/x-sitecore-searchdatasource"
    data-sc-require="/-/speak/v1/controls/searchdatasource.js"
</script>
```

Now, if you check the **Network** tab in the developer tools or **Firebug**, you will find a request being fired to the **Item Web API** as a result of the data source component being on the page, which will return the product details in the JSON format, as shown in the following image. Now, based on the JSON output, the data source is bound to `ListControl` asynchronously:

```
shell?search=&root=%7B28C65C97-5520-4C27-BB49-36AC3E1B8EF3%7D&sc_content=master&lang
/-/item/v1/sitecore

X   Headers   Preview   Response   Cookies   Timing

▼{statusCode: 200, result: {totalCount: 8, resultCount: 8,…}}
  ▼result: {totalCount: 8, resultCount: 8,…}
    ►items: [{Category: "Phones", Database: "master", DisplayName: "iPhone 6S"
    resultCount: 8
    totalCount: 8
  statusCode: 200
```

In the same way, while sorting, it will again request the Item Web API to retrieve the sorted data source based on the columns and bind this to `ListControl`.

SPEAK 1.1 provides many out-of-the-box components. In Sitecore 8.1, you can find them in `/sitecore/client/Business Component Library/<`**version number**`> /Layouts/Renderings` based on the SPEAK version number. In earlier Sitecore versions, renderings were available in `/sitecore/client/Business Component Library/Layouts/Renderings`.

In the next recipe, you will learn how to search and filter in order to extend our product listing page.

See also

You can learn SPEAK 2.0 at `http://goo.gl/xK67e5` and find out changes at `https://goo.gl/DU8yPY`.

Searching and filtering products using SPEAK

In the previous recipe, you learned how to list items and sort them using **ListControl** and **SearchDataSource** SPEAK components. We are going to extend the previous recipe to apply searching and filtering to them.

How to do it...

We will first implement search on the `ProductListing` page:

1. From Sitecore Rocks in the `core` database, select the **ProductListing** application item that we created under `/sitecore/client/Your Apps/Cookbook`.

2. Open **Layout Designer** for the item. Add a `SearchPanel` component to the `ApplicationContent.Main` placeholder.

3. Add a **TextBox** component to the `SearchPanel.Searches` placeholder, set its **ID** to `TextBoxProduct`, and give any watermark text.

4. We have already used the **SearchDataSource** component to retrieve product details named **ProductDataSource**. In its **Text** property, locate `{Binding TextProduct.Text}`.

5. Preview the application. In the textbox, enter a product name and press *Enter*. It will retrieve and display the searched product details only, as shown in the following image:

Product	Company	▲	Price	▲
iPhone 6	Apple		730	
iPhone 5S	Apple		530	

Now, we will implement facets or filtering products based on the company. In the **PageSettings** item, create a `Facets` folder. In this, create a child item `Company` using the **Facet** template. Set the **FieldName** field value as `Company`. This will work as a **Company** facet to list products, as shown in the following image:

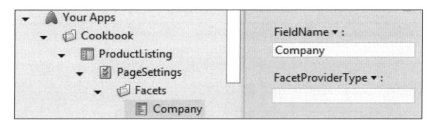

6. Select the **ProductListing** item. For the **ProductDataSource** component, set the **FacetRootItemId** property value to the created `Facets` folder item's **ItemId**. So, the data source will create filters based on the facets that we created in the `Facet` folder.

7. In the **ProductListing** item, add `FilterControl` to the `SearchPanel`. `Filters` placeholder and set **ID** as `FilterProducts`. On its **Facets** property, locate the **ProductDataSource** component's `Facet` property—{Binding `ProductDataSource.Facets`}.

8. Preview the page and see how the company filter control is rendered, as shown in the following image:

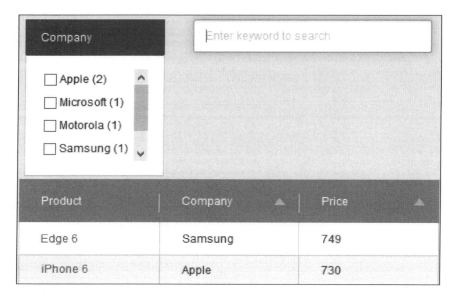

9. You will find that selecting the companies in the filter does not reflect on the product listing. To apply it, open the **ProductDataSource** rendering of the **ProductListing** item. Set the **SelectedFacets** property to {Binding FilterProducts. SelectedFacets} and try to apply the filter.

There's more...

We can also create multiple facets here such as Price or some specification of the product, and we can use different out-of-the-box **FacetProviders** such as **DimensionFacetProvider** and **UpdatedFacetProvider** based on our requirement. You can read more about facets and **FilterControl** at https://goo.gl/SNmmkX.

Building a custom form to bind product details using SPEAK

We achieved the listing, searching, and filtering of products without writing a single line of code using the SPEAK framework. In this recipe, we will create a form page to edit the selected product's details.

Getting ready

In the previous recipes, we created ListControl to render the product list, where we created a hyperlink in the **Product** column, as shown in the following image. So, clicking on it, we will now open a new form page to display and edit product details:

Product	Company	▲	Price
iPhone 5S	Apple		530

/sitecore/client/Your Apps/Cookbook/AddEditProduct?id={CB9C8524-4782-44DC-8E50-8422097EA

How to do it...

We will first create a custom form using the SPEAK application:

1. Using Sitecore Rocks in the core database, create a /sitecore/client/ Business Component Library/version 1/Templates/Branches/ Applications/**TaskPage** item—AddEditProduct—in the /sitecore/client/ Your Apps/Cookbook item.

2. You are already aware of how to add TextBox, Text, and other controls to **Layout Designer** of the item. Use the **RowPanel** rendering to add rows in order to add Label and TextBox for the **Title** field, as shown in the following image. Similarly, add `Price` and `Release Date` fields. For `Release Date`, we can use the **DatePicker** control:

Id	Rendering	Placeholder	Data Source
BackButton	BackButton	ApplicationHeader.Back	
SaveButton	Button	ApplicationHeader.Actions	
	ApplicationContentMl	ApplicationContent	
	GlobalFooter	GlobalFooter	
HeaderTitle	Text	ApplicationHeader.Title	
MainBorder	Border	ApplicationContent.Main	
RowTitle	RowPanel	MainBorder.Content	
ColumnTitleLabel	ColumnPanel	RowTitle.Content	
LabelTitle	Text	ColumnTitleLabel.Content	
ColumnTitleText	ColumnPanel	RowTitle.Content	
TextTitle	TextBox	ColumnTitleText.Content	

3. Now, open the application in the browser (`http://sitecorecookbook/ sitecore/client/Your%20Apps/Cookbook/AddEditProduct`), and you will find that a layout has been generated, as shown in the following image:

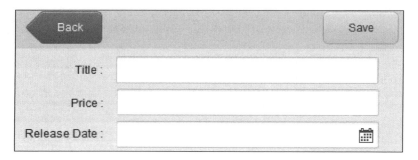

4. We have created a form; we will now create a controller to fetch the product details. In the `SitecoreCookbook` project, create a `Product` class in the `Models` folder and define its properties as follows:

```
public class Product
{
  public string Title { get; set; }
  public string Price { get; set; }
  public string ReleaseDate { get; set; }
}
```

5. In this project, create a `ProductController` controller in the `Controllers` folder and define a `GetProduct()` method, which expects `ItemId` as a query string parameter ID and will return a JSON object:

```
public ActionResult GetProduct()
{
    string productItemId = WebUtil.GetQueryString("id");
    Database db = Factory.GetDatabase("master");
    Item item = db.GetItem(new ID(productItemId));

    Product product = new Product();
    product.Title = item["Title"];
    product.Price = item["Price"];
    product.ReleaseDate = item["Release Date"].Replace("Z",
      "");
    return Json(product, JsonRequestBehavior.AllowGet);
}
```

6. Once we create this controller, the route will be set by default as `/api/sitecore/{controller}/{action}`. So, we can access it as follows:

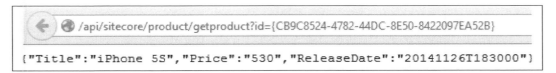

```
{"Title":"iPhone 5S","Price":"530","ReleaseDate":"20141126T183000"}
```

7. We will now create a custom **Page Code**, write code to fetch the product details from the preceding controller, and fill in the form. In the Visual Studio project, create a folder structure as `\sitecore\shell\client\YourApps\Cookbook\AddEditProduct`. Add a new Page Code component, as shown in the following image:

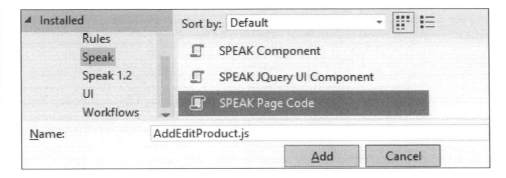

8. In this `AddEditProduct.js` file, you will find the `initialized()` function. Call the `getProduct()` function to fetch details from the preceding controller using an AJAX call. Once we get the product details in the JSON object, we will fill data in our form in the `fillForm()` function:

```
define(["sitecore"], function (Sitecore) {
  var AddEditProduct = Sitecore.Definitions.App.extend({
    initialized: function () {
      var id = Sitecore.Helpers.url.getQueryParameters(
        window.location.href)['id'];
      if (Sitecore.Helpers.id.isId(id)) {
        this.getProduct(id);
      }
    },

    getProduct: function (id) {
      var app = this;
      jQuery.ajax({
        type: "GET", dataType: "json",
        url: "/api/sitecore/Product/GetProduct",
        data: { 'id': id }, cache: false,
        success: function (data) {
          app.fillForm(data);
        },
        error: function () {
         alert("Error while fetching details!");
        }
      });
    },
    fillForm: function (data) {
      var app = this;
      app.TextTitle.set('text', data.Title);
      app.HeaderTitle.set('text', data.Title);
      app.TextPrice.set('text', data.Price);
      app.DateRelease.set('date', data.ReleaseDate);
    }
  });
  return AddEditProduct;
});
```

9. You have to link this JavaScript file to the page. For this, select the **AddEditProduct** item from Sitecore Explorer. Select the `Page Code` rendering and open the properties. Set the `PageCodeScriptFileName` property as `/sitecore/shell/client/YourApps/Cookbook/ProductListing/ProductListing.js`.

10. Now, open the **AddEditProduct** application by passing the item ID in the query string (`http://sitecorecookbook/sitecore/client/Your%20Apps/Cookbook/AddEditProduct?id={CB9C8524-4782-44DC-8E50-8422097EA52B}`). The page will look like the following image:

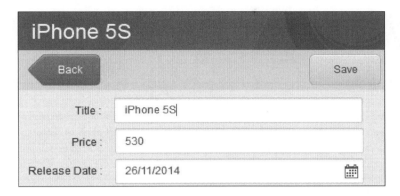

11. Using the same approach, we can save the modified product details. We can create a controller action to save product details. Clicking on the **Save** button, we can pass all the field details to the controller action using an AJAX request.

There's more...

In this recipe, we have bound the page form controls with product details using **SPEAK Page Code**. After understanding this, you should also be able to use **SPEAK Component** (view rendering); you can learn about it at `https://goo.gl/Y3ABM6`.

See also

SPEAK is a very vast framework, hence, we cannot cover it fully. You can learn more about it at `https://goo.gl/XBmN5F`.

Creating a custom editor tab in the Content Editor

The Sitecore Content Editor, by default, provides one editor tab—**Content**—for all items. If you select any `Folder` item, then we can get one additional tag, **Folder**, or, when you select any template, we get an additional tab of **Template Builder**.

Having a custom editor tab can be very useful if you want to show additional information to users. In this recipe, we will create a custom tab, **Product Details**, which will be visible on selecting any product category item. In this tab, we will show the product information (the Sheer UI application that we created in the previous recipe).

How to do it...

We will first create a custom editor tab:

1. From the desktop mode, switch to the `core` database. Open the Content Editor and select `/sitecore/Content/Applications/Content Editor/Editors/Items`. Create an item `Product Listing` using the `/sitecore/templates/Sitecore Client/Content editor/`**Editor** template, and fill in the details, as shown in the following image. Here, we set the URL of the XAML application created earlier in this chapter in the **Url** field:

2. Now, we will assign this editor tab to product category items. Open the Content Editor with the `master` database and select standard values of the `Product Category` template. In the ribbon, select the **Editors** button in the **Appearance** group from the **Configure** tab.

3. This will open a **Custom Editors** dialog, as shown in the following image. Select the **Product Listing** editor that we created:

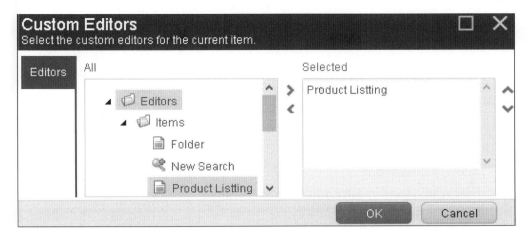

4. Now, you will see our custom **Product Listing** editor tab along with the **Content** tab for the product category items, as shown in the following image:

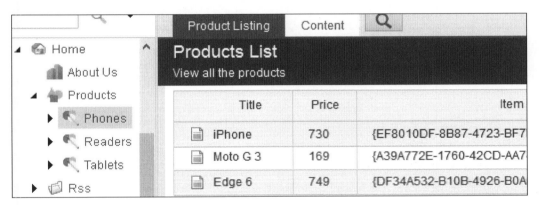

How it works...

You will be wondering how we can change the datasource dynamically based on the selected item. Sitecore has kept the provision to pass the item ID of the selected item to the editor in a query string with the ID key. Here, on clicking on any product category item, our editor URL will be `/sitecore/shell/default.aspx?xmlcontrol=ProductsListing&id=<item id>`. On clicking on any product category, we can show the products' list accordingly.

There's more...

Sitecore provides you with different types of built-in editors that are available under the /sitecore/Content/Applications/Content Editor/Editors folder in the core database. In this recipe, we created an Item Editor. There are other item editors available such as **Search**, **Folder**, and so on.

We can also use the following editors:

> ▶ **Layout Editor**: This can be the HTML viewer to show the HTML content of the sublayout and page designer to design and show sublayout controls. By default, both editors are hidden for all sublayouts.

> ▶ **Media Editor**: This can be a media folder, which is used to upload media files.

> ▶ **Template Editor**: This can be the template inheritance and template builder.

Creating a custom experience button using the Field Editor

The Experience Editor is an extremely efficient tool to edit content within Sitecore. Sitecore does not support in-line editing for Checkbox, Multilist, TreeList, and other fields, so it gets very difficult for content authors to find exact fields and items to modify them.

Just imagine if we could allow them to edit these fields not appearing anywhere on the page directly but still playing a role there. This is possible using the Field Editor, which we will use with the help of an experience button.

Getting ready

For this recipe, we will use the Site Root template, and we will make the Carousel Slides Multilist field (used to select multiple slides) editable from the Experience Editor.

How to do it...

We will first create a custom Field Editor button:

1. Open Sitecore in desktop mode and change the database to core. Open the Content Editor and select the /sitecore/Content/Applications/WebEdit/Custom Experience Buttons item. In it, create a Field Editor button, Product, using the /sitecore/templates/System/WebEdit/**Field Editor Button** template. Set values of the **Header**, **Icon**, **Tooltip**, and **Fields** fields. Enter a pipe-separated list of fields that you want to make editable in the **Fields** field, as shown in the following image:

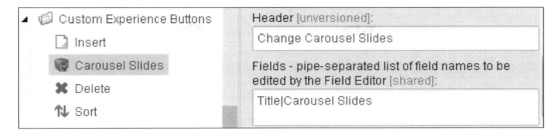

2. Now, go back to the `master` database, and select the `Carousel` rendering. In its **Experience Editor Buttons** (or Page Editor buttons for older Sitecore versions) field, choose the Field Editor button that you created in the previous step:

3. Open the `Home` page in the Experience Editor (or a page where you used the Carousel rendering) and select the **Carousel** rendering on it. You will find a new button, **Change Carousel Slides**, on the floating bar, as shown in the following image:

4. Clicking on the highlighted button will open the Field Editor dialog, which will allow us to edit preconfigured fields of the item itself, as shown in the following image:

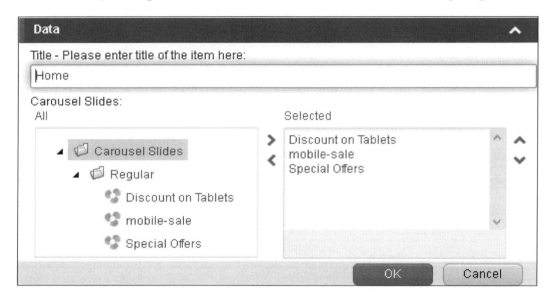

There's more...

The Experience Editor provides you with different types of buttons on the component floating bar to give flexibility to content owners. All the following types of buttons can be found in the `core` database under the `/sitecore/Content/Applications/WebEdit` item:

▶ Common Field Buttons

▶ Custom Experience Buttons

▶ Default Placeholder Buttons

▶ Default Rendering Buttons

▶ Edit Frame Buttons

Creating a custom rule to validate item fields

Being developers, we should provide an efficient interface to validate all information. Sitecore provides out-of-the-box validators that work both on the client side and server side, and also flexibility to create our own custom validators.

In this recipe, we will create an `Employee Information` form. Here, we will use some out-of-the-box validators to validate the required field, integer, and email. We will also create a custom validator to validate `Employee Joining Date` and `Relieving Date`.

How to do it...

We will first create a template with the required fields to achieve this recipe:

1. Create an `Employee` template with fields such as `Employee ID`, `Employee Name`, `Email Address`, `Date of Joining`, and `Date of Relieving`.

2. Now we will assign some out-of-the-box validators to some fields. From the field editor, select the **Employee ID** field in the **Validation Rules** section. In the **Validator Bar** field, select the **Required** and **Is Integer** field rules, as shown in the the following image:

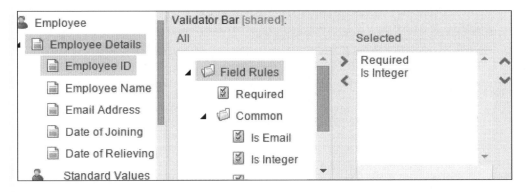

3. Similarly, for **Employee Name**, select the **Required** rule. For **Email Address**, select the **Required**, **Must be Lower Case**, and **Is Email** rules.

   Now we will create a custom validator. In the `SitecoreCookbook` project, create a `StartEndDateValidator` class in the `Validators` folder, and inherit it from the `Sitecore.Data.Validators.StandardValidator` class.

4. Sitecore expects the validator class to be serializable, so mark it with the `Serializable` attribute.

5. Define constructors of the validator class as follows:

```
public StartEndDateValidator() { }

public StartEndDateValidator(SerializationInfo info,
   StreamingContext context)
   : base(info, context){}
```

6. Override the `Evaluate()` method of the `StandardValidator` class as follows:

```
protected override ValidatorResult Evaluate()
{
  Item item = base.GetItem();
  string fieldStart = this.Parameters["StartDate"];
  string fieldEnd = this.Parameters["EndDate"];
  DateField startDate = item.Fields[fieldStart];
  DateField endDate = item.Fields[fieldEnd];

  if (startDate.DateTime != DateTime.MinValue &&
    startDate.DateTime > endDate.DateTime) {
    this.Text = String.Format(fieldStart + " ({0}) can't be
      greater than " + fieldEnd + " ({1})",
      startDate.DateTime, endDate.DateTime);
    return ValidatorResult.CriticalError;
  }
  return ValidatorResult.Valid;
}
```

7. Override the `GetMaxValidatorResult()` method and the `Name` property as follows:

```
protected override ValidatorResult GetMaxValidatorResult()
{
  return GetFailedResult(ValidatorResult.CriticalError);
}

public override string Name {
  get { return "Start Date cannot be greater than End
    Date";}
}
```

8. Register this validator in Sitecore by creating a new **Validation Rule** under `/sitecore/system/Settings/Validation Rules/Field Rules/Cookbook` named `Relieving Date should be greater than Joining Date` and fill in the information as follows. Our custom validator class expects two parameters, **StartDate** and **EndDate**. Pass the **Date of Joining** and **Date of Relieving** field names, as shown in the following image:

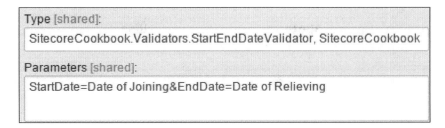

Type [shared]:

SitecoreCookbook.Validators.StartEndDateValidator, SitecoreCookbook

Parameters [shared]:

StartDate=Date of Joining&EndDate=Date of Relieving

9. Select the **Date of Relieving** field of the `Employee` template. Select the previously created rule in the **Quick Action Bar**, **Validation Button**, and **Validation Bar** fields.

10. Create a content item using the `Employee` template and fill in some invalid information; it will show validation messages in the Validation Bar, as shown in the following image:

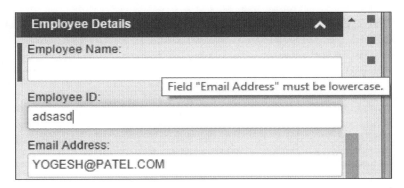

Here, you will see two types of validation bars. On the left-hand side of the **Employee Name** field, you can find a Validation Bar indicated by a vertical red bar. On the upper right-hand side, you can find the Validation Bar details indicated with red square icons. Both these bars show detailed information when hovered over as a tooltip. Additionally, the following image shows how our custom validator works:

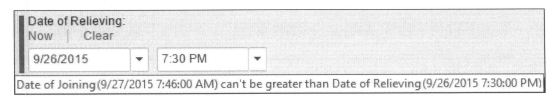

How it works...

In the custom validator class that we created, we passed two parameters, `StartDate` and `EndDate`, with the **Date of Joining** and **Date of Relieving** values, which are the field names that we want to validate. We could have created the validator without passing parameters by hardcoding these field names in the class. However, we used parameters to make this validator class generic. So, we can use the same validator for other `DateTime` fields as well, by just registering a new validator and passing different field names as parameters.

There's more...

In this recipe, you learned that by selecting validation rules in the Validator Bar field of the Template Field, as shown in step 2, we can show validations in a Validator Bar.

In the same way, by selecting validation rules in the Quick Action Bar field of the Template Field, we can show validation details of multiple items at the same time in the gutter area of the Content Editor tree list, as shown in the following image. We can see this bar by switching on the **Validation Rules** gutter:

By selecting validation rules in the **Validate Button** field of the Template Field, we can show validation details of all the fields at a time. To check this, select any item. In the ribbon, select the **Validation Button** in the **Proofing** section from the **Review** tab. This will open a new dialog showing validation results of all the fields of the item, as shown in the following image:

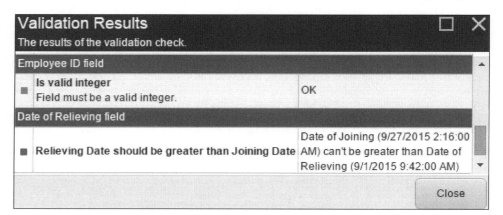

Creating a custom sorting routine to sort the content tree items

Sorting content items is a very useful feature for content authors when they have to work with a number of items in a common parent. Sitecore provides some out-of-the-box sorting rules such as **Created By**, **Display Name**, **Logical**, **Reverse**, **Updated**, and others.

However, sometimes content authors might need a custom rule of sorting. For example, they created a news items with the *dd-MM-yyyy* format, so content authors getting an invalid order of news items by applying out-of-the-box rules. In this recipe, you will learn how to create a custom sorting rule to sort by the News Date field.

Getting Ready

Create some news items under the 2015 folder, as shown on the left-hand side of the following image. These should have the News Date field with the DateTime field type. Now, we will achieve a sort order of the content items shown on the right-hand side of the image:

Default Order	Expected Order
⊿ 📄 2015	⊿ 📄 2015
📄 04-12-2015	📄 21-01-2015
📄 21-01-2015	📄 21-09-2015
📄 21-09-2015	📄 04-12-2015

How to do it...

We will create a class to make a sorting routine:

1. In the SitecoreCookbook project, create a DateFieldComparer class in the Data folder, and inherit it from the Sitecore.Data.Comparers. ExtractedKeysComparer class.

2. Override the DoCompare() method of the base class as follows:

```
static string DateField = "News Date";
protected override int DoCompare(Item item1, Item item2)
{
    DateTime date1 = GetDateTime(item1);
    DateTime date2 = GetDateTime(item2);
```

```
      return date1.CompareTo(date2);
    }
    private DateTime GetDateTime(Item item)
    {
      return DateUtil.ParseDateTime(item[DateField],
        DateTime.MinValue);
    }
```

3. Override the abstract methods `ExtractKeys()` and `CompareKeys()` as follows:

```
public override IKey ExtractKey(Item item)
{
  return (IKey)new KeyObj() {
    Item = item,
    Key = (object)GetDateTime(item)
  };
}
protected override int CompareKeys(IKey key1, IKey key2)
{
  return
    ((DateTime)key1.Key).CompareTo((DateTime)key2.Key);
}
```

4. Register this sorting routine class in Sitecore in `/sitecore/system/Settings/ Subitems Sorting`, as shown in the following image:

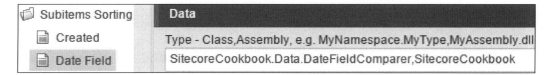

5. Now we will apply this custom routine to the parent folder item. From the Content Editor, right-click on the parent item. In the **Sorting** menu item, select **Subitems Sorting** (or from the ribbon in the **Home** tab, click on the **Sorting** section). This will open the **Sort order of Subitems** dialog, where you will find the previously created **Date Field** routine in the **Sorting** drop-down menu, as shown in the following image:

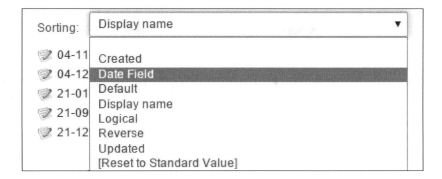

6. Select the **Date Field** routine; you will find that all the content items got sorted in the dialog. Saving this setting will reflect it on all the children in the content tree.

How it works...

Once we set the rules to the parent, all existing, newly created, and updated children will follow these rules. If you mention values in the **SortOrder** field (in the **Appearance** field section), they will override the parent sorting rules. Once we have applied a sort order to subitems, all the newly created items will get a relevant sorted place automatically. The same sort order will be reflected on the Experience Editor navigation bar and through APIs such as `item.GetChildren()` as well.

 It is always recommended to apply subitem sorting on standard values of the parent item template. Also, keep in mind that the **SortOrder** field is going to overrule any child sorting rules. You can set values to blank to get the child sorting back to effect.

Creating a custom field to save the date time with time zones

Different fields in a template have a data type that determines which control the Content Editor will provide for interactive manipulation of the associated data. Sitecore provides an extensive set of both simple and complex standard data types such as Single Line Text, Rich Text, Number, Image, Multilist, TreeList, and many others. Some requirements may not get fulfilled by these primitive data types and you may need to create custom fields.

Let's consider that we have a requirement to provide a time zone selection along with date time, which can be used to show upcoming events on different time zones. Sitecore provides a simple date time control without supporting time zones. In this recipe, we will create a custom field to fulfil this requirement.

How to do it...

We will first create the field class:

1. In the `SitecoreCookbook` project, create a `DateTimeWithTimeZone` class in the `Fields` folder. Inherit it from the `Sitecore.Web.UI.HtmlControls.Control` class and the `Sitecore.Shell.Applications.ContentEditor.IContentField` interface.

2. We need to show different standard field types such as `DateTimePicker` to select date time and `Combobox` to select the time zone, so declare them as follows. We will save all the fields' values combined in a common field with `fieldSeparator`:

```
private DateTimePicker _picker;
private Combobox _combo;
private string _fieldSeparator = "|";
```

3. Override the `OnInit()` method of the `Control` to load these standard fields. Here, we have a `FillTimeZones()` method to fill `Combobox`, which you can find from the code bundle provided with this book:

```
protected override void OnInit(EventArgs e)
{
  _picker = new DateTimePicker();
  _picker.ID = this.ID + "_picker";
  _picker.Changed += ((p0, p1) => this.SetModified());
  this.Controls.Add(_picker);

  _combo = new Combobox();
  _combo.ID = this.ID + "_combo";
  _combo.OnChange+= ((p0, p1) => this.SetModified());
  this.Controls.Add(_combo);
  FillTimeZones();
  base.OnInit(e);
}
```

4. Create a `SetModified()` method to inform `ClientPage` of any changes happening in the standard field value:

```
protected void SetModified()
{
  Sitecore.Context.ClientPage.Modified = true;
}
```

5. Here, the `IContentField` interface is expected to implement the `SetValue()` and `GetValue()` methods. Implement the `SetValue()` method, which will be invoked while loading the item to set the field values:

```
public void SetValue(string value)
{
  if (_picker == null || _combo == null)
    return;

  string[] dateTime = value.Split(new char[] {
    _fieldSeparator }, System.StringSplitOptions.None);
  if (dateTime.Length > 0)
    _picker.Value =
      DateUtil.IsoDateToServerTimeIsoDate(dateTime[0]);
  if (dateTime.Length == 2) {
    _combo.Value = dateTime[1];
    foreach (var listitem in _combo.Items) {
      if (listitem.Value == _combo.Value)
        listitem.Selected = true;
    }
  }
}
```

6. Implement the `GetValue()` method, which will be invoked while saving the item to store the field value to the database:

```
public string GetValue()
{
  if (this._picker != null)
    return _picker.Value + _fieldSeparator + _combo.Value;
  return "";
}
```

7. Now, we will register this custom field in Sitecore. Open the Content Editor with the `core` database. Create a new `Custom Types` folder in the `/sitecore/system/Field types` item. In this, create a new `Datetime With TimeZone` item using the `/sitecore/templates/System/Templates/Template field type` template and set value of fields, as shown in the following image:

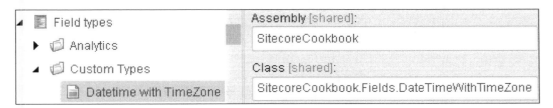

8. Open the Content Editor with the `master` database. Create an `Event` template and a field with the `Datetime With TimeZone` type, as shown in the following image:

9. Create content items based on this template; you will find our field working, as shown in the following image:

10. Now, we will add menu buttons to this field in order to fetch the current date time and clear field values. Open the Content Editor with the `core` database. Create a `Menu` folder in the custom field item that we created—`/sitecore/system/Field types/Custom Types/Datetime with TimeZone`. In this folder, create the `Clear` and `Now` menu items using the `/sitecore/templates/System/Menus/Menu item` template:

11. To handle these commands in the form of messages, override the `HandleMessage()` method of the `Control` class as follows:

```
public override void HandleMessage(Message message)
{
  base.HandleMessage(message);
  switch (message.Name){
    case "datetimezone:today": SetValue(
      System.DateTime.Now.ToString("yyyyMMddTHHmmss"));
      break;
    case "datetimezone:clear":
      SetValue("");
      break;
  }
}
```

12. Now, if you select the **Event** content item, you will find that these menu items have been added at the top of the field.

How it works...

There are two possible ways of creating a custom field in Sitecore:

  ▶ Inheriting the field class from the `Sitecore.Web.UI.HtmlControls.Control` class and creating HTML objects and functionalities inside it, which we implemented in this recipe

  ▶ Inheriting the field class from the Sitecore control itself, for example, Multilist, TreeList, or checklist, and performing further customizations on it

We can define, initialize, and add these controls to `HtmlControls.Control.Controls` by overriding the `OnInit()` method, which we did in step 3. You can also use the `OnLoad()` method to change control values. It's advisable to create or initialize controls during the first load, in other terms, when the `IsEvent` property of `Sitecore.Context.ClientPage` is set to `false`. You can use `OnPreRender()` and `OnRender()` methods to change control data and rendering respectively.

Sitecore stores any kind of field's values in plain text. So, while saving the multiple field values, we merged their values with the separator, pipe. You can see the preceding field's raw value, as shown in the following image. (To check raw values, select the item from the Content Editor. From the ribbon, select the **Raw values** checkbox in the **View** tab.)

Sitecore manages the `Sitecore.Context.ClientPage.Modified` property to indicate whether the item fields are changed or not. Here, in the `SetModified()` method, when we find that any value of the field gets changed, we set the modified property value to true so that before leaving the modified item in the Content Editor, Sitecore will check with the user whether to save or cancel the changes.

Making fields editable from the Experience Editor

To make this field editable from the Experience Editor, you can create `WebEdit` buttons using the `/sitecore/templates/System/WebEdit/WebEdit Button` template in the same way as we created **Menu** buttons, as shown in the following image:

This will add the `WebEdit` button to the floating bar, as shown in the following image. By clicking on this button (using a custom command), we can open our custom dialog to change date time with a time zone. You can refer to the example of a standard field date time to implement it yourself. You can find its configurations at `/sitecore/system/Field types/Simple Types/Datetime`.

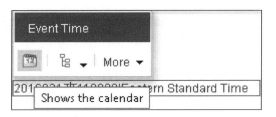

There's more...

When you render this field on a page, it will get rendered with its raw value such as `20160130T102525|Eastern Standard Time`. To show a valid date time value, we need to get strongly typed access for this field value, which requires creating additional mapping classes.

You can find the mapping classes for the preceding field from the code bundle provided with this book. Add the following listed files from the code bundle to the mentioned folders in the `SitecoreCookbook` project:

Filename (in the code bundle)	File location in the project
`DateTimeWithTimeZoneField.cs`	`\Fields`
`GetDateTimeZoneFieldValue.cs`	`\Pipelines`
`SitecoreCookbook.RenderDateTimeZone.config`	`\App_Config\Include\Cookbook`

The `DateTimeWithTimeZoneField` class will provide you with a strongly typed value of our custom field. You are required to map it in the `\App_Config\FieldTypes.config` file. In this file, you will find that all the Sitecore field classes have already been mapped.

```
<fieldType name="Datetime With TimeZone"
  type="SitecoreCookbook.Fields.DateTimeWithTimeZoneField,
  SitecoreCookbook" />
```

In the `SitecoreCookbook.RenderDateTimeZone.config` file, we registered the `GetDateTimeZoneFieldValue` class so that while rendering our custom field using the `@Html.Sitecore().Field()` or `FieldRenderer.Render()` methods, this class will get invoked and return a strongly typed value of this field using the `DateTimeWithTimeZoneField` class.

4
Leveraging the Sitecore Backend

In this chapter, we will cover the backbone topics of the Sitecore architecture. Sitecore's flexible and robust architecture enables you to extend any portion of its backend platform architecture to fulfil the requirements. In this chapter, we will cover the following topics:

- ► Working with multiple sites
- ► Customizing pipelines to achieve a custom 404 page
- ► Creating a custom event handler to auto-publish on an item save
- ► Achieving a site-specific URL pattern for a multisite environment
- ► Initializing hooks to subscribe events to prepare an audit trail
- ► Creating jobs to accomplish long-running operations
- ► Using a scheduling agent to delete older item versions
- ► Scheduling database tasks

Introduction

As we have seen in the previous chapters, everybody will feel that Sitecore is clearly designed with extensibility as a high priority. Developers can extend the Sitecore backend architecture using a variety of techniques. We can have multiple approaches to achieve one customization; it's just a matter of which one is the best suited.

Sitecore uses the `Sitecore.config` file almost like a dependency injection container. Most of the backend operations are defined in this file and are configurable and extendable as per requirement. You can override almost any feature defined in this configuration file such as pipelines, processors, handlers, agents, events, providers, event handlers, hooks, and others. You will also learn how to use a patch configuration file to override the `Sitecore.config` configurations.

Apart from this, we will also cover some more techniques of extending the Sitecore architecture in the next chapter.

Working with multiple sites

Sitecore is capable of allowing multiple different websites in a single installation, though the basic Sitecore installation contains only one physical website (a Sitecore instance) and contains a few virtual websites (managed by Sitecore internally) such as shell, login, admin, website, scheduler, system, and publisher.

The website definitions, including their properties, are defined in `Sitecore.config`. The site resolver determines the incoming HTTP requests and assigns an appropriate site based on the defined hostname.

In this recipe, we will create multiple sites that can be configured on both **content management** (**CM**) and **content delivery** (**CD**) Sitecore instances. We will also explore how to configure site-specific cache sizes and clear an HTML cache for all sites.

How to do it...

We will first achieve the creation of multiple sites in Sitecore:

1. In `Sitecore.config`, go to the `<sites>` section and you will see the following `<site>` node. Copy the `website` site node, paste it twice in the preceding line, and call it CM and CD site nodes respectively:

```
<site name="website" virtualFolder="/" physicalFolder="/" domain="extranet"
    rootPath="/sitecore/content" startItem="/home" database="master"
    allowDebug="true" enablePreview="true" enableWebEdit="true" />
```

2. First, let's configure a CM site node with the following properties and define other properties as per your requirement:

Property	Value
name	SitecoreStaging
hostname	staging.sitecorecookbook.com
rootPath	/sitecore/Content

Property	Value
startItem	/home
database	master
enablePreview	true
enableWebEdit	true

3. Now, let's configure the CD site node with the following properties and define other properties as per your requirement:

Property	Value
name	SitecoreLive
hostname	www.sitecorecookbook.com
rootPath	/sitecore/Content
startItem	/home
database	web
cacheHtml	true

4. In the `Sitecore.config` file, assign different cache sizes to different sites in the `<cacheSizes />` section:

```
<cacheSizes>
  <sites>
    <SitecoreLive>
      <html>10MB</html>
      <registry>0</registry>
      <viewState>0</viewState>
      <xsl>5MB</xsl>
    </SitecoreLive>
  </sites>
</cacheSizes>
```

5. You should be aware that on each publish, Sitecore clears the HTML cache on CD servers, so you will need to configure multiple sites to clear the HTML cache after each publish. For this, you need to mention your sites in `publish:end:remote` events as follows:

```
<event name="publish:end:remote">
  <handler type="Sitecore.Publishing.HtmlCacheClearer, Sitecore.Kernel"
           method="ClearCache">
    <sites hint="list">
      <site>website</site>
      <site>SitecoreLive</site>
      <site>Demo</site>
    </sites>
  </handler>
</event>
```

How it works...

Now you have multiple sites configured in your Sitecore instance. Using steps 2 and 3, you configured CM and CD sites respectively. The CM site should have Context Database as *master*, while all production sites should have Context Database as *web*. We created two sites here; in the same way, we can create multiple websites with a different `name`, `hostname`, `rootPath`, `startItem`, and other properties.

 All the new sites created in Sitecore must be configured above the `website` site node, otherwise requests with the unresolved site will be assigned the `website` site.

In Sitecore, sites are resolved by the `Sitecore.Pipelines.HttpRequest.SiteResolver` processor in the `<HttpRequestBegin />` pipeline. For each site in the `<sites>` list, Sitecore compares the `hostname` attribute (which may include wildcards) with the incoming URL. If multiple hostnames are pointing to a single site, then we can define multiple hosts pipe-separated in the `hostname` attribute for a site, as shown in the following line:

```
<site name="charity" hostname="charity.mydomain.com|donation.mydomain.com" />
```

Sitecore resolves the context site if the requested URL satisfies any of the following three criteria:

- When the `hostname` attribute of any site matches the incoming URL
- When the `hostname` attribute is empty and `virtualFolder` attribute of any site matches the incoming URL
- When the `name` attribute matches the `sc_site` query string parameter in the URL

In step 4, we assigned a site-specific cache size. We can tune it based on our website content and resource availability. This can play a good role in website performance.

By default, when any publishing occurs, Sitecore clears the HTML cache on the CD server by triggering the `publish:end:remote` event. While using multiple websites on Sitecore, we should define our multiple sites here so that on publishing, all sites will clear their HTML cache. However, this approach comes with a disadvantage: publishing of an item of one site leads to the clearing of the HTML cache of other sites. To overcome this issue, we can also do site-specific HTML cache clearing, which you will learn in *Chapter 7, Workflow and Publishing*.

There's more...

You learned that to add a site, we have to configure it in the `Sitecore.config` file. This means that the Sitecore instance will get restarted.

To overcome such a situation, write your custom site resolver to manage sites from a source other than `Sitecore.config`, that is, we can configure sites in Sitecore as an item itself. Read more about configuring sites at `http://goo.gl/D1hnbZ`. The **Multiple Sites Manager** module is already available on Sitecore Marketplace; you can install it and enjoy the power of multisites (`http://goo.gl/YHCVkC`).

 We can also add custom attributes to Sitecore sites, which we can retrieve using `Site.Properties[<property name>]`. You will see how to use it later in this chapter while achieving a site-specific URL patterns.

Customizing pipelines to achieve a custom 404 page

When we request for a web page that does not exist in the site, for example, `http://sitecorecookbook/test-page/`, Sitecore will redirect you to its default document not found page—`notfound.aspx` with a 302 HTTP status code. Here, we expect that the requested page itself should show page not found content with a 404 status without any redirection.

In this recipe, we will achieve this expected behavior by customizing the `<httpRequestBegin>` and `<httpRequestProcessed>` pipelines.

Getting ready

Create a content item, 404-Page, in side the Home item with Title and Body fields. Make sure that you have added *Title and Body* rendering on it. When the requested page does not exist in our site, we will show this page to the user with the 404 status.

How to do it...

We will first create a processor class to show 404-Page:

1. In the SitecoreCookbook project, create a PageNotFoundResolver class in the Pipelines folder and inherit it from the Sitecore.Pipelines.HttpRequest. HttpRequestProcessor class.

2. Override its Process() method as follows. Here, for invalid item requests, we will assign 404-Page to the Context item. For all other requests such as valid physical files or valid Sitecore content items, we will skip the further execution of our processor:

```
public override void Process(HttpRequestArgs args)
{
  string filePath =
    HttpContext.Current.Server.MapPath(args.Url.FilePath);

  if (IsValidItem()
    || args.LocalPath.StartsWith("/sitecore")
    || File.Exists(filePath))
    return;

  Context.Item = Get404Page();
  if (Context.Item != null)
    Sitecore.Context.Items["Is404Page"] = "true";
}
```

3. The preceding code requires the IsValidItem() method to check whether the Context item is valid or not. Create this method with the following code. Here, we consider that an item is valid only if it exists, if the requested language version exists on it, and layout details are also set:

```
protected virtual bool IsValidItem()
{
  if (Context.Item == null
    || Context.Item.Versions.Count == 0)
    return false;
  if (Context.Item.Visualization.Layout == null)
    return false;
  return true;
}
```

4. Create the `Get404Page()` method to get our created `404-Page` content item as follows:

```
private Item Get404Page()
{
    string itemPath = Context.Site.StartPath + "/404-Page";
    return Context.Database.GetItem(itemPath);
}
```

Now we will register this processor class in the `<httpRequestBegin>` pipeline after the `ItemResolver` processor.

5. From **Visual Studio**, create the `\App_Config\Include\Cookbook` folder. In this, create a patch configuration file—`SitecoreCookbook.CustomPageNotFound.config`—as follows:

```
<?xml version="1.0"?>
<configuration
    xmlns:patch="http://www.sitecore.net/xmlconfig/">
    <sitecore>
        <pipelines>
            <httpRequestBegin>
                <processor type=
                    "SitecoreCookbook.Pipelines.PageNotFoundResolver,
                    SitecoreCookbook"
                    patch:after="processor[@type=
                    'Sitecore.Pipelines.HttpRequest.ItemResolver,
                    Sitecore.Kernel']">
                </processor>
            </httpRequestBegin>
        </pipelines>
    </sitecore>
</configuration>
```

6. Now, request a page that does not exist, such as `http://sitecorecookbook/test-page`. You will find that it will show the content of `404-Page` but with a 200 status:

Now, we will show a 404 status code instead of 200 using following steps:

7. Create another `Set404Status` processor class and inherit it from `HttpRequestProcessor`, the same as the previously created class.

8. Override the `Process()` method to write 404 status code for page not found requests only, which we can identify using **Request cache**—`Sitecore.Context.Items[]` defined in `PageNotFoundResolver`:

```
public override void Process(HttpRequestArgs args)
{
  if (Sitecore.Context.Items["Is404Page"] != null
    && Sitecore.Context.Items["Is404Page"].ToString() ==
    "true") {
    HttpContext.Current.Response.StatusCode = 404;
    HttpContext.Current.Response.TrySkipIisCustomErrors =
      true;
  }
}
```

9. Open the `SitecoreCookbook.CustomPageNotFound.config` file; in the `<configuration/sitecore/pipelines>` node, register this processor in the `<httpRequestProcessed>` pipeline as follows:

```
<httpRequestProcessed>
  <processor type="SitecoreCookbook.Pipelines.Set404Status,
    SitecoreCookbook" />
</httpRequestProcessed>
```

10. Now, preview the same page; you will find that `404-Page` now returns 404 status code:

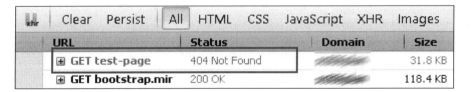

How it works...

An operation to be performed in multiple steps can be carried out using the pipeline system, where each individual step is defined as a processor. Data processed from one processor is then carried to the next processor in arguments. You can find default pipelines from the Sitecore.config file under the <pipelines> node (which are system processes) and the <processors> node (which are UI processes):

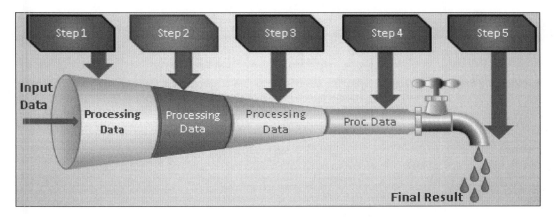

The <httpRequestBegin> pipeline is the heart of the Sitecore HTTP request execution process. It defines different processors to resolve the site, device, language, item, and layout sequentially. In our case, to check whether the requested item exists or not, the site, language, and item should be resolved before that. So, we added our custom processor— PageNotFoundResolver—after ItemResolver in the <httpRequestBegin> pipeline using the patch:after attribute in the patch configuration file. The <httpRequestProcessed> pipeline is invoked before the page response is sent to the browser. So, we created a custom processor—Set404Status—to set 404 HTTP status code for custom page not found requests. Read more about the <httpRequestBegin> pipeline at http://goo.gl/nM2kyv.

 To cancel the further execution of the current pipeline, you can call the AbortPipeline() method of the argument passed to the Process() method of the processor, for example, args.AbortPipeline().

Patch configuration

Instead of creating the `SitecoreCookbook.CustomPageNotFound.config` file in step 5, we could have also added this processor directly to `Sitecore.config` on an appropriate location, but it is advisable to keep custom configuration separate from Sitecore configuration, which is called distributed configuration or patch configuration. When Sitecore starts, it traverses the `/App_Config/Include` folder and its subfolder recursively, merges all the `*.config` files, and produces the resulting XML document, which can be found at `http://sitecorecookbook/sitecore/admin/showconfig.aspx`, where you can find our custom processor below `ItemResolver` (because of the `patch:after` attribute), as shown in the following image:

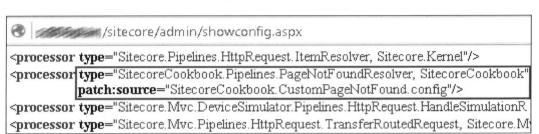

Configuration patching allows us to add, replace, and delete existing settings, properties, and configuration nodes. Learn more about it from from `https://goo.gl/fJOKrj`.

 Sitecore configuration nodes must be placed inside `/configuration/sitecore` path of the configuration file.

There's more...

A page request traverses through other pipelines as well such as `<preProcessRequest>`, `<renderLayout>`, and `<httpRequestEnd>`. We can achieve many requirements such as 301/302 redirections, language fallback, `sitemap.xml`, and `robots.txt` by customizing these pipelines. It's also possible to create our own pipelines. You can read more at `https://goo.gl/5JYlZV`.

You can monitor the performance and utilizations of all the Sitecore pipelines and processors used solutions using the Sitecore pipeline profiling tool (`http://sitecorecookbook/sitecore/admin/pipelines.aspx`). To enable this, enable the `\App_Config\Include\Sitecore.PipelineProfiling.config.disable` file (by removing the `.disable` extension).

Creating a custom event handler to auto-publish on an item save

Event handlers play a big role in Sitecore to intercept events being executed. When any event is raised, it executes multiple event handlers sequentially, which is the same that a pipeline does with its processors. We can create our own event handler to apply custom logic to events such as an item getting created, saved, published, or deleted, and many others.

Consider a case where our application pulls a new press release from external resources. It creates and saves a news item in Sitecore, which should get published immediately without delay. Otherwise, consider a case where we have to export the details to an external data source immediately. In this recipe, you will learn how to intercept events to publish an item after it is saved.

Getting ready

Create a `News` template with `Title`, `Body`, `Release Date`, and `Show in Menu` fields to display news on the site. Add one checkbox field—`Auto Publish`. So, any saved news item should get published automatically if this field is checked.

How to do it...

We will first create an `EventHandler` class, which will intercept an item-saving event and publish the item:

1. In the `SitecoreCookbook` project, create the `ItemPublishEventHandler` class in the `Handlers` folder. Create the `OnItemSaved()` method, which we will trigger when any item gets saved. Here, we can get the saved item from the first argument from `EventArgs`. When the item is of the `master` database and its `Auto Publish` field is checked, we will publish it:

```
protected void OnItemSaved(object sender, EventArgs args)
{
  if ((args != null)) {
    Item item = Event.ExtractParameter<Item>(args, 0);
    if (item != null && item.Database.Name == "master") {
      if (item["Auto Publish"] == "1") {
        using(new EditContext(item)) {
          item.Fields["Auto Publish"].Value = "0";
        }
        Database[] targetDBs = GetTargetDatabases();
```

```
            PublishManager.PublishItem(item, targetDBs,
              item.Languages, false, false);
          }
        }
      }
    }
```

2. Create the `GetTargetDatabases()` method to get publishing targets:

```
private static Database[] GetTargetDatabases()
{
  Item publishTarget = Client.GetItemNotNull(
    "/sitecore/system/publishing targets");
  List<Database> db = new List<Database>();
  foreach (Item item in publishTarget.Children)
    db.Add(Factory.GetDatabase(item["Target Database"]));
  return db.ToArray();
}
```

We have created a custom event handler. Now, we will register it in the `item:saved` event.

3. In the `\App_Config\Include\Cookbook` folder, create the `SitecoreCookbook.AutoPublishEventHandlers.config` file to register this handler as follows:

```
<sitecore>
  <events>
    <event name="item:saved">
      <handler type=
        "SitecoreCookbook.Handlers.ItemPublishEventHandler,
        SitecoreCookbook" method="OnItemSaved" />
    </event>
  </events>
</sitecore>
```

4. Create a news item manually or using an API; tick the `Auto Publish` field and set other field values. Now, on saving the item, you will find that it gets published automatically.

How it works...

Events in Sitecore are similar to events in other systems. This means that an action triggers an event and there can be multiple handlers to handle the event. The event handlers are similar to pipeline handlers that you learned in the previous recipe.

Sitecore uses the .NET framework's event model to handle its events. This means that you can use the `Event.ExtractParameter()` method to extract parameters from the `EventArgs` object parameter. To use this method, you must know the position of the parameter that you want to extract. Here, we will get an item from the first parameter using the following code:

```
Item item = Event.ExtractParameter<Item>(args, 0)
```

To get rid of this parameter numbering, you can cast event arguments to relevant event argument classes such as `ItemSavedEventArgs` for a saved event using the following code:

```
ItemSavedEventArgs saveArgs = args as ItemSavedEventArgs;
Item item = saveArgs.Item;
```

 While working with custom event handlers for a common event, you can create all handler methods in a single class. This will help maintain them easily.

There's more...

The `item:saved` event is raised after the item actually gets committed. So, in case you want to check some validations on the item name or any other fields, you can create a custom event handler in the `item:saving` event, which gets triggered before saving an item. Sitecore has many events such as `item:deleting`, `item:deleted`, `item:copying`, `item:copied`, `item:moving`, and `item:moved`.

All such events have remote events as well. These remote events are executed on remote servers using the Sitecore **event queue**. (See how the event queue works at `https://goo.gl/DfuLWo`.) Let's consider a real-time example. We have two or more CM servers. On one server, one item gets updated, and then the `item:saved` event is triggered on this server. Now, for the same item, the `item:saved:remote` event will get executed on all remote servers to update the cache for the saved item.

You can learn more about Sitecore events at `http://goo.gl/eSTf0v`.

See also

You can also create custom remote events while working on multiple Sitecore instances in a cluster. Refer to the post on how to create remote events at `http://goo.gl/USG2VY`.

Achieving a site-specific URL pattern for a multisite environment

Sitecore provides the **LinkProvider** class, which contains different properties to achieve different URL patterns such as adding a `.aspx` extension, location of language, language embedding, lowercase URLs, and so on. The **LinkManager** in Sitecore can contain multiple LinkProviders (multiple URL patterns), and any one LinkProvider can be set as the default. The URL configuration set in the default link provider will be applied to all the sites' URLs.

Consider a case where you are working on a multisite solution, and different websites need different URL patterns. One site is built with a single language, so its URLs will not contain language information; other multilingual sites may need language as `filePath` or `queryString`. In this recipe, we will allow the Sitecore solution to apply a website-specific URL pattern by creating a custom LinkProvider.

How to do it...

Let's first configure multiple URL configurations (link providers):

1. In the `\App_Config\Include\Cookbook` folder, create a patch configuration file named `SitecoreCookbook.MultisiteLinkProvider.config`. In the `<configuration/sitecore>` node, add different providers `link-pattern-1`, `link-pattern-2`, and so on with different URL configurations:

```
<linkManager>
  <providers>
    <add name="link-pattern-1" type=
      "Sitecore.Links.LinkProvider, Sitecore.Kernel"
      addAspxExtension="false"
      languageLocation="filePath" />
    <add name="link-pattern-2" type=
      "Sitecore.Links.LinkProvider, Sitecore.Kernel"
      addAspxExtension="true"
      languageLocation="queryString" />
  </providers>
</linkManager>
```

Now, we will assign the required link provider to individual sites.

2. In `Sitecore.config` or a patch configuration, add a custom `linkProvider` attribute to sites in the `<site>` node, which will specify which link provider the site will use. So, here, `website` and `website2` will use `link-pattern-1` and `link-pattern-2` link providers respectively:

```
<site name="website" linkProvider="link-pattern-1"
  virtualFolder="/" ... />
<site name="website2" linkProvider="link-pattern-2"
  virtualFolder="/" ... />
```

However, Sitecore does not understand this custom `linkProvider` attribute that we assigned to sites. It means that all sites will still serve the default provider, `sitecore`. So, we need to override the default link provider to switch to the provider based on the context site on-the-fly.

3. In the `SitecoreCookbook` project, create a `MultisiteLinkProvider` class in the `Providers` folder and inherit it from the `Sitecore.Links.LinkProvider` class.

4. When the URL of any item is generated, the default `GetDefaultUrlOptions()` method of `LinkProvider` is invoked to generate `UrlOptions` based on configurations. Here, to get `UrlOptions` for the link provider assigned to the context site, we will override this method:

```
public override UrlOptions GetDefaultUrlOptions()
{
  return GetMultiSiteLinkProvider().GetDefaultUrlOptions();
}
```

5. Create a `GetMultisiteLinkProvider()` method to get the provider assigned to the context site as follows:

```
private LinkProvider GetMultiSiteLinkProvider()
{
  if (Sitecore.Context.Site != null) {
    string siteName = Sitecore.Context.Site.Name.ToLower();

    var providerName =
      Sitecore.Context.Site.Properties["linkProvider"];
    if (!string.IsNullOrEmpty(providerName)) {
      var siteProvider =
        LinkManager.Providers[providerName];
      return siteProvider;
    }
  }
  return LinkManager.Providers["sitecore"];
}
```

Now, we will set this created link provider class as the default link provider.

6. Add the preceding link provider, name it `switcher` in the created patch configuration file, and set it as the default provider as follows:

```
<linkManager>
  <patch:attribute name="defaultProvider" value="switcher" />
  <providers>
    <add name="switcher"
    type="SitecoreCookbook.Providers.MultisiteLinkProvider,
      SitecoreCookbook" />

    . . .
  </providers>
</linkManager>
```

7. Now, preview the pages of the site `website` and `website2`; you will find that the links generated on both websites will have different URL patterns. On the page of the site `website`, we have the link provider as `link-pattern-1`, where it expects generated links without the `.aspx` extension and language location as `filePath`, such as `http://website/en/about-us`. For `website2`, `link-pattern-2` expects links with the `.aspx` extension and language as a query string, such as `http://website2/about-us.aspx?sc_lang=en`.

How it works...

When we generate a URL of any Sitecore item, we use a LinkManager API, such as `Sitecore.Links.LinkManager.GetItemUrl(item)`. In the backend, this method is implemented as follows:

```
public static string GetItemUrl(Item item) {
return Provider.GetItemUrl(item, GetDefaultUrlOptions());
}
```

This clearly shows that it collects `UrlOptions` from the `GetDefaultUrlOptions()` method of the provider. Here, we override the default provider to switch the provider on the fly based on the context site and collect `UrlOptions` accordingly.

The `UrlOptions` class provides you with strongly typed properties assigned to the link provider.

There's more...

We could have achieved the same recipe without creating multiple providers. For this, we can assign properties such as addAspxExtension, languageLocation, and others directly to sites in the <sites> node, and then from the GetDefaultUrlOptions() method of the overridden link provider class, we can directly read these properties and create our custom UrlOptions, as shown in the following code snippet. You can also get this code from the code bundle provided with this book:

```
public override UrlOptions GetDefaultUrlOptions()
{
  UrlOptions urlOptions = new UrlOptions();
  urlOptions.AddAspxExtension =
    (Sitecore.Context.Site.Properties["addAspxExtension"] ==
    "true");
  return urlOptions;
}
```

See also

When you generate links from a scheduled task, Sitecore will generate the link using the link provider set in the context site scheduler, even though the item relates to website or website2. So, this will lead to incorrect website URLs. To overcome this issue, we can use SiteContextSwitcher with the following code to switch the site for the code block:

```
SiteContext siteContext = Factory.GetSite("website");
using (new Sitecore.Sites.SiteContextSwitcher(siteContext)) {
  string url = Sitecore.Links.LinkManager.GetItemUrl(item);
}
```

Sitecore provides you with different providers such as ItemProvider, TemplateProvider, SiteProvider, DomainProvider, UserProvider, PublishProvider, PreviewProvider, and many more and the flexibility to override their behavior as well.

Initializing hooks to subscribe events to prepare an audit trail

Sitecore hooks provide you with an interface to invoke custom logic on system initialization before any HTTP web request is served. You can use hooks to subscribe to events dynamically, configure memory and health monitoring, switch MediaProviders and LinkProviders, interpret URLs, and much more.

In this recipe, you will learn how to use hooks to subscribe events to prepare an audit trail of different item operations such as create, delete, move, and others. You will also learn how to override MediaProvider using hooks.

How to do it...

We will first create an event handler class where we will create some event handling methods:

1. In the `SitecoreCookbook` project, create an event handler `AuditTrailEventHandler` class in the `Handlers` folder, and create a `WriteLogs` property in it:

```
public bool WriteLogs { get; set; }
```

2. Create the `OnItemCreated()` and `OnItemDeleted()` event methods as follows:

```
public void OnItemCreated(object sender, EventArgs args)
{
  ItemCreatedEventArgs eventArgs =
    Event.ExtractParameter<ItemCreatedEventArgs>(args, 0);
  if (eventArgs.Item != null)
    WriteAuditLog("created", eventArgs.Item);
}
public void OnItemDeleted(object sender, EventArgs args)
{
  Item item = Event.ExtractParameter(args, 0) as Item;
  if (item != null)
    WriteAuditLog("deleted", item);
}
```

3. Create the `WriteAuditLog()` method to write logs to the file or database. You can write the `StoreToDatabase()` method yourself to store data on the database.

```
public void WriteAuditLog(string operation, Item item)
{
  if (WriteLogs) {
    Log.Audit("Item " + operation + ":" + item.Paths.Path,
      this);
    StoreToDatase("Item " + operation, item);
  }
}
```

We created event handlers. However, instead of registering them in the patch configuration file, we will create a hook to subscribe events to invoke these created methods.

4. In the `SitecoreCookbook` project, create a `AuditTrailHook` class in the `Hooks` folder and implement the `IHook` interface. Create a `WriteLogs` property to decide whether we should write audit logs or not, and we will get its value from the hook's parameterized constructor as the `logActivity` parameter:

```
public bool WriteLogs { get; set; }
public AuditTrailHook(string logActivity)
{
   WriteLogs = (logActivity == "true");
}
```

5. Implement the `Initialize()` method to subscribe events:

```
public void Initialize()
{
   AuditTrailEventHandler handler = new
     AuditTrailEventHandler();
   handler.WriteLogs = WriteLogs;
   Event.Subscribe("item:created", new
     EventHandler(handler.OnItemCreated));
   Event.Subscribe("item:deleted", new
     EventHandler(handler.OnItemDeleted));
}
```

Now we will register the hook in patch configuration.

6. In the `\App_Config\Include\Cookbook` folder, create the `SitecoreCookbook.Hooks.config` file and patch a new hook in the `<configuration/sitecore>` node as follows. The hook that we created in the previous step expects one parameter, `logActivity`, in the constructor, which we passed in the `<param>` node.

```
<hooks>
   <hook type="SitecoreCookbook.Hooks.AuditTrailHook,
     SitecoreCookbook">
     <param desc="logActivity">true</param>
   </hook>
</hooks>
```

7. Now, create or delete an item from the content editor or experience editor, and perform any operation for which we have a subscribed event. You will find the audit logs as follows:

```
7192 09:46:22 INFO  AUDIT (sitecore\admin): Item created:
   /Hooks/test-item
7192 09:46:22 INFO  AUDIT (sitecore\admin): Item deleted:
   /Hooks/test-item
```

How it works...

The `Sitecore.Pipelines.Loader.LoadHooks` processor in the `<initialize>` pipeline iterates over the `/configuration/sitecore/hooks/hook` entries in `Sitecore.config`. Then, it creates an object of each specified type and invokes its `Initialize()` method of each hook defined there.

Hooks support parameters to the class' constructor. Here, we have `logActivity` as a parameter. We could also have used the `WriteLogs` property instead of using this parameterized constructor, as shown in the following code:

```
<hook type="SitecoreCookbook.Hooks.AuditTrailHook,
  SitecoreCookbook">
  <WriteLogs>true</WriteLogs>
</hook>
```

There's more...

Sitecore provides out-of-box hooks for health monitoring (`HealthMonitorHook`) and memory monitoring (`MemoryMonitorHook`), which you can find from `Sitecore.config`.

Creating jobs to accomplish long-running operations

When you need to do some long-running operations such as importing data from an external service, sending e-mails to subscribers, resetting content item layout details, and so on, we can use Sitecore jobs, which are asynchronous operations in the backend that you can monitor in a foreground thread (**Job Viewer**) of Sitecore Rocks or by creating a custom Sitecore application.

In this recipe, we will create a task of resetting content item layout details and execute it asynchronously by creating a Sitecore job.

Getting ready

This recipe assumes that you already have assigned layout and rendering details to templates as well as some content pages. Now, for reverting layout details changes for the content items, we will reset their values.

How to do it...

We will first create a job to execute a task asynchronously:

1. In `SitecoreCookbook`, create a `ResetLayoutDetailsJob` class in the `Tasks` folder. Define the `Job` property as follows:

```
private string _jobName = " Reset Layout Details Job";
public Job Job {
  get { return JobManager.GetJob(_jobName); }
}
```

2. Create the `Run()` method with a parameter to get root item. In this method, create a `JobOptions` object and start job using the `JobManager.Start()` method. So that, the task will be executed asynchronously. We will implement this task of resetting layout details of root item and its descendants in the `ResetLayoutDetails()` method in next step:

```
public void Run(Item rootItem)
{
  JobOptions options = new JobOptions(_jobName,
  "Reset Layout", Context.Site.Name, this", "ResetLayoutDetails",
new object[] { rootItem })
  {
    EnableSecurity = true,
    ContextUser = Sitecore.Context.User,
    Priority = ThreadPriority.AboveNormal
  };
  JobManager.Start(options);
}
```

3. Create a `ResetLayoutDetails()` task method to fetch all the descendant items and reset their layout (rendering) details:

```
private void ResetLayoutDetails(Item rootItem)
{
  if (Job != null && rootItem != null) {
    List<Item> itemList =
      rootItem.Axes.GetDescendants().ToList();
    itemList.Add(rootItem);

    Job.Status.Total = itemList.Count;
    Job.Status.State = JobState.Running;

    foreach (Item item in itemList) {
      using(new EditContext(item)) {
```

```
            item.Fields["__renderings"].Reset();
        }
        Job.Status.Processed++;
    }

    Job.Status.State = JobState.Finished;
    }
}
```

We have created a job. Now, we can invoke it by creating a custom command button from the ribbon, web page, or Sitecore scheduling agents (which you will learn in the next recipe).

4. To invoke the job, write the following code to the appropriate location:

```
ResetLayoutDetailsJob job = new ResetLayoutDetailsJob();

Item item = Sitecore.Configuration.Factory.GetDatabase(
    "master").GetItem("/sitecore/Content/Home");
job.Run(item);
```

5. From the Sitecore Rocks menu bar, click on the **Sitecore | Start Page** menu item. Make sure that you have selected the correct active database. Now, on the **Start Page**, find the **System** tab and click on **View running background jobs in the Job Viewer**, which will open **Job Viewer**. It will show you all the current jobs, as shown in the following image. Here, it shows that **Reset Layout Details Job** is running and it has reset **9** items out of **34**:

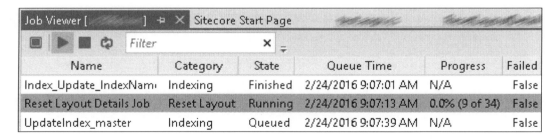

How it works...

Sitecore jobs have no **HttpContext** and get executed in **ManagedPoolThread** or, in terms of Sitecore, run in the `scheduler` context. This means that while it is executing, its context site will be `scheduler`.

Once the job is invoked, you can see its progress from **Job Viewer**. The **State** column will show its different status—**Initializing**, **Queued**, **Running**, or **Finished**. The **Progress** column shows you the number of units processed.

Let's first understand three primary classes involved in creating jobs:

- ▶ `Job`: This represents a job
- ▶ `JobOptions`: This represents information about the job such as the job name, job category, context site, method to invoke, and parameters passed to this method
- ▶ `JobManager`: This is a static class that invokes and manages jobs

Here, you will see interesting properties of `JobOptions` such as `EnableSecurity` and `Priority` that are responsible for enabling or disabling Sitecore security during the execution of the job and thread priority respectively. There are few more properties as follows:

- ▶ `AfterLife`: This is the length of time that Sitecore maintains information of a job after its completion.
- ▶ `AtomicExecution`: This enables/disables the concurrent execution of jobs. The default is true, which means that the concurrent execution of jobs is disabled.
- ▶ `ContextUser`: The job will get executed in the context of this user.

Here, we started the job in the context of the current user and enabled security so that only these items will be affected by which user has write access rights.

 If jobs are created for content owners (or for non-admin users), then it's advisable to enable security and run them with the current user's context only.

In step 3, you will find that we changed the status of a job using the `Job.Status.State` property. `Job.Status.Processed` provides you with the status of the number of operations that job is performing. `Job.Status.Total` shows you how many operations the job has to perform. So, based on this status, we can show users the real-time status of how much percent the job has been finished or we can provide an estimate too. You can find the job and unit details in logs too:

```
ManagedPoolThread #14 09:07:07 INFO  Job started: Reset Layout Details
Job
ManagedPoolThread #14 09:07:39 INFO  Job ended: Reset Layout Details
Job (units processed: 34)
```

 Runtime exceptions in jobs can lead to stopping of the job, so it's advisable to handle runtime exceptions and have proper logging.

The following image shows us that our job failed after resetting 10 items due to a runtime exception, so after that it stopped running and its state changed to **Finished**:

Name	Category	State	Queue Time	Progress	Failed
Reset Layout Details Job	Reset Layout	Finished	2/24/2016 9:40:55 AM	0.0% (10 of 35)	True
UpdateIndex_master	Indexing	Finished	2/24/2016 9:40:56 AM	N/A	False

See also

You can also intercept the jobs by customizing the `<Job>` pipeline or job events such as `job:starting`, `job:started`, or `job:ended`.

Using a scheduling agent to delete older item versions

You learned about Sitecore jobs, which we invoked on user action. Now, you will learn how we can schedule such jobs in Sitecore. Scheduling tasks is possible in Sitecore using two different techniques: **agents** and **database tasks**.

We will take a case of a Sitecore instance using Sitecore item versioning. Now think, what will happen when your items have a number of versions? Your content owners are facing difficulty in managing them, which will make the user interface slower and impact the overall Sitecore performance as well. So, we will create a Sitecore agent that will keep a few of the latest versions and delete all the older versions of items every 12 hours so that users do not need to do it manually for each item individually.

How to do it...

Now, we will first implement the task that we want an agent to run:

1. In the `SitecoreCookbook` project, create a `VersionDeletionAgent` class in the `Tasks` folder and declare properties as follows:

```
public string RootItem { get; set; }
public string DatabaseName { get; set; }
public int MaxVersions { get; set; }
```

2. Create the `Run()` method that will be invoked by a scheduling agent:

```
public void Run()
{
    Database database = Factory.GetDatabase(DatabaseName);
    Item item = database.GetItem(RootItem);
    if (item != null) {
```

```
    Item[] items = item.Axes.GetDescendants();
    foreach (Item child in items) {
      foreach (Language language in child.Languages) {
        Item langItem = database.GetItem(child.Paths.Path,
          language);
        if (langItem.Versions.Count > MaxVersions)
        DeleteOlderVersions(langItem);
      }
    }
  }
}
```

3. Create the `DeleteOlderVersions()` method to delete older versions:

```
private void DeleteOlderVersions(Item item)
{
  Sitecore.Data.Version[] versions =
    item.Versions.GetVersionNumbers();
  for (int i=0; i < versions.Length - MaxVersions; i++) {
    Item itemToDelete = item.Database.GetItem(item.Paths.Path,
      item.Language, versions[i]);
    itemToDelete.Versions[versions[i]].RecycleVersion();
  }
}
```

We will register this class in the scheduling agent.

4. In the `\App_Config\Include\Cookbook` folder, create the `SitecoreCookbook. Schedulers.config` file. In the `<configuration/sitecore/scheduling>` section, add a new agent node, register the preceding class, and assign its properties, as shown in the following code. Additionally, configure the interval attribute of the agent to run every 12 hours:

```
<scheduling>
  <agent type="SitecoreCookbook.Tasks.VersionDeletionAgent,
    SitecoreCookbook" method="Run" interval="12:00:00">
  <param desc="database">master</param>
  <param desc="root Item">/sitecore/Content/Home</param>
  <parm desc="maximum versions">3</parm>
  <LogActivity>true</LogActivity>
  </agent>
</scheduling>
```

5. Now this agent will get executed every 12 hours and delete the older versions.

6. To test agents quickly, you can set the agent interval and scheduling frequency to one minute (`00:01:00`) to invoke the agent every one minute.

How it works...

In the `Sitecore.config` file, you can find the `<initialize>` pipeline that includes a `Sitecore.Pipelines.Loader.InitializeScheduler` processor. This processor creates a new thread, which wakes up every predefined amount of time specified in `/configuration/sitecore/scheduling/frequency` and invokes those agents who are ready to get executed under `/configuration/sitecore/scheduling`. An agent cannot run more often than this frequency value set for the scheduling, but an agent can be set to run less often:

```
<scheduling>
    <!-- Time between checking for scheduled tasks waiting to execute -->
    <frequency>00:05:00</frequency>
```

 The format of the interval attribute should be *[days].HH:mm:ss*, and setting its value to `00:00:00` will disable the agent.

Every Sitecore agent creates a job to run the task. So, you will find the following logs when an agent gets executed. Remember, you can't get number of processed units in logs here unlike the job we created in previous recipe. That, you can achieve by creating your own job and invoking it from the `Run()` method of the `VersionDeletionAgent` class:

```
ManagedPoolThread #9 12:18:04 INFO  Job started: SitecoreCookbook.
Tasks.VersionDeletionAgent
ManagedPoolThread #9 12:18:14 INFO  Job ended: SitecoreCookbook.Tasks.
VersionDeletionAgent (units processed: )
```

 Scheduling agents can slow down a Sitecore instance if used frequently, so it is important to use them appropriately.

Scheduling database tasks

Sitecore provides you with the database task feature to schedule tasks, which comes with many advantages over scheduling agents. To make this recipe shorter, we will configure database task to reset layout details.

How to do...

We will first implement a task to reset layout details, which we already implemented while creating jobs:

1. In the `SitecoreCookbook` project, create a `ResetLayoutTask` class in the `Tasks` folder and implement the `Execute()` method. Database task expects a specific signature for this method as follows:

```
public void Execute(Item[] items, CommandItem command,
ScheduleItem schedule)
{
  foreach(Item rootItem in items) {
    ResetLayoutDetails(rootItem);
  }
}
```

2. Create the `ResetLayoutDetails()` method to reset layout details, which we already implemented while creating a job. You can also get the code from the code bundle provided with this book.

   Now we will create the database task.

3. From the content editor, select the `/sitecore/system/Tasks/Commands` item. In this, create a **Commands** item—`Delete Older Versions`. Set the **Type** and **Method** fields, as shown in the following image:

4. Inside the `/sitecore/system/Tasks/Schedules` item, create a `Schedule` item—`Version Deletion Schedule`. Select the command we just created in the **Command** field, root item path in the **Items** field, and set the **Schedule** field value, as shown in the following image. Setting values will run the database task every 12 hours. You will learn about creating the **Schedule** field value later in this recipe.

5. To test the database task, 12 hours will be too long. Set the **Schedule** field as `20140101|99990101|127|`**`00:10:00`** in order to invoke it every 10 minutes. Additionally, set the scheduling frequency to one minute if not set in the previous recipe.

 Remember that database tasks will consider a minimum interval of 10 minutes.

How it works...

A database agent needs two different items: `Command` and `Schedule`. The `Command` item defines the type of task we created, which expects three parameters: an array of `Item`, `CommandItem`, and `ScheduleItem`, as we implemented in step 1.

In the `Items` field, we can pass the path of a single item, paths of multiple items that are pipe-separated, or Sitecore query so that they are accessible as an array of `Items`. Now, it will simply perform the task that you have implemented.

The `Schedule` field value expects four parts. The first and second parts are the start date and end date of the task, which can be set in the `yyyyMMdd` or `yyyyMMddTHHmmss` format. Their part sets the days of the week when the task should run. Each day of the week is assigned a value (Mon-1, Tue-2, Wed-4, Thu-8, Fri-16, Sat-32, and Sun-64). The third part is the sum of values assigned to days on which we want to invoke the task. For example, to invoke it on Monday, Wednesday, and Friday, we should set the value to `1+4+16=21`. The fourth part is the interval to specify how frequently the task should get executed.

A database task provides you with many advantages over agents as follows:

▶ We get the flexibility of creating or deleting any number of scheduled tasks without any configuration changes, and so application restart is not required.

▶ We can also schedule a one-time task by selecting the **Auto Remove** checkbox field. This task will get deleted automatically once it's executed.

▶ We can create tasks in the master and core databases. If you publish these task items, they will get executed from the web database as well, but note that in doing so, tasks may get executed from all the CD servers.

5
Making Content Management More Efficient

In this chapter, we will cover how to improve the accessibility of content management users to achieve specified goals with effectiveness and efficiency. You will learn the following recipes:

- ▶ Using dictionary domains for multilingual sites on a multisite environment
- ▶ Creating vanity URLs for marketing purposes using an alias item
- ▶ Centralizing common content using a clone item
- ▶ Using a wildcard item to integrate external content
- ▶ Placing dynamic content in the Rich Text Editor by replacing tokens
- ▶ Adding a custom tool to the Rich Text Editor to generate tokens
- ▶ Dealing with user-generated content using an Item Web API
- ▶ Storing external content using a custom cache

Introduction

In this chapter, we will look at different techniques that are intended to make **content management system** (**CMS**) users' life easier by managing content efficiently. While none of the recipes in this chapter are mandatory for your CMS, having them in your Sitecore CMS will provide a lot of efficiency and accessibility to its users.

The recipes here are concerned with solving some real-world problems that developers, content authors, and marketers face. They give an explanation on how to make the multilingual experience better using dictionaries, different ways to serve or import external content faster using Wildcard items, custom caches, and Item Web APIs. This chapter also explains other different types of items such as clone items and alias items and their best usage to make the lives of content authors and marketers easier. A few recipes here are intended to show how we can customize the Rich Text Editor to provide great flexibility to CMS users.

Using dictionary domains for multilingual sites on a multisite environment

Content authors can easily create content items in multiple languages and show them without requiring major development, as we saw in the *Creating multilingual content pages* recipe of *Chapter 2, Extending Presentation Components*. Sometimes, we need to display some labels, common text, messages, or warnings on websites in multiple languages, which cannot be part of content items. Leveraging the Sitecore **dictionary** can help you prevent hardcoded labels or common text.

In this recipe, you will learn how to use the dictionary and dictionary domains to create site-wise dictionaries for a multisite environment.

How to do it...

We will first see how to create and use a dictionary:

1. In the Content Editor, navigate to the /sitecore/system/Dictionary item. Create a Cookbook dictionary folder in it. Under the folder, create a few dictionary entries, Email, First Name, Surname, and so on.

2. In each dictionary entry, enter a **Key** and **Phrase**. **Key** is the name that we will use as a key for the dictionary and **Phrase** is the text value that shows up for different languages. Here, we enter **Phrase** for English and Spanish languages, as shown in the following image: (**Key** will remain the same for all the languages.)

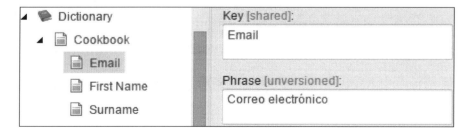

3. Create a view and add the following code to it:

    ```
    @using Sitecore.Globalization
    @model RenderingModel

    @Html.Raw(Translate.Text("Firstname"))  <br />
    @Html.Raw(Translate.Text("Surname"))  <br />
    @Html.Raw(Translate.Text("Email"))
    ```

4. Add this view to a page and preview the page in both English and Spanish languages; you will find that the labels get autoconverted, as shown in the following image:

English	Spanish
First Name	Nombre de pila
Surname	Apellido
Email	Correo electrónico

    We can create dictionary entries anywhere in the content tree outside of `/sitecore/System/Dictionary` to achieve a site-wise dictionary. Suppose that `Site-A` has a start path as `/sitecore/Content/Site-A`, then we can create a dictionary domain as `/sitecore/Content/Site-A/Site-A Dictionary` and the same for other sites.

5. In the site folder item (that is, `/sitecore/Content/Site-A`), create a dictionary domain item using the `/sitecore/templates/System/Dictionary/Dictionary Domain` template. Create dictionary folders or dictionary entries in the same way as we created in steps 1 and 2.

6. You can read dictionary entries for any site using its domain name. In the previously created view, you used the `Translate.Text()` method. Instead of this, use the `Translate.TextByDomain()` method as follows:

    ```
    @Html.Raw(Translate.TextByDomain("Site-A Dictionary",
      "Firstname"))
    ```

7. Here, you will feel that both the `Translate.Text()` and `TranslateTextByDomain()` methods are reading phrases from different dictionary items for the same **Key**.

8. In the same way, you can create *n* number of dictionary domains and have different keys with the same name in each.

How it works...

Sitecore maintains a filesystem cache for the dictionaries in the `\temp\dictionary.dat` file, which gets updated whenever any modifications happen to the dictionary. So, we get the flexibility to create a dictionary domain and its entries anywhere in the content tree.

Bind a dictionary to a site

As you learned, we can use the `Translate.TextByDomain()` method to read dictionary phrases for a dictionary related to the domain (or site). However, it requires a hardcoded domain name. To avoid this, we can directly bind the dictionary to the site using the `dictionaryDomain` attribute in the `<site>` section in the `\App_Config\Sitecore.Config` file. Refer to the following configuration for reference. So, once we have configured the dictionary domain to the site, we can use it as a context dictionary using the `Translate.Text()` method only:

```
<site name="Site-A" dictionaryDomain="Site-A Dictionary"
  rootPath="/sitecore/Content/Site-A" … />

<site name="Site-B" dictionaryDomain="Site-B Dictionary"
  rootPath="/sitecore/Content/Site-B" … />
```

A fallback dictionary domain

While working with multiple sites on an instance, it's not a good practice to create duplicate dictionary entries for each site. For dictionary reusability, you can have most of your content in the global dictionary, smaller site-specific content in the site's local dictionary, and the global dictionary as its fallback:

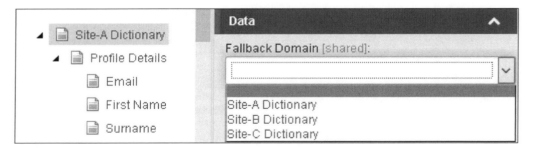

While working on a multisite environment, it's always recommended to bind the dictionary domain to the site and have a global dictionary as a fallback for dictionary reusability.

We can make dictionaries editable by creating it outside `/sitecore/system/`. To make them editable from the Experience Editor, you can refer to `http://goo.gl/HIy6xJ`.

Creating vanity URLs for marketing purposes using an alias item

An **alias** is an alternate path for an item to get accessed or, you can say, a shorter and alternate URL to access an item that has a long URL. It is often called **vanity URL** when used for marketing purposes. In this recipe, we will create an alias URL for an item.

How to do...

Let's create an alias for a content item:

1. Open the Content Editor and select a content item. Here, we select the `/sitecore/Content/Home/investors/financial-news/2016/25-02-2016` item, which shows the latest trading updates of the company.

2. From the ribbon in the **PRESENTATION** tab, click on the **Aliases** button in the **URL** section, which will open the **Aliases** dialog, as shown in the following image:

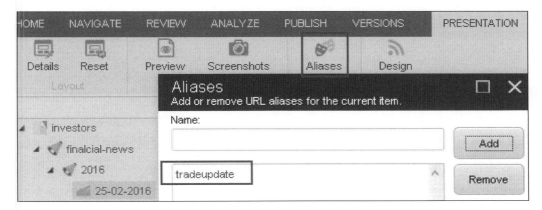

3. Enter the name of the alias and click on the **Add** button. Here, we set it as `tradeupdate`.

4. That's it. Now access this item using the alias URL, `http://sitecorecookbook/tradeupdate`.

How it works...

When you create an item alias, it gets created in the `/sitecore/system/Aliases` item, as shown in the following image, so that you can create alias items from here as well:

Sitecore resolves aliases before context item get resolved so that if `AliasResolver` finds an alias for the requested URL, Sitecore assigns the **Linked item** to the context item.

Using item alias, we will have multiple URLs for a single content page. It is generally advisable to prevent search engines from indexing multiple URLs for a single content item. So, we can take advantage of **canonical URL** (`https://goo.gl/GQc8br`) to tell search engines to index only one URL.

See also

Currently, Sitecore supports aliases for content items only. You can help your marketing team by providing aliases for media items as well. For that, refer to `http://goo.gl/8leHxv`.

By default, one alias can be assigned to a single content item only. In case you need to have a common alias name on multiple sites, it's quite possible by some customizations, which you can find at `http://goo.gl/04bx78`.

Centralizing common content using a clone item

A cloning item is a very flexible and well-designed feature of the Sitecore architecture, which allows us to reuse the content of an item or the whole content tree. It can be very useful for both single site and multisite instances for various purposes.

Let's consider a case where we have multiple sites hosted in a Sitecore environment, and we are creating and managing the same duplicate content for each individual site. Here, we will create source items on one site and clone them on another site.

Getting ready

For better understanding, this recipe is explained in the context of multiple sites, but it's not necessary for you to have multiple sites to work on it.

How to do it...

Let's see how to create clone items:

1. From the Content Editor, select a source item that we need to clone.

2. From the ribbon in the **Configure** tab, click on the **Clone** button in the **Clones** section. This will open the **Clone Item** dialog.

3. In this dialog, select the destination parent item in which you want to clone the selected item.

4. That's it. You will find a replica of the source item as a child of the destination item, as shown in the following image:

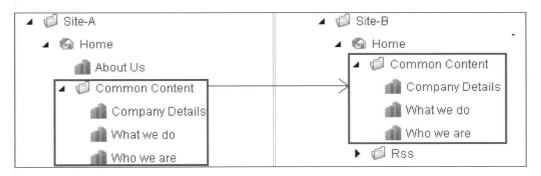

5. Here, the /site-A/Home/Common Content item was the source item that we selected in step 1 and /Site-B/Home was the destination item that we selected in step 3. Now, you can access these cloned items in Site-B in the same way as normal physical items to read, write, or access them through APIs.

How it works...

A clone is a separate Sitecore item whose field values are inherited (not copied) from the source item. This is similar to how standard values work, so modifying the source item will reflect it in cloned items. However, if you modify the cloned item directly, then later changes in the source item will not get reflected in cloned items. The cloned items will have their own workflow to approve or reject changes done in the source item.

Publishing a source item does not publish cloned items. Creating a new item in source items does not get reflected in cloned items.

Once you publish the cloned items, they are created as physical items in the content delivery database as such clone items are more useful in managing common content in a content management environment and have nothing for live sites. You can read more on managing clone items in the workflow and publishing perspective at `https://goo.gl/VZJfQS`.

See also

Before clone items were introduced in Sitecore, there was a feature of creating proxy items, which is still available in the latest Sitecore versions. You can read more about it at `http://goo.gl/xmyCcJ`.

Using a wildcard item to integrate external content

You have learned different ways to render the Sitecore content, but sometimes, we may need to fetch some data from external systems such as an external database, feeds, and so on, and render them on Sitecore.

In this recipe, we will consider an example of pulling news from an external database. On requesting, `http://sitecorecookbook/News/2015` will pull news details of the year 2015.

Getting ready

In this recipe, we are pulling news details from an external database. Create a `News` table, as shown in the following image:

Column Name	Data Type	Allow Nulls
ID	int	✔
NewsDate	datetime	✔
Title	varchar(300)	✔
Description	varchar(MAX)	✔
UrlTitle	varchar(300)	✔

How to do it...

We will see how a wildcard item can support any virtual request on Sitecore:

1. In the `SitecoreCookbook` project, create a new controller `NewsController` class to fetch news details from an external database and register it in Sitecore:

```
public class NewsController : Controller
{
  public ActionResult NewsListing()
  {
    string year = WebUtil.GetUrlName(0);
    string strSQL = "SELECT * FROM News WHERE
      year(NewsDate)=" + year;
    DataSet dataset = GetNewsFromDatabase(strSQL);

    return View(dataset.Tables[0].Rows);
  }
}
```

2. In this class, create the `GetNewsFromDatabase()` function that returns `DataSet` for the given SQL query for the table you created, or you can also get it from the code bundle provided with this book.

3. Create a `NewsListing.cshtml` view with the following code and register it:

```
@model System.Data.DataRowCollection
<div class="newslist">
  @foreach (System.Data.DataRow news in Model)
  {
    <div>@news["NewsDate"]</div>
    <div>
      <a href='@news["UrlTitle"]'>@news["Title"]</a>
    </div>
    <div>@news["Description"]</div> <hr />
  }
</div>
```

4. Create a wildcard item (an item with a single asterisk in its name) under the `/sitecore/Content/Home/News` item as follows:

5. For the wildcard item, assign the main layout, add the `News Listing` controller, and place it in the `main-content` placeholder.

6. Preview news pages such as the following:

   `http://sitecorecookbook/News/2015`

   `http://sitecorecookbook/News/2014`

   It will render the list of news of the given year as follows:

2015

Aug 26 2015
Programmers with security in mind are better developers
According to security researchers from North Carolina State University and Microsoft productive and influential workers who other coders strive to emulate.

Aug 03 2015
Windows 10 ups market share in July
According to ratings firms NetMarketShare and StatCounter, and against all odds, world's PC operating systems.

Jul 29 2015
Internet security flaw discovered in Linux OS
Earlier today, a new programming language survey reveals that Apple's Swift language is breaking into the top twenty for the first time.

How it works...

Any item with name of asterisk (*) is called a wildcard item, which is just like any other item, mostly used to integrate data from external systems.

Here, the /Home/News item contains a wildcard item (/News/*) and has no other children. So, Sitecore sets the context item to /News/* for any URL that corresponds to a child of the /News item, such as /News/2015.aspx.

It's also possible to use nested wildcard items, but you might need to add a custom processor in the <httpRequestBegin> pipeline to resolve nested wildcard items.

There's more...

You can also achieve this recipe by customizing the <mvc.getRenderer> pipeline, explained at http://goo.gl/f0wnXq. Additionally, while using wildcard items, you might need to rework renderings such as breadcrumb, side menu, and others as they can't understand wildcard items.

Placing dynamic content in the Rich Text Editor by replacing tokens

Content authors sometimes get stuck when they need to put dynamic content in the **Rich Text Editor** (**RTE**). Let's suppose that they want to place some advertisements, embed some videos, and update stock quotes or any other content that gets changed frequently. In all such situations, they become handicapped and have to modify the Rich Text content very frequently or manage content using multiple fields.

In this recipe, you will learn about replacing tokens mentioned in the Rich Text field of one item to render the share price information configured in other items.

Getting Ready

Here, we will create a <token> tag that will have the item and field attributes, which specify the item path or item ID and field name and place it in the Rich Text content. For the following mentioned <token> tag, it should render the value of the Company field from the specified item:

```
<token field="Company"
item="/sitecore/Content/Home/Global/Share Price" ></token>
```

In its first impression, you will find it very difficult to manage for content authors. However, you can make it simpler by creating a custom dialog in the RTE to select the item and field and autogenerate the <token> tag, which you will learn in the next recipe.

How to do it...

For the token substitution, we will first create a `<renderLayout>` pipeline processor:

1. In the `SitecoreCookbook` project, create a `ReplaceRTETokens` class and the `Process()` method in the `Pipelines` folder as follows:

```
public void Process(RenderFieldArgs args)
{
  string TOKEN_PATTERN = @"<token[\s\S]*?/token>";
  Regex rgx = new Regex(TOKEN_PATTERN);
  if (args.FieldTypeKey == "rich text") {
    string fieldValue = args.FieldValue;
    foreach (Match match in rgx.Matches(fieldValue))
    {
      fieldValue = ReplaceTokens(fieldValue, match, args);
    }
    args.Result.FirstPart = fieldValue;
  }
}
```

2. Create the `ReplaceTokens()` method, which reads each token of this field and replaces it with an actual field value:

```
private static string ReplaceTokens(string fieldValue, Match
match, RenderFieldArgs args)
{
  XElement xElement = XElement.Parse(match.ToString());
  if (xElement.Attribute("field") != null
    && xElement.Attribute("item") != null) {
    string item = xElement.Attribute("item").Value;
    string field = xElement.Attribute("field").Value;

    Item tokenItem = Context.Database.GetItem(item);
    if (tokenItem != null && !(tokenItem.ID == args.Item.ID
      && string.Equals(field, args.FieldName,
      System.StringComparison.OrdinalIgnoreCase)))
      fieldValue = fieldValue.Replace(match.ToString(),
        FieldRenderer.Render(tokenItem, field));
  }
  return fieldValue;
}
```

3. In the `\App_Config\Include\Cookbook\` folder, create a patch configuration file, `SitecoreCookbook.RTEToken.config`, and in the `<configuration/sitecore>` node, add the previously created processor after the `GetFieldValue` processor as follows:

```
<pipelines>
  <renderField>
  <processor type="SitecoreCookbook.
    Pipelines.ReplaceRTETokens, SitecoreCookbook"
    patch:after="processor[@type='Sitecore.Pipelines.
      RenderField.GetFieldValue, Sitecore.Kernel']" />
  </renderField>
</pipelines>
```

4. Create a `Share Price` item in the `Home` item (that is, `/sitecore/Content/Home/Global/Share Price`) and fill in the following details:

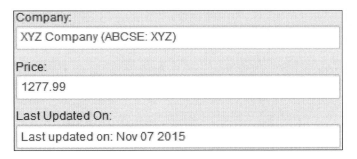

5. Create another item with a Rich Text field—`Description`—and enter the following content in it in HTML mode. We added two tokens to replace the value of the `Company` and `Price` fields of the item created previously:

```
<p><strong>SHARE PRICE</strong></p>
<token item="/sitecore/Content/Home/Global/Share Price"
  field="Company">Share Price-Company</token>
<hr/>
$<token item="{1F2BFD7A-39BC-41F9-96B8-EB15549762B7}"
  field="Price">Share Price-Price</token>
```

6. Create a view with the following code and add it to the presentation details:

```
@model RenderingModel
@Html.Sitecore().Field("Description", Model.Item)
```

7. Preview the item created in step 5; you will find that all the tokens have been replaced with the share price information in the page source, as shown in the following image:

```
<p><strong>SHARE PRICE</strong></p>
XYZ Company (ABCSE: XYZ)
<hr>
$1277.99
```

How it works...

You are already aware of how pipelines and processors work. The `<renderField>` pipeline is responsible for rendering a field value in any page mode. It contains different processors such as `SetParameters` (renders the field value based on input parameters), `GetFieldValue` (gets the field value), `AddBeforeAndAfterValues` (adds HTML tags before and after the field value based on input parameters), and `RenderWebEditing` (appends a JavaScript wrapper to make content editable in the Experience Editor). It also contains different processors to read values of different types of field types.

For token substitution we must have a field value, so we added our processor after the `GetFieldValue` processor. Here, we replaced tokens for the Rich Text field only. We can find the field type from the `RenderFieldArgs` object using `args.FieldTypeKey`.

Ignore replacing tokens that are referring to the same item and field to avoid infinite token substitution, which we have already taken care of here.

Here, we replaced tokens using the `FieldRenderer.Render()` method so that it will replace the rendered output of the Single Line, Rich Text, Image, and other fields.

You will find that along with the Rich Text field value, you can also modify the share price information replaced by the token from inline editing of the Experience Editor; this is really amazing stuff that we can get in Sitecore!

There's more...

We can also apply this recipe to other field types to modify a field's renderings or even fetch and replace content from external systems as well.

Customizing the `<renderField>` pipeline, we can render the field value of a custom created field type, apply wrappers to the rendered field values or modify them, and introduce custom rendering parameters such as `EnclosingTag`, and `DisableWebEditing`, achieve field-level fallbacks, change the behavior of renderings in different page modes, and so on.

Adding a custom tool to the Rich Text Editor to generate tokens

Sitecore provides you with multiple HTML editor profiles, and each provides different sorts of toolbar buttons. It also gives a provision to add a custom button to the editor toolbar and interact with a custom tool as well.

In the previous recipe, we used tokens to replace values of selected items. In this recipe, you will learn how to create a user interface to select items and fields, generate these token tags, and display them in better visuals in **Design** mode of the RTE.

Getting Ready

Just as a recap, in the previous recipe, we created tokens as shown in the following command. We will continue this recipe in reference to that:

```
<token field="Company"
item="/sitecore/Content/Home/Global/Share Price" ></token>
```

 In this recipe, we will modify Sitecore's out-of-the-box JavaScript and stylesheet files, so after changing them, don't forget to clear the browser cache every time.

How to do it...

First, we will create a custom button in the RTE toolbar:

1. Open the Content Editor with the `core` database and select the toolbar item of your default HTML editor profile. You can find your default editor profile in the `HtmlEditor.DefaultProfile` setting in `Sitecore.config`, that is, `/sitecore/system/Settings/Html Editor Profiles/Rich Text Default/Toolbar 1`.

2. Create a new HTML editor button, **Insert Token** inside it, enter the command name as `InsertToken` in the **Click** field, and set an icon as required. Open the RTE; you will find our created button, as shown in the following image:

Now, we have to open a tool to select tokens by clicking on this button. For this, we need to append our RTE script to the RTE page in order to handle the preceding `InsertToken` command.

3. From Visual Studio, create a new JavaScript file, `CustomRTECommands.js`, in the `/Sitecore/shell/Override` folder and add the following content:

```
var scEditor = null;

Telerik.Web.UI.Editor.CommandList["InsertToken"] =
  function (commandName, editor, args) {
  var url = "/sitecore/shell/default.aspx?
    xmlcontrol=RichText.InsertToken&la=" + scLanguage;

  scEditor = editor;
  editor.showExternalDialog( url, null, 600, 500,
    scInsertToken, null, "Insert Token", true,
    Telerik.Web.UI.WindowBehaviors.Close, false, false
  );
};

function scInsertToken(sender, returnValue) {
  if (returnValue) {
    scEditor.pasteHtml(returnValue.media);
  }
}
```

4. In the `\App_Config\Include\Cookbook` folder, create a patch configuration file, `SitecoreCookbook.RTETokenButton.config`. Add this JavaScript file to the RTE page by registering it as follows so that we do not need to add the preceding JavaScript code in the Sitecore RTE `RichText Commands.js` command file or the RTE page:

```
<clientscripts>
  <htmleditor>
  <script language="javascript"
    src="/sitecore/shell/Override/CustomRTECommands.js" />
  </htmleditor>
</clientscripts>
```

5. We will now create the custom tool using `xmlControl` named `RichText.InsertToken`. You are already aware of how to create `xmlControl`. Create an `InsertToken.xml` XML file in the `\sitecore modules\Shell\InsertToken` folder. Use `FormDialog` with `xmlControl—RichText.InsertToken—`in it as follows:

```
<RichText.InsertToken>
  <FormDialog OKButton="Insert">
```

```
    <CodeBeside Type="SitecoreCookbook.XAML.
       InsertTokenForm,SitecoreCookbook"/>
  </FormDialog>
</RichText.InsertToken>
```

6. Add a `TreeViewEx` control to select an item and assign a `DataContext` control to it so that we can apply a root item to treeview. You can set the site's `Home` item as the root of the `DataContext` control:

```
<DataContext ID="RootItem" Root=
  "{110D559F-DEA5-42EA-9C1C-8A5DF7E70EF9}"/>
<Scrollbox>
  <TreeviewEx ID="TokenTree" DataContext="RootItem"
    Root="true" />
</Scrollbox>
<Border>
  <GridPanel>
    <Literal Text="Field Name:"/> <Edit ID="TextField" />
  </GridPanel>
</Border>
```

7. In the `SitecoreCookbook` project, create an `InsertTokenForm` class in the `XAML` folder and inherit it from `DialogForm`.

8. Override the `OnLoad()` method as follows:

```
protected Edit TextField;
protected TreeviewEx TokenTree;
protected DataContext RootItem;
protected override void OnLoad(EventArgs e)
{
  base.OnLoad(e);
  if (Context.ClientPage.IsEvent)
    return;
  this.RootItem.GetFromQueryString();
}
```

9. Override the `OnOK()` event method to generate a `<token>` tag with the item and field details and return to RTE:

```
protected override void OnOK(object sender, EventArgs args)
{
  string tokenString = "<token item=\"{0}\"
    field=\"{1}\">{2}</token>";

  Item selectedItem = TokenTree.GetSelectionItem();
  string tokenText = selectedItem.DisplayName + ":" +
    TextField.Value;
```

```
tokenString = string.Format(tokenString,
    selectedItem.Paths.Path, TextField.Value, tokenText);

SheerResponse.SetDialogValue(tokenString);
base.OnOK(sender, args);
}
```

10. Now, open RTE from any item's Rich Text field. Click on the **Insert Token** button that we created previously. It will open the tool as follows:

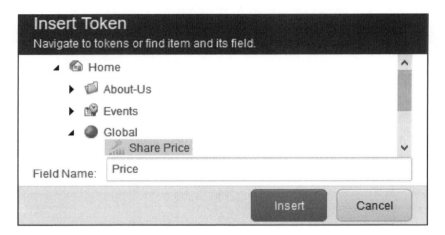

11. Select any item, say **Share Price**, and enter a field name, say `Price`, to read from this item, and click on **Insert**. You will find a `<token>` tag inserted in RTE, wrapped around the **Share Price:Price** text, which signifies `<Item Name>:<Field Name>` for better visibility in Design mode:

```
<token item="/sitecore/content/Home/Global/Share Price" field="Price">Share Price:Price</token>
```

You will find this token in Design mode as follows:

```
Share Price:Price
```

12. To make this token more realistic, you can add a style sheet class in the `\sitecore\shell\Controls\Rich Text Editor\Editor.css` file or a custom CSS file as follows:

```
token { background: #F5F5F5
    url('/~/icon/Software/16x16/component.png') no-repeat;
    padding: 0 5px 0 20px; border: 1px dashed #d35400; }
```

13. Check the token in Design mode:

How it works...

Here, we created a custom button for the RTE default `Rich Text Default` profile; in the same way, Sitecore provides different profiles in the `core` database in `/sitecore/system/Settings/Html Editor Profiles/`. You can learn more customizations on RTE at `https://goo.gl/HCGGbd`.

All RTE commands are mentioned in the `\sitecore\shell\Controls\Rich Text Editor\RichText Commands.js` file. We can add the code of our custom `InsertToken` command in this file itself. Luckily, Sitecore provides better flexibility to keep our scripting files separate from Sitecore files and injects them into applications dynamically. Here, we injected our custom JavaScript file into the RTE page by registering it in the `Sitecore.config` file in the `<sitecore/clientscripts/htmleditor>` node. Similarly, we can add a custom JavaScript file to all the pages of Sitecore by registering it in the `<sitecore/clientscripts/everypage>` node.

It's time to make content authors happier by giving them RTE tokens, which we achieved in these two recipes.

Dealing with user-generated content using an Item Web API

Sometimes, we have a requirement to implement **user-generated content** (**UGC**) creation, that is, comments or feedback to products, events, and so on, on a live site and yet it might require a proper workflow set up with comment moderation before making the content live.

The best approach would be to store this content in the master database so that reviewers can moderate it and make it live by publishing. It also needs a security-hardened architecture as the master database cannot be accessed directly from content delivery servers. In this recipe, you will learn how to create UGC along with the workflow or autopublish feature using the Sitecore **Item Web API** framework.

Getting Ready

This recipe assumes that you have already created a product details page along with comment submission, which is live (or in a content delivery environment). On comment creation, we will create a comments item under the current page (product or event) in the master database using the Sitecore Item Web API.

How to do it...

We will first create a `Comment` template and assign a workflow state:

1. Create a `/sitecore/templates/Cookbook/Comment` template with the `Username`, `Email`, `Comment`, and `Commented On` fields. In its standard values, keep the `Workflow` field in **Waiting Approval** state. So, whenever any comment gets created, it will be sent to the workflow automatically.

   We will create comment items using Web APIs from content delivery servers. So, we will make the Web API accessible from outside of content management servers with standard Sitecore security.

2. On the content management server, set the security mode to **StandardSecurity** with **ReadWrite** access to your site from `\App_Config\Include\Sitecore Cookbook.ItemWebApi.config` or from a custom patch configuration. Disallow access to any anonymous users as follows:

```
<site name="website">
  <patch:attribute name="itemwebapi.mode">
    StandardSecurity</patch:attribute>
  <patch:attribute name="itemwebapi.access">
    ReadWrite</patch:attribute>
  <patch:attribute name="itemwebapi.allowanonymousaccess">
    false</patch:attribute>
</site>
```

3. We will now create comment items by passing comment-related fields using Web API requests. In the `SitecoreCookbook` project, create a `Comment` class and an `AddComment()` method in the `Data` folder. This method expects the current (`Context`) item, username, e-mail, and comments filled in the **Comments** section of the page. Using these parameters, we will create a Web API request:

```
public void AddComment(Sitecore.Data.Items.Item product,
  string userName, string email, string comment)
{
  string host = "sitecorecookbook", database = "master";

  string url = String.Format("http://{0}/-/item/
    v1/?sc_itemid={1}&template={2}&name={3}" +
    "&sc_database={4}&payload=content",
    host, product.ID.ToString(),"Cookbook/Comment",
    Guid.NewGuid().ToString(), database);

  HttpWebRequest request =
    (HttpWebRequest)WebRequest.Create(url);
  SetRequestHeaders(request);
  SendFieldValues(request, userName, email, comment);
}
```

4. Create a `SendFieldValues()` method to pass field names and relevant values in the POST request body for item creation as follows:

```
private static void SendFieldValues(HttpWebRequest request,
    string userName, string email, string comment)
{
    string fields = string.Format("User
        name={0}&Email={1}&comment={2}&Commented On={3}",
        userName, email, comment,
        DateTime.Now.ToString("yyyyMMddTHHmmss"));

    byte[] data = Encoding.ASCII.GetBytes(fields);
    request.ContentLength = data.Length;
    request.ContentType = "application/x-www-form-
        urlencoded";
    request.Method = "POST";
    request.KeepAlive = false;

    using (Stream stream = request.GetRequestStream())
    {
        stream.Write(data, 0, data.Length);
    }
}
```

5. As we are creating secure access to Web APIs on the content management server, we need to pass user credentials in request headers. Here, we can use credentials with limited write access rights:

```
private static void SetRequestHeaders(HttpWebRequest request)
{
    request.Headers.Add("X-Scitemwebapi-Username",
        "sitecore\\comment_creator");
    request.Headers.Add("X-Scitemwebapi-Password", "b");
}
```

6. Now, invoke the `AddComment()` method that we created in step 3. When any end user submits the comment, you will find a new comment item gets created:

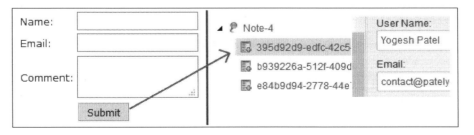

7. Now, content reviewers can moderate the comments and publish to live websites so that comments will be visible on the page where end users submit.

There's more...

Here, we set a workflow for comment moderation before becoming visible to live pages. Sometimes, we might have a requirement that comments should get published automatically, which means that no comment moderation is required. For these comment items, we can ignore the workflow and set an item for autopublishing. We have already covered such a recipe to autopublish any newly created and saved item using custom event handlers in the *Creating a custom event handler to auto-publish on an item save* recipe of *Chapter 4, Leveraging the Sitecore Backend*.

Here, we published the comments to the web content database itself. If we do not want to merge both site content and UGC into a common database, we can use a fresh copy of the web database as a user-generated content (ugc) database. So, whenever we publish the comments or any other UGC items, they should get published to the ugc database only, not on actual web databases. Additionally, normal site content publishing to a ugc database should be restricted.

We can also add these items to a bucket if we are getting lots of comments; you will learn using buckets in the *Managing millions of items using an item bucket* recipe of *Chapter 9, Sitecore Search*.

We used the Item Web API, which we can use to manipulate the content items through HTTP requests. The API gives access to content through item paths, IDs, and Sitecore queries. You can learn more on Item Web APIs at `https://goo.gl/2Iwj2U`.

Storing external content using a custom cache

While developing a Sitecore solution, you may sometimes face a situation where you have to fetch some data from external resources frequently. So, you want to save them in a cache for some time as they get changed frequently. If you have CSS and JS items in Sitecore and want to cache their merged and minified content output to avoid doing it on every request, you can use Sitecore's custom cache.

In this recipe, you will learn how to use Sitecore's **custom cache** mechanism.

Getting Ready

In this recipe, we will consider a case where we want to show some share price details from an external web service. Here, to gain better performance of the website, we will avoid fetching the share price on every request and serve the share price delayed by a maximum of two minutes by caching it for two minutes.

How to do it...

We will first create a `CustomCache` to store share price details:

1. In the `SitecoreCookbook` project, create a `SharePriceCache` class in the `Caching` folder and inherit it from `Sitecore.Caching.CustomCache`. This inheritance is required as the `CustomCache` is an abstract class, so we cannot use it directly.

2. Initialize constructor of `CustomCache` to pass the cache name and maximum cache size to Sitecore's cache manager as follows:

```
public SharePriceCache(string name, long maxSize)
  : base(name, maxSize) { }
```

3. Create a new instance of the `SetString()` and `GetString()` methods. Here, the `SetString()` method expects three parameters—key, string, and time—when the cache will expire:

```
new public void SetString(string key, string value,
  DateTime expiry)
{
  base.SetString(key, value, expiry);
}

new public string GetString(string key)
{
  return base.GetString(key);
}
```

4. Now, we will need a static cache manager to manage `SharePriceCache` that will instantiate the `CustomCache` object in the constructor. Create another `SharePriceCacheManager` class and keep a static constructor as follows. Here, we hardcoded the cache name and maximum size of the cache in the constructor for ease of code; otherwise, you can define them in settings if required:

```
private static readonly SharePriceCache Cache;

static SharePriceCacheManager()
{
```

```
    Cache = new SharePriceCache("SharePriceCache",
      StringUtil.ParseSizeString("10MB"));
  }
```

5. Create the `SetCache()` and `GetCache()` methods to read and write the cache as follows:

```
public static string GetCache(string key)
{
  return Cache.GetString(key);
}

public static void SetCache(string key, string value,
  DateTime expiry)
{
  Cache.SetString(key, value, expiry);
}
```

6. Now, you can use the `SharePriceCacheManager` class anywhere to read and write the cache. In the `SitecoreCookbook` project, create a `SharePriceController` class and an `ActionResult ShowSharePriceDetails()` method in the `Controllers` folder. Here, we are getting the share price information for the company code from an external service through the `FetchSharePriceFromExternalSystem()` method, which you can implement yourself:

```
public ActionResult ShowSharePriceDetails()
{
  string code = RenderingContext.Current.Rendering.Item[
    "Company Code"];

  string shareprice =
    SharePriceCacheManager.GetCache(code);
  if (string.IsNullOrEmpty(shareprice))
  {
    DateTime expiresOn = DateTime.Now.AddMinutes(2);
    shareprice = FetchSharePriceFromExternalSystem(code);
    SharePriceCacheManager.SetCache(code, shareprice,
      expiresOn);
  }

  return Content(shareprice);
}
```

7. You can now get the share price information stored for different code (companies) faster as we are storing it in the Sitecore custom cache for two minutes and reducing requests to the external service.

How it works...

In the backend, `SharePriceCache` or `Sitecore.Caching.CustomCache` manages the `Sitecore.Caching.Cache` object, which contains a collection of all the caches that we create. So, when we add a cache object to `SharePriceCacheManager`, it makes a cache entry in the local collection of the cache object.

Here, we named the custom cache `SharePriceCache` and set its maximum size as 10 MB. This means that when memory allocation for this cache exceeds 10 MB, it will automatically clear 50% of the cache, that is, 5 MB, for further cache creation. You can monitor caches using the `http://sitecorecookbook/sitecore/admin/cache.aspx` tool. Here, you can see that **SharePriceCache** has **6** caching entries that occupy a total of **1.9 MB** out of the maximum size of **10 MB**:

Name	Count	Size	Delta	MaxSize
service[xsl]	0	0	0	50MB
SharePriceCache	6	1.9MB	1.9MB	10MB
shell[filtered items]	0	0	0	10MB

You will also find that the cache value will get cleared automatically after two minutes of its creation but the cache entry exists in the Sitecore cache.

There's more...

You can clear all `SharePriceCache` by invoking the `Clear()` method of the `CustomCache` class. For this, you can create a method in the `SharePriceCacheManager` class and invoke it when necessary:

```
public static void ClearSharePriceCache()
{
    Cache.Clear();
}
```

It works in the same way where you can clear any specific cache or even all the caches using the following APIs:

```
CacheManager.ClearAccessResultCache();
CacheManager.ClearAllCaches();
```

We can store a cache in various ways. Here, we created a cache that was time-dependent. In the same way, we can create a cache that will get cached permanently (until it gets cleared) using `SetString(string key, string value)`. The `CustomCache` class also has a provision to store objects as a cache using the `SetObject()` method.

See also

You can learn more about caching fundamentals and different ways of implementing a custom cache at `http://goo.gl/5mKJ5w`.

6

Working with Media

In this chapter, we will cover some interesting tasks related to Sitecore media items. You will learn the following recipes:

- ▶ Restricting malicious files being uploaded to the media library
- ▶ Downloading the media library folder
- ▶ Protecting media files under a disclaimer
- ▶ Achieving responsive images
- ▶ Serving media files from CDN or external storage

Introduction

In this chapter, you will see different techniques that are required to make media management secure, such as restricting malicious file uploads, preventing **denial-of-service** (**DoS**) attacks while media downloads, and preventing direct access of media files from search engines or bots using disclaimers.

Responsive web design and CDN have become a necessity of major websites. Recipes in this chapter also cover achieving responsive images, publishing them to CDN, and serving images from CDN domains to get the maximum benefit of **domain sharding**.

Restricting malicious files being uploaded to the media library

Sitecore has the facility of uploading media files that does not validate the extension or MIME type of file being uploaded. This would enable an adversary to upload a malicious file to the web server and attempt to execute it. To have restrictions over this, Sitecore provides the **Upload Filter** tool, which allows us to restrict certain extensions. You can download it from `https://goo.gl/DxnwBk`. However, is only restricting extensions enough? An adversary can rename the EXE file to JPG and upload it. Here, the file is still malicious. This recipe explains how we can restrict the file from being uploaded by checking its extensions, MIME types, and magic numbers.

How to do it...

Let's see how we can secure Sitecore's upload files mechanism:

1. In the `SitecoreCookbook` project, create a new `UploadRestrictions` class in the `Pipelines` folder and inherit it from `Sitecore.Pipelines.Upload.UploadProcessor`.

2. Create two methods, `AddRestrictedContentType()` and `AddRestrictedExtension()`, in the class:

```
private List<string> restrictedContentType = new
  List<string>();
private List<string> restrictedExtensions = new
  List<string>();

protected virtual void AddRestrictedContentType(XmlNode
  configNode)
{
  restrictedContentType.Add(configNode.InnerText);
}
protected virtual void AddRestrictedExtension(XmlNode
  configNode)
{
  string[] extensions = configNode.InnerText.Split(new
    string[] { "," }, StringSplitOptions.RemoveEmptyEntries);
  foreach (string extension in extensions)
    restrictedExtensions.Add("." + extension);
}
```

3. Add two more methods, `IsRestrictedExtension()` and `IsRestrictedContentType()`, as follows:

```
private bool IsRestrictedExtension(string extension)
{
  return restrictedExtensions.Exists(ext =>
    string.Equals(ext, extension,
    StringComparison.CurrentCultureIgnoreCase));
}
private bool IsRestrictedContentType(string contentType)
{
  return restrictedContentType.Exists(type =>
    string.Equals(type, contentType,
    StringComparison.CurrentCultureIgnoreCase));
}
```

4. Add the `Process()` method as follows:

```
public void Process(UploadArgs args)
{
  foreach (string fileKey in args.Files)
  {
    string fileName = args.Files[fileKey].FileName;
    string contentType = args.Files[fileKey].ContentType;
    string extension = Path.GetExtension(fileName);

    if (IsRestrictedExtension(extension) ||
      IsRestrictedContentType(contentType)) {
      args.ErrorText = "Upload of this file restricted.";
      args.AbortPipeline(); break;
    }
  }
}
```

5. In the `\App_Config\Include\Cookbook` folder, create a patch configuration `SitecoreCookbook.UploadRestrictions.config` file and add the previously created custom processor in the `<configuration/sitecore/processors/uiUpload>` node above the `CheckPermissions` processor or place it as the first processor in the `<uiUpload>` pipeline using `patch:before="*[1]"`. Configure restricted extensions and content types in the `processor` section as follows:

```
<uiUpload>
  <processor mode="on" patch:before="*[1]"
    type="SitecoreCookbook.Media.UploadRestrictions,
    SitecoreCookbook">
    <restrictedExtensions
      hint="raw:AddRestrictedExtension">
      <extensions>exe,msi,dll,bat,html,aspx</extensions>
```

```
    </restrictedExtensions>
    <restrictedContentTypes
      hint="raw:AddRestrictedContentType">
      <contentType>application/octet-stream</contentType>
    </restrictedContentTypes>
  </processor>
</uiUpload>
```

6. Now upload any file with a restricted extension or content type and see how it will restrict that file from being uploaded:

The file "Setup.bat" cannot be uploaded.

OK

How it works...

The `<uiUpload>` pipeline is executed while uploading a media file to Sitecore. We kept our custom processor first in this pipeline so that before uploading any file, Sitecore will take the first action to check extensions and content types, and if it finds a restricted file getting uploaded, it will abort the pipeline execution using `args.AbortPipeline()`.

Here, we mentioned extensions to restrict in the `<restrictedExtensions>` section. The `<restrictedExtensions hint="row:AddRestrictedExtension">` section allows you to implement custom logic yourself to extract content from the section itself. In the same way, we can configure content types to restrict in the `<restrictedContentTypes>` section.

There's more...

ASP.NET finds the content type from the file request headers. However, when we have **Flash** installed on the browser and Sitecore uploads files using the Flash upload mechanism, we will not get the exact content type of the file at that time.

To get the exact content type for the Flash upload, we can use magic numbers of the files by reading the first few bytes of the contents of the file being uploaded. Refer to `http://goo.gl/qZcR0U` for better understanding and implementation of the content type validation using magic numbers.

Downloading the media library folder

Sitecore provides you with the facility to download individual files from the Content Editor. Sometimes, content authors might need to download the whole media library or media files of any selected folders in a ZIP file. In this recipe, you will learn how to use Sitecore APIs to download the whole media library folder along with media metadata.

How to do it...

We will first create a Command class to download the media library folder:

1. In the SitecoreCookbook project, create a new DownloadMediaLibraryFolder class in the Commands folder and inherit it from the Command class.

2. Override the Execute() method of the class as follows:

```
public override void Execute(CommandContext context)
{
  if (context.Items.Length == 1) {
    Item currentItem = context.Items[0];
    DownloadMediaFolder(currentItem);
  }
  return;
}
```

3. Create the DownloadMediaFolder() method. Here, we create a ZIP file in the MediaDownload directory in the temp directory of Sitecore. Here, we have collected only the immediate child items and added them to ZipWriter. To use ZipWriter, add the Sitecore.Zip.dll assembly to the project:

```
private void DownloadMediaFolder(Item item)
{
  string folder = Settings.TempFolderPath +
    "/MediaDownload/" +
  item.Name + DateTime.Now.ToString("HHmmss");
  string zipFile = FileUtil.MapPath(folder + ".zip");

  if (!Directory.Exists(FileUtil.MapPath(folder)))
    Directory.CreateDirectory(FileUtil.MapPath(folder));

  ChildList images = item.GetChildren();
  using (ZipWriter zipWriter = new ZipWriter(zipFile))
  {
    foreach (Item image in images)
      AddFileToZip(zipWriter, image);
  }
```

```
Sitecore.Context.ClientPage.ClientResponse.Download(
  zipFile);
}
```

4. Create the `AddFileToZip()` method to get a media stream for each media item, save the file to a physical disk, and add each individual file to the ZIP archive:

```
private static void AddFileToZip(ZipWriter zipWriter, Item
  image)
{
  string fileName = image.Name + "." + image["extension"];
  MediaStream mediaStream =
    MediaManager.GetMedia(image).GetStream();
  if (mediaStream!=null)
    zipWriter.AddEntry(fileName, mediaStream.Stream);
}
```

5. Create a `Content Editor` button and assign a command to it with the previously created `Command` class.

6. Select any media library folder from the Content Editor that contains media files and click on the button that you created. You will find that a ZIP file will get downloaded, which contains all the media files of the immediate children.

How it works...

In step 2, we collected the selected media library folder item from the `CommandContext` object passed in the `Execute()` method using `context.Items[0]`.

Here, we have collected only the immediate children of the selected media library folder. However, you can change the code as per your requirement to have all the descendants.

From the media item, we retrieved `MediaStream` using the `MediaManager.GetMedia(mediaItem).GetStream()` API. This stream is created based on the media cache. If there is no media cache created for the media item, it will first fetch blob data from the database, then create a media cache. It means that if you download the media library, it's not necessary that it will fetch all blob data from the database, but will serve from the media cache only, which is stored in the `\App_Data\MediaCache\` folder on the server.

See also

▶ You can read more on how a media cache works at `http://goo.gl/RmbnYP`.

Protecting media files under a disclaimer

Sometimes, we get a requirement to protect media files by showing a disclaimer, which means we need to put a disclaimer before viewing any media file to prevent abuse by setting governing laws, owning the content, protecting documents from search engines, and so on. In such cases, the user will first agree to the disclaimer and then will be able to view the media documents.

In this recipe, you will learn showing disclaimers on media items using MediaRequestHandler.

How to do it...

We will first create a Disclaimer Content Page, which will be opened when a user opens a protected media item:

1. Create a Disclaimer Page template with two fields, Title and Description. Create a content page, /Home/Privacy-Disclaimer, using this template.

2. Create another Disclaimer Settings template with two fields, Media To Protect as Treelist and Disclaimer Page as Droptree. Set the **Media To Protect** field source to an appropriate media path, for example, /sitecore/media library/Files. This setting defines which disclaimer page should be opened when a protected media file gets accessed. Create a disclaimer setting using this template. We can have multiple settings as follows:

3. Let's see how we can achieve a media disclaimer using MediaRequestHandler. In SitecoreCookbook, create a MediaDisclaimerHandler class in the Handlers folder and inherit it from Sitecore.Resources.Media.MediaRequestHandler. We will achieve this disclaimer functionality using an ASP.NET session, so we must implement the System.Web.SessionState.IRequiresSessionState interface here.

4. Override the `DoProcessRequest()` method of `MediaRequestHandler`. Here, we will check whether the requested media item is a protected item or not. If it's protected, we will show the disclaimer page. Here, we ignored checking for disclaimers when the `Context` database is `core`, as we need to protect media items of content database only:

```
protected override bool DoProcessRequest(HttpContext
  context, MediaRequest request,
  Sitecore.Resources.Media.Media media)
{
  if (Context.Database.Name.ToLower() != "core") {
    string mediaId =
      media.MediaData.MediaItem.ID.ToString();

    Item disclaimerFolder = Context.Database.GetItem(
      "/sitecore/Content/Global/Settings/Disclaimers");
    if (disclaimerFolder != null)
    {
      foreach (Item disc in disclaimerFolder.Children)
      {
        if (disc["Media To Protect"].IndexOf(mediaId) >= 0) {
          string disclaimerPageId = disc["Disclaimer Page"];
          Item item = Context.Database.GetItem(new
            ID(disclaimerPageId));
          string url = LinkManager.GetItemUrl(item);

          ShowDisclaimer(mediaId, url);
          break;
        }
      }
    }
  }
  return base.DoProcessRequest(context, request, media);
}
```

5. Add the `ShowDisclaimer()` method to redirect the user to the relevant `Disclaimer` Page. To know whether the user has accepted the disclaimer or not, we check the `ProtectedMedia+<MediaId>` session. If the session is null, the user has not accepted the media yet so we will redirect to the disclaimer page that we will create in later steps; otherwise, we will directly show the requested media file:

```
private void ShowDisclaimer(string mediaId, string
  disclaimerUrl)
{
  HttpContext context = HttpContext.Current;
  if (context.Session["ProtectedMedia" + mediaId] == null){
    context.Session["ProtectedMedia"] = mediaId;
    context.Session["ProtectedMediaUrl"] =
      context.Request.Url.ToString();
```

```
    context.Response.Redirect(disclaimerUrl, true);
  }
}
```

6. Let's create the `Disclaimer Content` page. Create a `Disclaimer.cshtml` view file. Write code to show the disclaimer page's `Title` and `Description`. Also add two buttons, `Accept` and `Reject`:

```
<h3> @Html.Sitecore().Field("Title", Model.Item) </h3>
<p> @Html.Sitecore().Field("Description", Model.Item) </p>

@using (Html.BeginForm("Submit", "Disclaimer",
  FormMethod.Post)) {
  <p>
    <input type="submit" name="submitButton" value="Accept" />
    <input type="submit" name="submitButton" value="Reject" />
  </p>
}
```

7. In the `SitecoreCookbook` project, create a `DisclaimerController` class with a `ActionResult` method, `Submit()`, in the `Controllers` folder. Here, if the user has accepted the disclaimer, we will update the protected media session and redirect the user to the media file:

```
[AcceptVerbs(HttpVerbs.Post)]
public ActionResult Submit(string submitButton)
{
  string MediaId =
    HttpContext.Session["ProtectedMedia"].ToString();
  string mediaUrl =
    HttpContext.Session["ProtectedMediaUrl"].ToString();
  if (submitButton == "Accept")
    HttpContext.Session["ProtectedMedia" + MediaId] = "1";
  else
    HttpContext.Session["ProtectedMedia" + MediaId] = null;

  return Redirect(mediaUrl);
}
```

8. Add the created disclaimer view to the presentation details of the `Disclaimer Content` page, `/Home/Privacy-Disclaimer`, which we created in step 1.

9. From the `Web.config` file, in the `<system.webServer/handlers>` section, comment the existing `sitecore_media.ashx` handler. Instead of this handler, add the created custom `MediaRequestHandler` as follows:

```
<add verb="*" name="DisclaimerHandler"
  type="SitecoreCookbook.Handlers.MediaDisclaimerHandler,
  SitecoreCookbook" path="sitecore_media.ashx" />
```

10. Now, open the media that is selected in the **Media To Protect** field, as shown in step 2 (that is, `http://sitecorecookbook/~/media/files/patents.pdf`). It should redirect you to the disclaimer page. Clicking on the **Accept** button will allow you to download/view the media file.

From Sitecore 8.1, the media request prefix has been changed from tilde (~) to a hyphen (-) by default in order to boost performance. So, you can request the preceding URL as `http://sitecorecookbook/-/media/files/patents.pdf`.

Disclaimer

This page lists several **disclaimer statements**. The disclaimer notices you use will depend on which legal aspects are important to the company.

| Accept | Reject |

How it works...

Sitecore serves media items using a custom handler, `sitecore_media.ashx`. By default, `MediaRequestHandler` does not implement a session, but to achieve the media disclaimer, we implemented the `IRequiresSessionState` interface so that it will allow us to use the ASP.NET session to manage disclaimer session values.

Sitecore has a few other custom handlers such as `sitecore_api.ashx`, `sitecore_xaml.ashx`, `sitecore_icon.ashx`, and `sitecore_feed.ashx`. The custom handlers are first identified by the `CustomHandlers` processor of the `<httpRequestBegin>` pipeline. It resolves the custom handler if the requested URL pattern matches any custom handler trigger defined in the `<sitecore/customHandlers>` section in `Sitecore.config`. For example, you can find a custom handler for media defined as `<handler` **`trigger="~/media/"`** `handler="sitecore_media.ashx"/>`.

Once the custom handler is resolved, it continues execution with handler we defined in `Web.config`, in the `<system.webServer/handler>` section, which we did in step 9.

Using `IRequiresSessionState` in a media handler can slow down the media requests as session state access requires that the handler runs sequentially using a lock on it so that all media files (images) on a page will be served sequentially. To overcome this issue, you can refer to `http://goo.gl/NdfHY3`.

Achieving responsive images

In responsive websites, getting different sized images based on the screen size (viewport) would be a great option to serve optimized images to make pages faster and provide better user experience.

In this recipe, you will learn rendering different sized images dynamically using `MediaUrlOptions`. We will render the `<picture>` element to achieve responsive images in HTML 5.

Getting ready

A Sitecore image will be rendered as `<img src="/~/media/Images/image.jpg" />`. To get a responsive image, we will render the `<picture>` tag as follows. If you are not aware of it, get some basic knowledge from `http://goo.gl/GmHprC`.

```
<picture>
  <source media="(min-width: 800px)"
    srcset="/~/media/Images/Cookbook/myimage.jpg?w=200">
  <source media="(min-width: 500px)"
    srcset="/~/media/Images/Cookbook/myimage.jpg?w=150">
  <img srcset="/~/media/Images/Cookbook/myimage.jpg?w=300">
</picture>
```

How to do it...

We will first create an extension method to generate the expected modified image tag:

1. In the `SitecoreCookbook` project, create a `Dimensions` class in the `Helpers` folder, and create properties and constructors as follows:

```
public class Dimensions
{
  public int ScreenSize { get; set; }
  public int Width { get; set; }
  public int Height { get; set; }
  public Dimensions(int screenSize, int width, int height)
  {
    ScreenSize = screenSize;
    Width = width;
    Height = height;
  }
}
```

2. In the same folder, create another `SitecoreHelperExtensions` class, and add an extension method, `RenderResponsivePicture()`:

```
public static HtmlString RenderResponsivePicture(this
  SitecoreHelper helper, string fieldName, Item item =
  null, bool isEditable = false, List<Dimensions>
  dimensions = null)
{
  if (item.Fields[fieldName] == null)
    return new HtmlString(string.Empty);

  var mediaItem = new
    ImageField(item.Fields[fieldName]).MediaItem;
  if (mediaItem == null)
    return new HtmlString(string.Empty);

  if (Sitecore.Context.PageMode.IsExperienceEditor)
    return helper.Field(fieldName, item);

  return GeneratePictureTag(dimensions, mediaItem);
}
```

3. Create the `GeneratePictureTag()` method to generate the `<picture>` tag:

```
private static HtmlString GeneratePictureTag(
  List<Dimensions> dimensions, Item mediaItem)
{
  if (dimensions == null || dimensions.Count == 0)
    return new HtmlString(string.Empty);

  StringBuilder html = new StringBuilder("<picture>");
  foreach (Dimensions param in
    dimensions.Take(dimensions.Count - 1))
  {
    string mediaUrl = GetMediaUrl(mediaItem, param.Width,
      param.Height);
    html.AppendFormat("<source media=\"(min-width: {0}px)\"
      srcset=\"{1}\">", param.ScreenSize, mediaUrl);
  }

  Dimensions lastParam = dimensions.Last();
  string imgUrl = GetMediaUrl(mediaItem, lastParam.Width,
    lastParam.Height);
  html.AppendFormat("<img src=\"{0}\" alt=\"{1}\">",
    imgUrl, mediaItem["Alt"]);

  html.Append("</picture>");
  return new HtmlString(html.ToString());
}
```

4. Create the `GetMediaUrl()` method to generate media URLs to serve an image with the passed `height` and `width` of the image:

```
private static string GetMediaUrl(Item mediaItem, int
  width, int height)
{
  MediaUrlOptions mediaUrlOptions = new MediaUrlOptions();
  if (width > 0)
    mediaUrlOptions.Width = width;
  if (height > 0)
    mediaUrlOptions.Height = height;
  return MediaManager.GetMediaUrl(mediaItem,
    mediaUrlOptions);
}
```

5. Create an `Image-Gallery.cshtml` view and write the following code to render responsive images:

```
@using SitecoreCookbook.Helpers
@using Sitecore.Data.Items
@model RenderingModel
@foreach (Item item in Model.Item.Children)
{
  <div>
    @Html.Sitecore().RenderResponsivePicture("Image", item,
      false,
      new List<Dimensions>{
        new Dimensions(800, 200,0),
        new Dimensions(500, 150,0),
        new Dimensions(300, 100,0)
      })
  </div>
}
```

6. Add this view rendering to a page, and make sure that its children have the `Image` field to render the image.

Do not forget to include the following `<meta>` viewport element to your main layout to support HTML 5:

```
<meta name="viewport" content="width=device-width,
  initial-scale=1.0" />
```

7. Preview the page using device emulators from your browser to test with different devices; you will find that different sized images are getting served for different sized devices. You will find images loaded as follows:

How it works...

Here, the `<picture>` tag expects different sized images for different screen sizes of devices. To achieve this, we need different media URLs that can serve the same image in different sizes.

Luckily, Sitecore provides out-of-the-box features to resize, scaling, and so on on the fly. We can perform these transformations by providing different query string parameters to a Sitecore image URL, such as h (height), w (width), and so on. For example, `http://sitecorecookbook/~/media/myimage.jpg` is an original image. While, `http://sitecorecookbook/~/media/myimage.jpg?w=200` will serve the same image by resizing it to a width of 200 pixels.

To generate a media URL, you can define different parameters to an object of `MediaUrlOptions` and pass it to the `MediaManager.GetMediaUrl(MediaItem, MediaUrlOptions)` method, which is what we did in step 4.

To check how we are getting responsive images from the local system, you can use device emulators from modern browsers such as Chrome or Firefox. From the emulator, select different devices and request the page; you will find that different sized images will be served as per `Dimensions` that we defined in step 5.

 Image parameters can be used to make a DoS attack by creating and requesting different media options that will keep the Sitecore server fully busy in image transformation activities. To avoid this, it's strongly recommended to keep media request protection enabled.

You can enable media request protection and configure the related settings from the `\App_ Config\Include\Sitecore.Media.RequestProtection.config` file.

By default, Sitecore generates media URLs with the `.ashx` extension. You can switch to its relevant extension by changing the following setting to `Sitecore.config`:

```
<setting name="Media.RequestExtension" value=""/>
```

There's more...

You can learn different image transformation parameters from `http://goo.gl/eoljwG`. It also explains how you can perform this recipe without using HTML 5. Apart from these out-of-the-box transformation parameters, you can also create your custom parameters. You can learn how to create custom transformation parameters from `https://goo.gl/jZI9Wk`.

Sitecore provides different algorithms and settings for image resizing and quality. You can learn these settings to get optimized responsive images from `http://goo.gl/h0n5mk`.

Serving media files from CDN or external storage

Sometimes, we use **content delivery network** (**CDN**) as a reverse proxy from where it can serve content and all media files by caching them on it.

Sometimes, we use CDN just to serve media files using multiple domains (domain sharding), that is, your content will get served from `http://sitecorecookbook.com/` and your images or files will get served from `http://sitecorecookbook.cdn.com/`. So, page rendering would be even faster as browsers will be able to download more resources simultaneously, resulting in faster user experience.

In this recipe, you will learn how we can publish media files to CDN storage while publishing them and access these media files from the CDN domain.

How to do it...

First of all, we will intercept the `<publishItem>` pipeline to copy media files to the CDN server:

1. In the `SitecoreCookbook` project, create a class file named `PublishToCDN` in the `Publishing` folder and inherit it from `PublishItemProcessor`.

2. Override the `Process()` method to upload media to the CDN server on media item publishing:

```
public override void Process(PublishItemContext context)
{
  var item = context.PublishHelper.GetSourceItem(
    context.ItemId);
  if (item != null && item.ID != ItemIDs.MediaLibraryRoot
    && item.TemplateID != TemplateIDs.MediaFolder &&
    item.Paths.IsMediaItem)
  {
    string mediaPath = item.Paths.MediaPath;
    if (context.Action == PublishAction.DeleteTargetItem)
      DeleteMediaFile(mediaPath);
    else
    {
      MediaStream mediaStream =
        MediaManager.GetMedia(item).GetStream();
      UploadMediaFile(mediaPath, mediaStream.Stream);
    }
  }
}
```

3. Implement `UploadMediaFile()` and `DeleteMediaFile()` methods to upload or delete media files. For this, you can use an API provided by the CDN provider. Here, we passed the media stream to create a file on the destination media path.

 For local testing purposes, you can copy the publishing media items to another directory of your local system, assuming that it's a CDN drive.

4. In the `\App_Config\Include\Cookbook` folder, create a patch configuration `SitecoreCookbook.CDNPublishing.config` file. In the `<configuration/sitecore/pipelines>` section, add this processor to the `<publishItem>` pipeline after the `PerformAction` processor section follows:

```
<publishItem>
  <processor type="SitecoreCookbook.Publishing.
    PublishToCDN, SitecoreCookbook" patch:after=
    "processor[@type='Sitecore.Publishing.
    Pipelines.PublishItem.PerformAction, Sitecore.Kernel']"
  />
</publishItem>
```

5. Publish your media items and check whether they have been uploaded to the CDN server or not!

Now, our media items are published to CDN and, to serve them, media URLs must have the domain name mapped to the CDN server. Let's see how to achieve this by customizing `MediaProvider`. In the `SitecoreCookbook` project, create another `CDNMediaProvider` class in the `Providers` folder. Inherit it from `Sitecore.Resources.Media.MediaProvider` and implement `Sitecore.Events.Hooks.IHook`. Add the `CDNDomain` property to it:

```
public string CDNDomain { get; set; }
```

6. Implement the `Initialize()` method to make our provider default `MediaProvider`:

```
public void Initialize()
{
  MediaManager.Provider = this;
}
```

7. Override the `GetMediaUrl()` method to generate a media URL with the CDN domain:

```
public override string GetMediaUrl(MediaItem item,
  MediaUrlOptions options)
{
  string mediaUrl = item.MediaPath + "." + item.Extension;
  return string.Format("{0}{1}", CDNDomain, mediaUrl);
}
```

8. In the patch configuration file that we created, add the hook to the `<configuration/sitecore/hooks>` section:

```
<hook type="SitecoreCookbook.Providers.CDNMediaProvider,
  SitecoreCookbook">
  <CDNDomain>http://sitecorecookbook.cdn.com</CDNDomain>
</hook>
```

> For local testing purposes, if you are publishing media files to the local directory, you can set it as a physical root path for another website from IIS and bind it with the `sitecorecookbook.cdn.com` hostname to serve these images.

9. View your website page and see your images getting rendered using the CDN domain. For example, your Sitecore image URL `/~/images/cookbook/coffee.jpg` will be rendered as a CDN image URL `http://sitecorecookbook.cdn.com/images/cookbook/coffee.jpg`!

How it works...

We split the recipe into two tasks. First, we uploaded the media files to CDN on their publishing, and second, we changed the media URL of all the media files getting rendered from pages.

The <publishItem> pipeline is invoked for each individual item publish; you will learn more recipes about this in *Chapter 7, Workflow and Publishing*. In our custom processor, we checked whether the publishing item is a media item, then we retrieved the media file path, and uploaded the physical file to CDN using an API provided by the CDN provider.

> If we have multiple publishing targets or multiple languages, then this processor will get called multiple times, so our code will upload the same media file multiple times. In such cases, we can configure this processor to get executed on specific publishing targets only.

The second task of this recipe was creating our custom media provider that modifies the media URL by appending the CDN domain name. For this, we created a hook to override Sitecore's default MediaProvider with our own CDNMediaProvider.

There's more...

We can also use the domain sharding technique to split resources across multiple domains. This means that website resources will get served through multiple domains. Using domain sharding, browsers will be able to download more resources simultaneously, resulting in a faster user experience. Refer to https://goo.gl/m1mgBq to know more about it.

For domain sharding, you can prepare an algorithm that will assign a domain name to each media item's URL based on the item ID or media ID.

See also

By default, Sitecore stores media files to the database. It is also possible to store media files as physical files; for this, do the following setting in the Sitecore.config file:

```
<setting name="Media.UploadAsFiles" value="true"/>
```

Once you upload media as a physical file, you can find its path in the **File Path** field of the item, as shown in the following image:

7
Workflow and Publishing

In this chapter, we will cover some different and interesting tasks related to workflow and publishing. You will learn the following recipes:

- ▶ Creating a custom action using workflow
- ▶ Achieving time-based automated publishing
- ▶ Unpublishing of items
- ▶ Using publishing events to send a publish completion e-mail
- ▶ Publishing file-based items using web deploy
- ▶ Clearing an HTML cache based on published items for a multisite environment
- ▶ Customizing the publishItem pipeline to avoid duplicate names on a live site

Introduction

This chapter assumes that you have a basic understanding of the Sitecore workflow and publishing interfaces. Here, you will learn some interesting recipes of workflow and publishing. We will see how both are interrelated with each other and how we can maximize their use to make them achieve real-life needs.

Sitecore workflow is designed in a very flexible and scalable way so we can mostly customize it without custom development. Still, in real-life workflows, we might need some customizations that need development. You will learn how to customize workflow actions using workflow APIs.

Sitecore publishing is a very essential part of Sitecore and for any website as well. There are lots of customizations that we can do with publishing for performance and scalability. You will learn doing some real-life needs such as unpublishing items, automating publishing, publishing at a specific time, using publishing events, publishing physical files along with items, and clearing site-specific caches with publishing. After learning these recipes, you will have a very clear picture of the customizing publishing architecture.

Creating a custom action using workflow

Workflows ensure that items move through a predefined set of states before they become publishable. Sometimes, to meet business requirements, we might need to add or modify states, commands, or their respective actions.

Sitecore provides an e-mail action command that uses predefined parameters such as sender, recipient, and so on to send e-mails, which is not a practical way while working with multiple editors and reviewers. In real life, business users demand that when the reviewer rejects the changes done by the editor, an e-mail should be sent to the editor who did the changes with information regarding the item along with the reviewer's comments. In this recipe, we will achieve this requirement by creating a custom action using workflow APIs.

Getting ready

This recipe assumes that you are aware of how Sitecore workflow works. For a basic understanding, you can refer to *Sitecore Workflow QuickStart Guide* at `http://goo.gl/7HSKqR`.

How to do it...

To achieve this, we will create a new `Action` template to define this customized action and related parameters. Then, we will use APIs to determine the sender and recipient to send an e-mail.

1. Create a `Reject Email Action` template in `/sitecore/templates/System/Workflow` and add fields as follows:

2. From the Content Editor, select the out-of-the-box **Sample Workflow** item, `/sitecore/system/Workflows/Sample Workflow`. In the **Awaiting Approval** state, create a `Reject Email Action` item in the **Reject** command item using the previously created template, and fill in the editing rejection e-mail information, as shown in the following image. Here, `$to$`, `$from$`, `$itempath$`, `$comments$`, and others are token variables, which will get replaced by actual values in the e-mail:

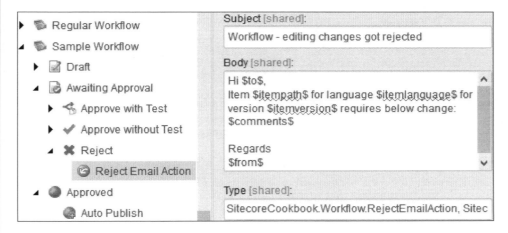

3. Now, we will create the `RejectEmailAction` class mentioned in the **Type** field in the preceding image, which will be responsible for sending an e-mail with the token details. In the `SitecoreCookbook` project, create a class named `RejectEmailAction` in the `Workflow` folder.

4. In this class, implement the `Process()` method, as shown in the following code. Here, the context user will be the reviewer user and we can get an editor user from the workflow history. We can get subject, message, comment, item, and other details from the workflow pipeline arguments:

```
public void Process(WorkflowPipelineArgs args)
{
  User editorUser = GetEditorUser(args);
  if (editorUser != null) {
```

```
     User reviewerUser = Sitecore.Context.User;

     Item innerItem = args.ProcessorItem.InnerItem;
     string subject = innerItem["subject"];
     string message = innerItem["message"];

     string comment = args.CommentFields["Comments"];
     message = message.Replace("$to$",
       editorUser.Profile.FullName)
       .Replace("$from$", reviewerUser.Profile.FullName)
       .Replace("$itempath$", args.DataItem.Paths.Path)
       .Replace("$itemlanguage$",
         args.DataItem.Language.Name)
       .Replace("$itemversion$",
         args.DataItem.Version.ToString())
       .Replace("$comments$", comment);

     SendEmail(reviewerUser.Profile.Email,
       editorUser.Profile.Email, subject, message);
   }
 }
```

5. Add the `GetEditorUser()` method to find the editor who submitted the changes in workflow. Here, we found the details of the user who did the last action from the workflow history:

```
private User GetEditorUser(WorkflowPipelineArgs args)
{
  Item item = args.DataItem;
  IWorkflow itemWorkflow =
    item.Database.WorkflowProvider.GetWorkflow(item);
  WorkflowEvent[] workflowHistory =
    itemWorkflow.GetHistory(item);

  if (workflowHistory.Any()) {
    string userName = workflowHistory.Last().User;
    return User.FromName(userName, false);
  }
  return null;
}
```

6. Implement the `SendEmail()` method to send the e-mail that we used in step 4.

7. Assign `Sample Workflow` in the **Default workflow** field in the content template's standard values, as shown in the following image:

8. Create a content item using this template, make some changes, and submit the item to workflow for the reviewing.

9. Now, when a reviewer rejects the changes with appropriate comments, the editor will get an e-mail as follows:

```
Hi Editor 1,
Item /sitecore/content/Home/News/2015-10-9 for language en for version
2 requires below change:
The time of this event should be corrected from 8:00 PM to 9:00 PM PST.

Regards
Reviewer 2
```

How it works...

Sitecore has some predefined workflow actions such as **Auto Submit**, **Validation Action**, **Auto Publish**, and others. You can use the `/sitecore/templates/System/Workflow/Action` template to create custom actions.

If a workflow action definition item is created under a workflow state item, the action is performed when an item enters the workflow state, for example, **Auto Publish**. If a workflow action definition item is created under a workflow command item, the action is executed when the command is triggered, for example, **Auto Submit** and **Validating Action**. In step 2, we created **Reject Email Action** under the **Reject** workflow command item.

To send an e-mail back to the editor, we needed user details of the current user, reviewer, editor, and item details along with comments. We can find all these details in the custom action, which Sitecore command passes through the `WorkflowPipelineArgs` parameters.

We can also pass custom parameters to workflow actions through the arguments. If you see the **Auto Publish** action item, you will find the **Parameters** field, as shown in the following image, and you can read it using the `args.Parameters()` method from the `Process()` method of the defined action class:

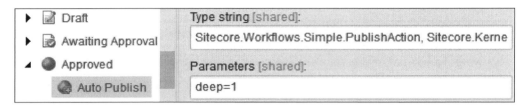

Sitecore keeps track of all workflow activities and writes everything in the `WorkflowHistory` table, which we can retrieve using APIs. This is what we achieved in step 5 to find the last workflow activity on the item.

There's more...

In this recipe, we involved only the editor and reviewer. Sometimes, business requirement comes with a more flexible requirement that when an editor submits the workflow, an e-mail should be sent to all the reviewers. To achieve this, we can apply different roles to editors and reviewers. So, when an item gets in the workflow, we can find out all the reviewers using roles and send e-mails to all of them.

There could be a further requirement that, while making a revision of the workflow item, the e-mail should not be sent to all reviewers but should be sent to that specific reviewer only. We can achieve this by checking the workflow history again for that item and identifying the last reviewer in the same way that we identified the editor.

It is always advisable to assign proper role-based rights to states. In our case, states such as **Editing**, **Awaiting Approval**, and **Approved** should be given rights for appropriate roles such as **Workflow Editor**, **Reviewer**, and **Publisher**.

Achieving time-based automated publishing

Sometimes, we need to change the web page contents frequently and publish them on or at a later specific date and time. In the daily routine, it gets very critical and time-consuming to achieve this as it requires a lot of manual work to remember at what time what content should be changed and published accurately.

This recipe will cover how we can automatically publish content based on time. It will also give us the freedom of remembering publishing items and doing the publishing in and out of office hours as well as weekends; in short, no manual publishing at all!

How to do it...

1. Create multiple versions of an item with different content, as shown in the following image:

3. Modified **10/17/2015 3:03 PM** by **sitecore\admin**.

2. Modified **10/14/2015 1:04 PM** by **sitecore\admin**.

1. Modified **10/09/2015 6:58 PM** by **sitecore\admin**.

Add version

2. Select this item from the Content Editor; in the ribbon, click on the **Change** button in the **Restriction** group from the **Publish** menu.

3. This will open the **Publishing Settings** dialog. Now, restrict the publishing of individual versions of the item based on date and time, as shown in the following image:

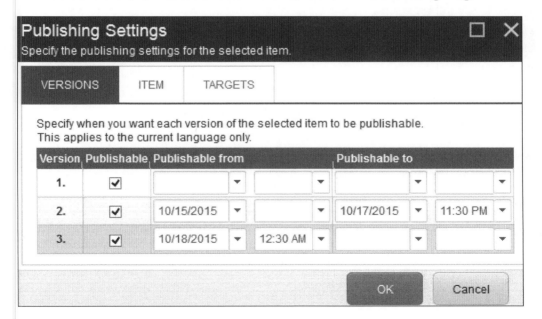

Publishing Settings

Specify the publishing settings for the selected item.

VERSIONS	ITEM	TARGETS

Specify when you want each version of the selected item to be publishable. This applies to the current language only.

Version	Publishable	Publishable from		Publishable to	
1.	✔				
2.	✔	10/15/2015		10/17/2015	11:30 PM
3.	✔	10/18/2015	12:30 AM		

OK   Cancel

4. Now, we will set up a publishing agent that will run every 30 minutes. Open the `\App_Config\Sitecore.config` file. Find the agent named `Sitecore.Tasks.PublishAgent` in the `<scheduling>` section. Set the interval of executing this agent, publication mode, and languages as per need, as shown in the following image:

```
<agent type="Sitecore.Tasks.PublishAgent" method="Run" interval="00:30:00">
  <param desc="source database">master</param>
  <param desc="target database">web</param>
  <param desc="mode (full or smart or incremental)">smart</param>
  <param desc="languages">en, en-GB, it-IT</param>
</agent>
```

5. Do not forget to set `frequency` of the Sitecore agent to less than 30 minutes; here, we set it as five minutes:

```
<!-- SCHEDULING -->
<scheduling>
  <!-- Time between checking for scheduled tasks waiting to execute -->
  <frequency>00:05:00</frequency>
```

6. That's it. You have now automated publishing with time-based restrictions.

How it works...

Here, to achieve time-based automated publishing, we used three different functionalities of Sitecore: versioning, publishing settings, and scheduling agent.

In step 1, we created different versions of an item. In each version, we kept different content, which will need to get published at a specific time.

In step 3, we set a specific time at which the version of the item should get published. Here, the publishing restrictions will be applied to the current language versions only.

In the image shown in this step, version **1** will be publishable before 10/15/2015. Version **2** will be publishable between 10/15/2015 and 10/17/2015 11:30 PM only and the same for version **3** as per the values set to it. So, while publishing the item, Sitecore will find the appropriate version to be published based on time restrictions that we have set.

In step 4, we automated the publishing of the site. Sitecore provides a publishing agent, which is disabled by default. We enabled it by setting its execution interval to the required time, say, 30 minutes (HH:mm:ss). So, this agent will get executed every 30 minutes and publish the full site.

The following are some recommended tips while using automated publishing:

> ▶ It is good practice to keep a limited number of versions, say, 10 to 15, for better CMS performance. We should delete irrelevant or older versions regularly, which we learned in the *Using a scheduling agent to delete older item versions* recipe of *Chapter 4, Leveraging the Sitecore Backend*.

> ▶ We should set the scheduling agent interval as high as possible as each publication clears the full HTML cache on live sites, which will slow down live sites until new caches are generated.

> ▶ Sitecore scheduling agents do not work when the Sitecore instance is down, so configure IIS application pool settings and Sitecore settings to keep it available all the time, which you will learn in *Chapter 11, Securing, Scaling, Optimizing, and Troubleshooting*.

There's more...

We can also set automated publishing for media items to publish them before the content pages that refer them actually get published. For this, we can customize `Sitecore.Tasks.PublishAgent` agents to publish only media items. We can pass an additional parameter of items to publish so that our custom publish agent will publish only publishable items instead of the incremental publish.

> It is recommended to have a proper workflow set up before using automatic publishing to make sure that your work-in-progress items don't get published.

Using a scheduling agent can create an overhead of publishing unnecessarily at regular intervals. To overcome this, you can also use **database task** to schedule publishing at a specific time only. For this, you can create a user interface from where content authors or publishers can schedule the publishing, which will create a database task in the background, as shown in the following image. To learn more about database tasks, you can refer to *Chapter 4, Leveraging the Sitecore Backend*:

To achieve even more accurate publishing, you can use Windows **Task Scheduler** to invoke publishing.

Unpublishing of items

While working with some important content pages, which are not yet ready to *go live*, such as press releases or limited time offers, somehow, these get published and appear on live sites by mistake or due to improper workflows. In such cases, users will delete these pages from the content management environment and publish its parent to make sure that the pages get deleted from live. However, this is not a recommended practice, which is time-consuming and risky as well.

Luckily, Sitecore provides you with a facility to unpublish items. Let's see how to use it.

How to do it...

Let's see the steps to unpublish an item:

1. Open the Content Editor and navigate to the content page that you want to unpublish.

2. In the ribbon, click on the **Change** button in the **Restrictions** group from the **Publish** tab, which will open a dialog of **Publishing Settings**. Here, select the **Item** tab. Untick the **Publishable** checkbox and click on the **OK** button:

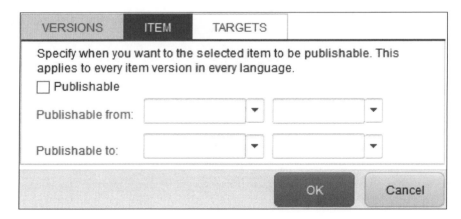

3. Publish the item.

4. Now, check whether the page has been deleted or unpublished. You will see that the live site will not show the content of this page and show a **404 Page Not found** error.

How it works...

Each Sitecore item contains a standard field named **Never publish**. While performing step 2, it actually checks the **Never publish** field of that item in the background. So, while publishing the item, Sitecore first reads this field. If it is checked, the item will get deleted from the target databases if it exists.

We can also take a simpler approach to tick/untick the **Never publish** field for any item in order to unpublish/publish the item without opening the **Restriction** dialog:

Publishing this item again by unchecking this field will make the item live again.

There's more...

It would be so convenient if Sitecore also provided some mechanism to restrict such unwanted publishing rather than being dependent on unpublishing items.

Actually, Sitecore itself provides time-based publishing restrictions. With this, we can prevent the publishing of such items in advance, which is what you learned in the previous recipe. To achieve this, open the **Publishing Settings** dialog's **ITEM** tab and select **Publishable from** and **Publishable to** fields, as shown in the following image. We can also restrict the publishing using any one or both of these fields, depending on our need:

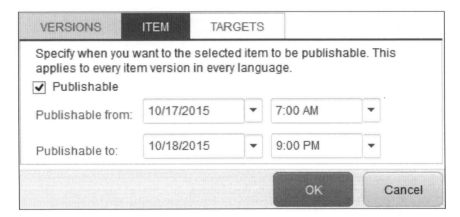

As shown in the preceding image, publishing for the item is allowed only in the time slot selected here. Publishing out of this time will be ignored by Sitecore.

> Remember to uncheck the **Never publish** field before using time-based restrictions. It is a shared field, so changing its value will affect the entire item publishing (all language versions).

Using publishing events to send a publish completion e-mail

Sitecore has no out-of-the-box provision to notify content authors when publishing gets completed or fails. Notifying users becomes very important when a longer publishing gets completed and, even more importantly, when it fails in order to remind them to publish it again.

In this recipe, you will learn how we can send e-mails to the publisher user on publishing completion using the `publish:complete` event. After this, you will be able to send e-mails after publishing fails or expires.

How to do it...

We will first create an event handler class that will extract all publishing parameters and send an e-mail with publishing details:

1. In the `SitecoreCookbook` project, create a new `SendEmail` class in the `Publishing` folder.

2. Create the `OnPublishComplete()` method as follows:

```
public void OnPublishComplete(object sender, EventArgs
  args)
{
  SitecoreEventArgs pubArgs = (SitecoreEventArgs)args;
  var optionsList = Event.ExtractParameter(pubArgs, 0) as
    IEnumerable<DistributedPublishOptions>;
  DistributedPublishOptions options = optionsList.First();

  Database database =
    Factory.GetDatabase(options.SourceDatabaseName);
  string ItemPath= string.Empty, Languages = string.Empty;
  string ItemId = options.RootItemId.ToString();
  Item item = database.GetItem(new ID(ItemId));
  if (item != null)
    return;
  ItemPath = item.Paths.Path;

  foreach (DistributedPublishOptions opts in optionsList)
  {
```

```
        Languages += opts.LanguageName + ",";
    }

    SendPublishCompletionEmail(Context.User.Name,
        Context.User.Profile.Email, ItemPath, Languages,
        options.Deep, options.PublishRelatedItems,
        options.PublishDate);
    }
```

3. Create the `SendPublishCompletionEmail()` method to send an e-mail with the required details that you invoked from the preceding step.

4. We will now register this event handler to the publish completion event. In the `\App_Config\Include\Cookbook` folder, create a patch configuration file, `SitecoreCookbook.PublishingEmail.config`, and register the handler in the `<configuration/sitecore/events>` section as follows:

```
<events>
  <event name="publish:complete">
    <handler type="SitecoreCookbook.Publishing.SendEmail,
      SitecoreCookbook" method="OnPublishComplete" />
  </event>
</events>
```

5. Now publish an item; you will get an e-mail once the publishing is finished.

How it works...

Sitecore raises many events during the publishing process. When the publishing for all publishing languages and publishing targets is completed, the `publish:complete` event gets executed. Here, in the event handler that we created in the `OnPublishComplete()` method, we can get publishing details. `SitecoreEventArgs` contains multiple parameters. In the first parameter, we can get a collection of `Sitecore.Publishing.DistributedPublishOptions` using the following code:

```
SitecoreEventArgs pubArgs = (SitecoreEventArgs)args;
var optionsList = Event.ExtractParameter(pubArgs, 0) as
  IEnumerable<DistributedPublishOptions>;
```

The collection length will be the multiplication of selected languages and publishing targets. This means that if we have published one or more items in three languages with two publishing targets, the arguments will have a total of six `DistributedPublishOptions`.

We can get all common publishing details such as the publishing item, publishing mode (**Republish / Smart publish / Incremental publish**) with subitems, related items, and so on, and publishing date from the first `DistributedPublishOptions`. We can get selected databases and publishing targets by iterating the enumerable, which is what we did in step 2.

`Sitecore.Context.User` provides us with details of the publisher user that provides the username and e-mail address, which we will use to send the e-mail.

There's more...

We can use the `publish:fail` event when the publishing fails. If publishing faces a database network connectivity issue or any other runtime error, the publishing gets stopped and raises this event.

We can use the `publish:expired` event when the publishing gets expired in case it does not get finished after a certain period of time. The default period is two hours, which is configured in `\App_Config\Sitecore.config` as follows:

```
<setting name="Publishing.TimeBeforeStatusExpires" value="02:00:00"/>
```

Sending an e-mail on publishing failure or expiry will be helpful to content authors to publish those items again.

As an alternate, you can also override the **Publishing** dialog by overriding `Sitecore.Shell.Applications.Dialogs.Publish.PublishForm`, and you can get the status in the `CheckStatus()` method and send an e-mail.

Publishing file-based items using web deploy

In Sitecore, a few types of items get stored in the filesystem, such as sublayouts, XSLT, layouts, and others. Sitecore also allows you to store media on the filesystem. To publish such items, we can use the out-of-the-box feature of `WebDeploy` to publish physical files from the **content management** (**CM**) server to the **content delivery** (**CD**) server.

By default, web deploy synchronizes folders between source and destination instances. So, on publishing, Sitecore invokes web deploy and all the configured folders get published or synced between CM and CD. Consider a case where we are working with such a Sitecore instance where we need to publish a specific sublayout or media file, which is not achievable, out of the box, in Sitecore.

In this recipe, you will learn publishing selected sublayout files.

Getting ready

This recipe assumes that you have already installed web deploy on the CM and CD servers. Assume that we have the `D:\Sitecore\Website\` directory as the web root of the Sitecore instance. We have all sublayouts stored in a directory, say, `D:\Sitecore\Website\layouts\Sublayouts`. We will create another directory, say, `D:\Sitecore\FilesToPublish\layouts\Sublayouts`, where we will copy all publishing sublayouts and sync it with the live sublayouts directory using web deploy so that recent changes in other sublayouts of the primary directory will not get published.

How to do it...

1. In the `SitecoreCookbook` project, add a reference of the `Sitecore.Publishing.WebDeploy.dll` file, which you can find in the `bin` folder of your website.

2. In the `SitecoreCookbook` project, create a `BeginWebDeploy` class in the `Publishing` folder and inherit it from `Sitecore.Publishing.WebDeploy.PublishHandler`.

3. Create a `PublishSublayouts()` method as follows:

```
string siteRoot = @"D:\Sitecore\Website";
string deployFolder = @"D:\Sitecore\FilesToPublish";
string sublayoutPath = "/sitecore/layout/Sublayouts";

protected void PublishSublayouts(object Sender, EventArgs
  args)
{
  Publisher publisher = ((Publisher)
    (((SitecoreEventArgs)(args)).Parameters[0]));
  Item rootItem = publisher.Options.RootItem;
  if (rootItem.Paths.Path.IndexOf(sublayoutPath) >= 0)
  {
    string sourceFile = siteRoot + rootItem["Path"];
    string targetFile = deployFolder + rootItem["Path"];
    string directory = Path.GetDirectoryName(targetFile);
    Directory.CreateDirectory(directory);
    File.Copy(sourceFile, targetFile, true);

    base.OnPublish(Sender, args);
  }
}
```

4. In the `\App_Config\Include\Cookbook` folder, create a patch configuration file, `SitecoreCookbook.PublishSublayouts.config`. In the `<configuration/sitecore/events>` section, add the preceding event handler to the `publish:begin` event and set the following configurations:

```
<event name="publish:begin">
  <handler type="SitecoreCookbook.Publishing.
    BeginWebDeploy, SitecoreCookbook"
    method="PublishSublayouts">
    <tasks hint="list:AddTask">
      <default type="Sitecore.Publishing.WebDeploy.Task">
        <targetDatabase>web</targetDatabase>
        <targetServer>192.168.225.111</targetServer>
        <userName>sitecorecookbook\yogesh.patel</userName>
        <password>ICantShareIt</password>
        <localRoot>D:\Sitecore\FilesToPublish</localRoot>
        <remoteRoot>E:\Live-Sitecore\Website</remoteRoot>
        <items hint="list:AddPath">
          <sublayouts>layouts/Sublayouts</sublayouts>
        </items>
      </default>
    </tasks>
  </handler>
</event>
```

5. Select a sublayout from the Content Editor and publish it.

6. Now, it should get copied from its actual location to the `D:\Sitecore\FilesToPublish` folder on the CM or the `Publishing` instance. Also, it should get synchronized to the CD server in the `E:\Live-Sitecore\Website\layouts\Sublayouts` folder, as configured in the preceding step.

If you are not able to publish sublayouts, there could be many reasons behind it; your Sitecore logs will help you troubleshoot the issues. To troubleshoot common problems that happen with web deploy, you can refer to `http://goo.gl/4PSAuz`. If the web deploy is working well, then you might need to check Sitecore logs if there might be changes of an invalid configuration in the `publish:begin` event.

How it works...

Sitecore provides integration with web deploy for scalability to synchronize files across different domains.

In steps 1 to 3, we created an event handler that contains a `PublishSublayouts()` method, which will get invoked before the publishing starts, as we configured its handler in the `publish:begin` event. In this method, we are checking whether the root item getting published is the sublayout. We copy this sublayout file to a local folder outside the web root. Then, we invoked the `base.OnPublish(Sender, args)` method that invokes web deployment using one or more background threads to synchronize the configured sublayout folder between the CM and CD servers.

In step 4, we configured the web deploy task, which requires the following configuration nodes:

Node	Value
targetDatabase	While publishing on this database, web deploy will get invoked.
targetServer	CD server IP/domain name where the sublayouts will get synced.
username	The username, which we created with admin access to be used by web deploy.
Password	The password of this user.
localRoot	The local folder of CM from where the sublayouts will get synced.
remoteRoot	The remote folder of CD to where sublayouts will get synced.
Items /*	The relative path of folders to get synced in the `localRoot`. We can have any number of items here to synchronize. The names of elements within the `<items>` element are arbitrary.

The following image shows how we have configured the architecture to publish sublayout files:

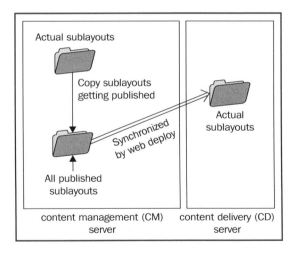

There's more...

Mostly, CM and CD servers have different domains, so we have to use web deploy to synchronize folders across different domains. If the servers are in the same domain/network, then we can use **Distributed File System** (**DFS**) to synchronize these folders and files.

The event handler contains the `<synchronous>` node. Its value decides whether to run the web deploy synchronously or not. If it's set as `true`, then Sitecore will first publish the item and then start syncing the files; otherwise, both operations will be performed concurrently. Learn more about configuring web deploy from the Sitecore *Scaling Guide* at `https://goo.gl/uNe6dO`.

Clearing an HTML cache based on published items for a multisite environment

Each Sitecore site contains its own HTML cache; its full utilization is really necessary to improve website performance. On each publish, Sitecore clears the HTML cache on the CD server of all the sites specified in the `publish:end:remote` event's `HtmlCacheClearer` handler as follows:

```
<event name="publish:end:remote">
  <handler type="Sitecore.Publishing.HtmlCacheClearer, Sitecore.Kernel"
           method="ClearCache">
    <sites hint="list">
      <site>website</site>
      <site>live-usa</site>
      <site>live-uk</site>
    </sites>
  </handler>
</event>
```

It is not a good practice that we clear the cache of all sites when publishing happens for a single site item as this can impact the performance of all the sites, and after this, each site will go to build an HTML cache again. This becomes critical when we have a large number of sites and publishing happens very frequently.

This recipe will explain how we can clear a site-specific HTML cache based on items that got published. This recipe will be very useful to improve the performance of sites when there are multiple sites hosted on a single Sitecore instance.

Getting ready

Before stepping into the recipe, make sure that you have created a separate Content Delivery instance other than the content management instance for better understanding. For this, refer to the *Configuring the Content Delivery Environment* section at `https://goo.gl/uNe6dO`. This recipe is still valid if you have a single Sitecore instance.

On the CD Sitecore instance, make sure that you have created multiple sites with different `rootPath`, enabled **Html Cache**, and pointed them to the `web` database, as shown in the following code:

```
<site name="sitecorelive" hostname="sitecorelive" database="web"
cacheHtml="true" rootPath="/sitecore/Content/"  />
```

How to do it...

Let's achieve this in simple steps as follows:

1. In the `SitecoreCookbook` project, create a class named `HtmlCacheClear` in the `Publishing` folder.

2. Create a function named `ClearCache()` in the class and write the following code:

```
protected void ClearCache(object Sender, EventArgs args)
{
  PublishEndRemoteEventArgs pubArgs =
    (PublishEndRemoteEventArgs)args;
  string rootID = pubArgs.RootItemId.ToString();

  Database db =
    Database.GetDatabase(pubArgs.TargetDatabaseName);
  Item rootItem = db.GetItem(rootID);
  if (rootItem != null)
    ClearHtmlCache(rootItem);
}
```

3. Add the `ClearHtmlCache()` function to the class:

```
private static void ClearHtmlCache(Item rootItem)
{
  List<SiteInfo> sites = Factory.GetSiteInfoList();
  var selectedSites = sites
    .Where(s => rootItem.Paths.Path.ToLower().StartsWith(
      s.RootPath.ToLower()) && s.Database.ToLower() ==
      "web");
  foreach (SiteInfo site in selectedSites) {
    ClearSiteHtmlCache(site);
  }
}
```

4. Add the `ClearSiteHtmlCache()` function to the class as follows:

```
private static void ClearSiteHtmlCache(SiteInfo site)
{
  string cacheName = site.Name + "[html]";
  Cache cache = CacheManager.FindCacheByName(cacheName);
  if (cache != null)
    cache.Clear();
}
```

5. In the `\App_Config\Include\Cookbook` folder, create a patch configuration file, `SitecoreCookbook.HtmlCacheClear.config`. In the `<configuration/sitecore/events>` section, add the preceding event handler to the `publish:remote:end` event, as shown in the following code. Make sure that you put this file in the CD environment.

```
<events>
  <event name="publish:end:remote">
  <handler type=
    "SitecoreCookbook.Publishing.HtmlCacheClear,
    SitecoreCookbook" method="ClearCache" />
  </event>
</events>
```

 If you have a common Sitecore instance serving both CM and CD, you should use `publish:end` event instead, and cast the publishing arguments with `PublishEndEventArgs` type in step 2.

6. Publish an item of any site from the CM environment and check whether the cache of that site only gets cleared from the CD environment using the `cache.aspx` tool (`http://sitecorelive/sitecore/admin/cache.aspx`). Here, you will see that the **sitecorelive[html]** site got cleared and the **Delta** found was **-1 MB**. This means that the HTML cache was 1 MB before publishing happened and it got cleared:

sitecorelive[filtered items]	0	0	0	2MB
sitecorelive[html]	0	0	-1MB	10MB
sitecorelive[registry]	0	0	0	0

How it works...

When publishing ends, the CM server executes `publish:end` event, and each CD server executes the `publish:end:remote` event. Each event in Sitecore provides its own set of arguments. The `publish:end:remote` event passes publishing-related information in the arguments, which is of the `PublishEndRemoteEventArgs` type.

In step 2, we created a `ClearCache()` function and identified the root item of the publishing that has happened using `pubArgs.RootItemId`. Similarly, we can also find the publishing language and target database information too, using these arguments.

In step 3, we created the `ClearHtmlCache()` function, which finds sites that this publishing item relates to. For this, we collected the sites list from our Sitecore instance using `Factory.GetSiteInfoList()` and filtered sites having the root item as an ancestor of the Publish root item by checking its item path. For example, `Site-A` has the `/sitecore/Content/Site-A` root path and `Site-B` has the `/sitecore/Content/Site-B` root path. Now, when a `/sitecore/Content/Site-A/Home/Careers` item gets published, then we can surely say that the item of `Site-A` has been published.

In step 4, we created a `ClearSiteHtmlCache()` function to clear the HTML cache. Sitecore stores each site's HTML cache with the name `site.Name + "[html]"`, and we obtained the object of the site's HTML cache using `CacheManager.FindCacheByName()`. If the object is valid, we will clear the cache.

There's more...

Sitecore updates item cache and data cache by default on each publish as they are application-level caches, whereas the HTML cache is a site-specific cache and the HTML output combines values of multiple items. So, while publishing any item, it is necessary to clear the HTML cache for that particular site.

Remember a few points when you are working at clearing the HTML cache:

▶ While working with XSLT files, clear the XSLT cache in the same way that we cleared the HTML cache.

▶ On publishing common templates, renderings, and so on (shared among multiple sites), always clear all the sites' HTML caches.

Customizing the publishItem pipeline to avoid duplicate names on a live site

Sitecore has a very powerful publishing architecture, which is perfect for almost all cases, but sometimes, we may need to override the publishing engine as per our requirement. The <publishItem> pipeline contains many processors playing different roles in publishing items.

A very common challenge in Sitecore is to deal with duplicate item names in a single parent. In this recipe, you will learn how we can achieve a unique item name in a single parent after publishing.

How to do it...

We will create a custom processor in the <publishItem> pipeline:

1. In the SitecoreCookbook project, create a RemoveDuplicateItems class in the Publishing folder and inherit it from PublishItemProcessor.

2. Override the Process() method of the PublishItemProcessor class:

```
public override void Process(PublishItemContext context)
{
  Item sourceItem =
    context.PublishHelper.GetSourceItem(context.ItemId);
  if (sourceItem != null) {
    Item targetItem = context.PublishOptions.
      TargetDatabase.GetItem(sourceItem.Paths.Path);

    if (targetItem != null && targetItem.ID !=
      sourceItem.ID) {
      context.PublishHelper.DeleteTargetItem(
        targetItem.ID);
      Log.Info("Deleted duplicate item: " +
        targetItem.Paths.Path, this);
    }
  }
}
```

3. In the `\App_Config\Include\Cookbook` folder, create a patch configuration file, `SitecoreCookbook.UniqueItemPublishing.config`. In the `<configuration/sitecore/pipelines>` section, add the preceding processor to the `<publishItem>` pipeline before the `DetermineAction` processor as follows:

```
<pipelines>
  <publishItem>
    <processor type="SitecoreCookbook.Publishing.
      RemoveDuplicateItems, SitecoreCookbook"
      patch:before="processor[@type='Sitecore.Publishing.
      Pipelines.PublishItem.DetermineAction,
      Sitecore.Kernel']" />
  </publishItem>
</pipelines>
```

4. We will now check how the processor will delete the duplicate item. Create one item, say, `Test` under `Home`, and set the appropriate field value. After publishing the item, you will find the same item in both the `master` and `web` databases:

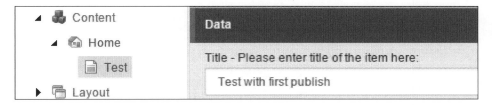

5. Delete the `Test` item from the `master` database.

6. Create another item in `Home` named `Test` and set a different field value as follows and publish this item:

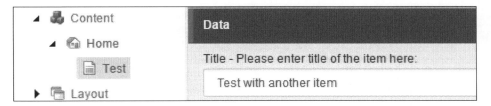

7. Now check the `web` database and find the `Test` item. You will find that the `Test` item that we published in the preceding step exists there and the older `Test` item that we published in step 4 has been deleted by our processor.

How it works...

If you remove our custom processor and perform steps 4 to 7, you will find multiple items in the web database, as shown in the following image. So, previewing the live content of the http://sitecorecookbook/Test page may serve the content of the older Test page, whereas we will be expecting content from the newly published item:

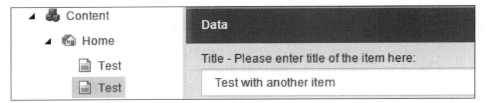

When we send any item to be published, the <publish> pipeline gets executed, which adds the selected item and languages to the publishing context and passes the context to the <publishItem> pipeline for further publishing actions. This pipeline has different processors that check the security for the publishing user for the publishing item, and determine actions on what to do—insert, update, or delete the publishing item, add related items, update publishing statistics, and so on.

In the processor that we created, we got the current item in publishing using context. PublishHelper.GetSourceItem(context.ItemId).

Using this item's path, we found the duplicate (older) item with the same name from the target database using context.PublishOptions.TargetDatabase.GetItem().

We deleted this duplicate item from the target database using the context. PublishHelper.DeleteTargetItem() method.

There's more...

We can do many publishing customizations by overriding the <publishItem> pipeline, such as making an audit trail for each publishing item, moving media files to CDN or any remote location, exporting some content items of publishing items, and many more.

Any runtime exception in the custom processor will stop further execution of the pipeline and can stop publishing job as well.

8

Security

In this chapter, we will cover some different and interesting development tasks related to Sitecore security. You will learn the following recipes:

- ▶ Working with a custom user profile
- ▶ Creating custom access rights for an item
- ▶ Achieving a single sign-on by creating a virtual user with custom roles and rights
- ▶ Preventing Sitecore from applying security
- ▶ Implementing extranet login

Introduction

Sitecore has a reputation of being very easy to set up the security of users, roles, access rights, and so on. Sitecore follows the .NET security model, so we will get all basic information of the .NET membership in Sitecore.

This chapter assumes that you have a basic understanding of User Manager, Domain Manager, Role Manager, Security Editor, and Access Viewer to create domains and users and apply roles and rights. In this chapter, you will learn some recipes that are needed in Sitecore environments to customize the Sitecore architecture, such as the user profile and access rights management, different ways we can get authenticated to Sitecore CMS such as single sign-on, impersonating users, leveraging the switching of users, and extranet login.

You can get an overview of Sitecore Security APIs from `https://goo.gl/n0nHOa`.

Working with a custom user profile

The Sitecore user profile provides all the basic information that we expect, such as the username, full name, password, e-mail, and so on. Most of the time, our requirements will get satisfied with these properties, but sometimes we might need to add more fields to the user profile. In such cases, we will create a custom user profile.

Configuring user profiles in .NET needs `Web.config` level configurations, which require application restart. In Sitecore, the dynamic user profile structure and role management is possible just through the user interface, which is simpler and easier. In this recipe, you will learn how to create a custom user profile to store a user's social media account details.

How to do it...

We will create a custom template with fields of social media account information and, using this, we will create a new social media user profile:

1. From the desktop view, select the `core` database and open the Content Editor.

2. Select `/sitecore/templates/System/Security`. In this, create a `Social Media User` template with some social media fields as follows:

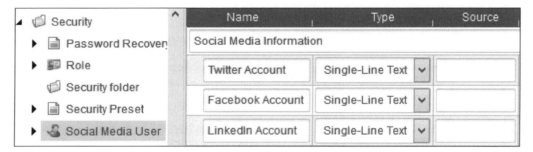

3. Select `/sitecore/system/Settings/Security/Profiles`. In this, create a new user profile, `Social Media User`, using the template created in the preceding step.

4. We will now create a new user with the user profile that we created in the preceding steps. Open **User Manager**. This will open the user creation wizard.

5. In this user creation wizard, you will see the **Social Media User** profile added. Select it, fill in all other details, and create a new user:

6. After creating a user, open **User Editor**, and click on the **Profile** tab in the wizard. You will see all custom properties set for the profile here. You can edit their values by clicking on the edit button.

How it works...

Each user has a profile and we can define a number of properties to it. In steps 1 and 2, we created a custom template allowing different fields that we want to use for the social media account details of users.

In step 3, we created a custom profile same as the existing user profile by inheriting the Social Media User template that we created in step 2. Doing this will create a new profile with these custom properties and keeping all the default fields that the user profile provides.

 Creating a user from this custom profile will contain all the .NET security membership attributes plus the fields that we declared in the template.

There's more...

We can apply values to these custom additional properties of the profile using the following code:

```
UserProfile currentUser = User.Current.Profile;
currentUser.SetCustomProperty("Twitter Account",
   "patelyogesh_in");
currentUser.SetCustomProperty("LinkedIn Account", "yspatel");
currentUser.Save();
```

We can use the GetCustomProperty and RemoveCustomProperty methods to retrieve and delete custom properties' values respectively.

If you cannot create a separate user profile, you can also add these additional properties to the existing user profile by adding these fields to the /sitecore/templates/System/Security/User template.

Creating custom access rights for an item

Sitecore's standard authorization model provides you with the ability to control permissions based on the item, field, language, site, and workflow. An item has different access rights such as read, write, delete, and so on. Most of the time, these access rights are enough to match all requirements. Sometimes, we might need to create our own custom access rights to meet business requirements.

In this recipe, we will create a custom access right to control the publishing of users. So, before publishing, we will use APIs to find out whether the user has publishing rights or not.

How to do it...

We will first configure the access rights in the Sitecore configuration:

1. In the `\App_Config\include\Cookbook` folder, create a patch configuration file, `SitecoreCookbook.CustomAccessRights.config`. In the `<configuration/sitecore/accessRights>` section, create an `item:publish` custom right as follows:

    ```
    <accessRights>
      <rights>
        <add name="item:publish" title="Publish"
          comment="Publishing rights for items."
          modifiesData="true" patch:before="*[2]" />
      </rights>
    </accessRights>
    ```

2. Click on any item in the Content Editor. In the **Fields** pane, go to the **Security** section and check the **Security** field (or from the ribbon, select the **Security** tab, and click on the **Assign** button in the **Security** group). You will see a new access right named **Publish** as follows:

3. Apply rights to the **Item** or **Descendants** as per requirement.

    We will now create a class that will help us set and get publishing rights to the item.

4. In the `SitecoreCookbook` project, create a `CustomAccessRightsManager` class in the `Security` folder and a `IsPublishAllowed` property that will tell us whether the user has publishing rights for the provided item in the constructor or not:

```
string publishAccessRightName = "item:publish";
public Item Item { get; private set; }

public CustomAccessRightsManager(Item item)
{
  this.Item = item;
}

public virtual bool IsPublishAllowed
{
  get
  {
    var right =
      AccessRight.FromName(publishAccessRightName);
    if (right == null)
      return false;
    var allowed = AuthorizationManager.IsAllowed(this.Item,
      right, Sitecore.Context.User);
    return allowed;
  }
}
```

5. We will override the **Publish** button command to make it visible based on the publishing rights of the selected item in the Content Editor. In the `SitecoreCookbook` project, create another `PublishItem` class in the `Security` folder and inherit it from the `Sitecore.Shell.Framework.Commands.PublishItem` class.

6. Override the `QueryState()` method of this class as follows:

```
public override CommandState QueryState(CommandContext
  context)
{
  if (context.Items.Length != 1)
    return CommandState.Hidden;

  CustomAccessRightsManager manager = new
    CustomAccessRightsManager(context.Items[0]);
  if(manager.IsPublishAllowed)
    return base.QueryState(context);
  else
    return CommandState.Hidden;
}
```

7. In the patch configuration file that we created in step 1, add the `item:publish` command with the previously created class to the `<configuration/sitecore/commands>` section as follows:

```
<commands>
  <command name="item:publishnow"
    type="Sitecore.Shell.Framework.Commands.PublishItem,
      Sitecore.Kernel">
    <patch:attribute name="type">
      SitecoreCookbook.Security.PublishItem,
        SitecoreCookbook
    </patch:attribute>
  </command>
</commands>
```

In this step, we override the `item:publish` command, which is totally different from the `item:publish` access right that we created in step 1. To avoid confusion, you can also rename the access right.

8. Now, check the **PUBLISH** menu from the ribbon for both the items with and without the publish access right. You will see that the **Publish** menu item will be hidden for the item that doesn't have publishing rights, as follows:

How it works...

Access rights are controlled in the `<sitecore/accessRights/rights>` section in the configuration file. There are many out-of-the-box access rights such as `item:read`, `item:write`, `item:rename`, and others, item-level access rights, `field:read`, `field:write`, and field-level access rights. In the same way, we created a new `item:publish` right in step 1 and, after doing this, **Publish** access rights will get reflected to **Security Editor** or **Access Viewer** immediately as shown in step 2.

In step 4, we created a custom access rights provider, which will help you know whether the user has publish rights to the specific item or not. The `AccessRight.FromName("item:publish")` method provides the access rights definition from the access rights name that we provided. The `AuthorizationManager.IsAllowed()` method tells us whether the user has publish rights for the item or not.

In steps 5 to 7, we overrode Sitecore's default `item:publish` command, which opens the **Item Publish** wizard. In the `QueryState` method of the command, we checked whether the user has publishing rights for the item or not. If the user does not have publish access rights, then we hide or disable the menu. Similarly, you can also override other publishing commands such as `item:publishnow`.

There's more...

In this recipe, we checked publishing access rights just to show or hide the publish item button. But, it can not restrict publishing of any subitem or related item if it does not have publishing access rights. So, to have a proper implementation of publishing access rights, we can modify the publishing process to enforce checking `item:publish` access rights before publishing individual items. For this, perform the following steps:

1. In the `Sitecore.config` file, add a new custom processor after the Sitecore's default `CheckSecurity` processor to the `<publishItem>` pipeline.

2. In this processor, check whether the item getting published has `item:publish` access rights for the current user or not.

3. If the user does not have publishing rights for the item, then skip that item's publishing.

 The administrators have complete control over everything and can publish any item, regardless of how you configure security, the same as all other access rights.

Achieving a single sign-on by creating a virtual user with custom roles and rights

Sometimes, we may be in a situation where we need to authenticate users against an external security system before providing them access to secured pages or media items of the Sitecore website; this can be achieved by creating virtual users in Sitecore.

In some cases, virtual users are easier and simpler to implement than authentication providers. In this recipe, we will create a virtual user for an authenticated user of an external system, apply some predefined roles and permissions, and log in that user to access website resources.

Getting ready

This recipe assumes that a previewer user is already authenticated in any external application, and we will log in this user as a virtual user with the provided access of Sitecore website resources based on predefined roles. We have already created a custom `external\External Previewer` role with proper access rights that we need to provide to the external previewer.

How to do it...

We have some predefined roles that we will provide to the virtual user, that is, `Sitecore\Sitecore Client Users` and `external\External Previewer`. Once the user is authenticated via an external application or database, we will first create a virtual user:

1. In the `SitecoreCookbook` project, create a `SingleSignOn` class in the `Security` folder. Create a `LoginWithVirtualUser()` method as follows:

```
public void LoginWithVirtualUser(string userName, string
  fullName, string emailAddress)
{
  string[] roles = new string[] {
    @"sitecore\Sitecore Client Users",
    @"external\Preview User"};

  string[] revokedItems = new string[]{
    @"/sitecore/Content/Home/Events",
    @"/sitecore/Content/Home/News"};

  User user = AuthenticationManager.BuildVirtualUser(
    userName, true);
  if (user != null) {
    AssignRoles(user, roles);
    RevokeItemAccessRights(user, revokedItems);
    SetProfile(user, fullName, emailAddress);
    AuthenticationManager.Login(user);
  }
}
```

2. Create the `AssignRoles()` method to assign our predefined roles to the user as follows:

```
private static void AssignRoles(User user, string[] roles)
{
  foreach (string role in roles) {
    if (Role.Exists(role))
      user.Roles.Add(Role.FromName(role));
  }
}
```

3. Create the `RevokeItemAccessRights()` method to revoke the access of selected items for the user as follows:

```
private static void RevokeItemAccessRights(User user,
   string[] items)
{
  Database database = Factory.GetDatabase("master");
  foreach (string itempath in items) {
    Item item = database.GetItem(itempath);
    if (item != null) {
      AccessRuleCollection accessRules =
        item.Security.GetAccessRules();
      accessRules.Helper.AddAccessPermission(user,
        AccessRight.ItemRead, PropagationType.Descendants,
        AccessPermission.Deny);
    }
  }
}
```

4. Create the `SetProfile()` method to assign a full name and e-mail address to the virtual user's profile:

```
private static void SetProfile(User user, string fullName,
   string emailAddress)
{
  UserProfile profile = user.Profile;
  profile.FullName = fullName;
  profile.Email = emailAddress;
  profile.Save();
}
```

5. Invoke the `LoginWithVirtualUser()` method from the coding where an external user has been authenticated, that is, the login page. Once the user is logged in with the virtual user, redirect the user to the required Sitecore content or media item.

6. You have now authenticated the Sitecore system without actually having a physical Sitecore user and bypassing the login page.

How it works...

In step 1, we created a virtual user using the `Sitecore.Security.Authentication.AuthenticationManager.BuildVirtualUser()` method. The virtual user is actually nothing but a `Sitecore.Security.Accounts.User` object stored in the application memory, just like the physical users. The virtual users persist information only for that browsing session, unlike physical users. So, once the user session expires, the user also gets destroyed.

In step 2, we assigned predefined native roles to the virtual users.

In step 3, we denied read permission to the user for some predefined items. In the same way, we can set or deny access read/write/delete rights to the users. We can collect an item's access rules using `item.Security.GetAccessRules()`. The `accessRules.Helper.AddAccessPermission()` method has four parameters:

- ▶ First is for the user
- ▶ Second is for the access right (`ItemRead`/`ItemWrite`/`ItemDelete` and many others)
- ▶ Third is for the propagation type (`Any`/`Entity`/`Descendants`/`Unknown`)
- ▶ Fourth is for access permission (`Allow`/`Deny`/`NotSet`)

In the same way, we can also assign roles and access rights of permissions to physical users programmatically; the only difference is that these roles or rights will get stored in Sitecore's security database for physical users.

In step 4, we updated the user's profile. The `UserProfile` object that we retrieved through `user.Profile` will help us get or set user profile information such as the username, e-mail address, culture, content language, and others.

There's more...

To provide a more secure solution, some applications or architects may not allow us to authenticate an external user from Sitecore itself. In such cases, they may host the login page on their system and, on each login, they generate a random and unique token and store it temporarily along with the user details and redirect to a custom secured page of Sitecore, where we can verify and authenticate that random ticket from the system and log in the user to Sitecore by creating a virtual user.

We achieved a secured login bypass into Sitecore without a username and password. Sometimes, we may have a user created in Sitecore with different roles and rights. In such cases, we can log in the user without a password using `AuthenticationManager.Login(user)`.

The role of virtual users becomes very crucial when working with **Federated Authentication**, Claim/Token-based, or **Windows Identity Foundation**. Read more on this at `https://goo.gl/2oU5lx`.

Preventing Sitecore from applying security

Sometimes, content authors need to perform some necessary operations for which they do not have access rights. Giving additional rights to them is not a permanent solution as requirements can vary from user to user or case to case. Sitecore gives freedom to developers by providing a security context switching feature so that users can perform some secured item or field-level changes in the security context of other users.

Let's consider a case where some super content author needs a facility to unlock pages locked by other content authors. So, instead of giving them rights to unlock the pages, we can do this impersonating the user and disabling security.

Getting ready

Create two different buttons in the Content Editor from the `core` database and define two respective command names for them. One button will be performing the item unlock using **User Impersonation** and another will be performing the item unlock using **Security Disabler**.

How to do it...

Let's first create a `command` class to impersonate a user:

1. In the `SitecoreCookbook` project, create a `UnlockImpersonate` class in the `Commands` folder and inherit it from the `Command` class.

2. Override the `Execute()` method and switch the user context for the code block using the `UserSwitcher()` class constructor to unlock items:

```
string UnlockUsingUser = @"sitecore\admin";
public override void Execute(CommandContext context)
{
  using (new UserSwitcher(UnlockUsingUser, true))
  {
    if (context.Items[0].Locking.CanUnlock())
    {
      context.Items[0].Locking.Unlock();
      SheerResponse.Alert("Item unlocked", true);
    }
  }
}
```

3. Let's create another command class to disable security. In the `SitecoreCookbook` project, create a `UnlockDisableSecurity` class in the `Commands` folder and inherit it from the `Command` class.

4. Override the `Execute()` method where we will disable security for the code block using the `SecurityDisabler()` class constructor:

```
public override void Execute(CommandContext context)
{
  using (new SecurityDisabler())
  {
    if (context.Items[0].Locking.CanUnlock())
    {
      context.Items[0].Locking.Unlock();
```

```
              SheerResponse.Alert("Item unlocked", true);
        }
      }
   }
```

5. Register these created commands in `Commands.config` or using a patch configuration file.

6. Open the Content Editor using an administrator account, lock a few items, and log out.

7. Log in using content author credentials and open the Content Editor.

8. Select one item that was locked by the administrator account and click on any command buttons that we created. You will find that we are able to unlock the items with user impersonation and disabling security.

How it works...

In step 2, we used `UserSwitcher` to unlock items, which allows a segment of code to run under a specific user regardless of the context user, so for the whole block, all rights will be applied to this specific user itself. Here, `sitecore\admin` has full rights to unlock any item locked by any user, so we used it in `UserSwitcher` to unlock items. When the block ends, the using statement causes the .NET runtime engine to invoke `Sitecore.Security.Accounts.UserSwitcher.Dispose()`, which resets the context user to the original context user.

In step 4, we used the `SecurityDisabler` class to cause the segment of code to run in the context of a user with administrative rights, regardless of the context user. The code within the using statement block has full control of the entire system and can take any action on any item or field. Here, we unlocked items using administrative privileges.

Implementing extranet login

Sometimes, we get a requirement to have password-protected pages on public-facing websites. Sitecore provides an out-of-the-box extranet login functionality, which is very simple and easy to achieve compared to ASP.NET.

In this recipe, we will implement extranet login for public-facing websites.

Getting ready

In our site, we have a **Members** section, which should be accessible only by authenticated or logged in users. All other pages should be accessible to everyone. So, the site structure looks like the following image:

If you have implemented the 404 Page Not Found handler, it will show the 404 page on the request of these restricted pages as anonymous users do not have read rights on them. So, to make this recipe work, you either disable this handler or modify it to not show a 404 page for these pages.

How to do it...

First, we will revoke access rights from the restricted **Members** pages:

1. From the Content Editor, select the **Members** item. From the ribbon, click on the **Assign** button in the **Security** group from the **Security** tab. This will open the **Assign Security Rights** dialog, as shown in the following image:

2. Here, add an **extranet\Anonymous** user and deny **Read** access to it and its **Descendants**, as shown in the preceding image.

3. Now, view the **Members** or any of its child pages from a private browser window (as an anonymous user), you will be redirected to the noaccess page, http:// sitecorecookbook/sitecore/service/noaccess.aspx. Here, we should redirect the user to the login page instead. For this, configure the requireLogin and loginPage attributes in the <site> section in the Sitecore.config file as follows. You can set any physical file or Sitecore item as the login page. Make sure that this page is accessible to anonymous users:

```
<site name="website" requireLogin="true" loginPage="/login" ... />
```

4. Now, when you request a page of the **Members** section, you will find that you are redirected to the login page.

5. Now you can render login control. However, after a successful login, you have to redirect the user to the originally requested **Member** section page. For this, you have to remember the URL of that page. Let's see how to remember it. From the Sitecore.config file, find the Authentication.SaveRawUrl setting and set its value to true:

```
<setting name="Authentication.SaveRawUrl" value="true"/>
```

6. Now, access the **Member** section page; you will find that you are redirected to the login page, and the original request is passed in a query string, that is, http://sc806plain/login?returnUrl=%2Fmembers%2Fmyorders.

7. We have applied security for extranet anonymous users. Now, we will create register (signup) control. In the SitecoreCookbook project, create a SecurityController class in the Controllers folder.

8. Create an ActionResult method, Register(). Here, we have simply created an extranet domain user, logged with the same credentials and redirected it to the original URL:

```
[AcceptVerbs(HttpVerbs.Post)]
public ActionResult Register(string userName, string
  password, string confirmPassword)
{
  string domainUser = Context.Domain.GetFullName(userName);

  System.Web.Security.Membership.CreateUser(domainUser,
    password);
  if (AuthenticationManager.Login(domainUser, password)) {
    string returnUrl =
      System.Web.HttpContext.Current.Request["url"];
    if (!Url.IsLocalUrl(returnUrl))
      returnUrl = "/";
    return Redirect(returnUrl);
  }
  return View();
}
```

9. Similarly, you can now create login control and relevant view files. You can also get the full source code from the code bundle provided with this book.

How it works...

Extranet domain is a website security domain that contains the user accounts that correspond to the visitors to the website. In step 1, we restricted the **Members** section for extranet anonymous users.

In steps 3 to 5, we enforced anonymous users to get redirected to the configured login page. For this, we used the `requireLogin` and `loginPage` attributes of the `<site>` element. We also maintained the original restricted URL by enabling the `Authentication.SaveRawUrl` setting.

There is one more way to achieve this behavior. Revert steps 3 to 5. Now, you know that anonymous users get redirected to the *No Access* URL on requesting restricted pages. You can set your login page URL in the `NoAccessUrl` setting in `Sitecore.config` as follows:

```
<setting name="NoAccessUrl" value="/Login"/>
```

This will take care of redirecting the user to the login page along with the originally requested URL as `http://sitecorecookbook/Login?item=%2fmembers%2fmyorders&user=extranet%5cAnonymous&site=website`. Using this setting, Sitecore will also pass the current username and site name along with the original URL.

By default, Sitecore assigns extranet as the default domain to the site, which you can find `domain="extranet"` in the `<site>` element. While working with a multisite environment, we may have to work with site-specific domains. In such cases, you can get a fully-qualified username (`domain\username`) using the `Context.Domain.GetFullName()` method.

For **Sitecore Client Authoring**, extranet domain users can also be members of relevant Sitecore roles to use client tools and edit the content of the website.

9
Sitecore Search

In this chapter, we will cover different types of search techniques, using Sitecore content search and **Lucene**. You will learn the following recipes:

- ▶ Indexing, searching, sorting, and paging content using a search query
- ▶ Creating a computed index field for categorization
- ▶ Refining search results by tagging based facets
- ▶ Achieving the autocomplete feature with a wildcard
- ▶ Influencing search results with boosting
- ▶ Hunting MoreLikeThis results
- ▶ Correcting a search with did you mean
- ▶ Managing millions of items using an item bucket

Introduction

So far, we used Sitecore data APIs to fetch item details from the Sitecore content tree. In this chapter, you will learn how we can save selected Sitecore item and field values to Lucene index files and read them. The Sitecore search engine lets you search quickly through millions of items of the content tree with the help of different types of queries with Lucene or **Solr** indexes.

The recipes in this chapter are concerned with providing different types of searching techniques available today, like Google, for example, indexing content items, searching them based on keywords or phrases with custom conditions, providing facets to refine searches, auto-suggest, similar searches, prioritizing search results, and so on. This chapter also covers techniques to create custom fields with calculated field values. It also explains how easy it is to manage millions of items in Sitecore using an item bucket.

This chapter does not explain how to search content in the content management environment through the Content Editor or Experience Editor as that can be easily learned from `https://goo.gl/aSd2Qw`. You can also find search- and Lucene-related configurations at `https://goo.gl/cX2Ad2`. Also, all the recipes are prepared in Lucene as it is the default search provider for Sitecore. You can easily convert them to Solr just by doing some small configuration-level changes.

Indexing, searching, sorting, and paging content using a search query

While working with a large number of content items, it's always recommended to use the content search API with Lucene or Solr indexing.

In this recipe, we will create a listing page for products, where we will search products by their name, order them by product fields, and page the results using the Sitecore **ContentSearch LINQ** API.

Getting ready

This recipe assumes that you are using Sitecore 8 or a later version. For this recipe, create a `Book` template with a few fields such as `Title`, `Author`, `Price`, and so on and create multiple book items using this template. Also, make sure that you have indexed all these items. From the **Content Editor** ribbon, you can find different options to index items in the **Indexing tools** group from the **Developer** tab.

How to do it...

We will write a **language-integrated query** (**LINQ**) API to make queries in order to search and apply sorting and paging the results:

1. In the `SitecoreCookbook` project, reference the `Sitecore.ContentSearch.dll` and `Sitecore.ContentSearch.Linq.dll` assemblies.

2. In your sublayout or any other rendering, create a `Search()` method as follows:

```
public List<SearchResultItem> SearchBook(string str, string
  orderBy, int pageSize, int pageNo, out int totalResults)
{
  string index = string.Format("sitecore_{0}_index",
    Sitecore.Context.Database.Name);
  using (var context = ContentSearchManager.GetIndex(
    index).CreateSearchContext())
  {
    var query = context.GetQueryable<SearchResultItem>()
```

```
        .Where(p => p.Path.StartsWith(
          "/sitecore/Content/home"))
        .Where(p => p.TemplateName == "book")
        .Where(p => p.Name.Contains(str));

        totalResults = query.Count();

        if (!string.IsNullOrEmpty(orderBy)) {
          if (orderBy == "name")
            query = query.OrderBy(p => p.Name);
          else if (orderBy == "date")
            query = query.OrderBy(p => p.Updated);
        }

        query = query.Page(pageNo - 1, pageSize);
        return query.ToList();
      }
    }
```

3. Invoke the preceding method with inputs provided by users, that is, to fetch results for search keyword – `truth`, page size – 3, sort on a field = `name`, page number to show – 1, you can call the preceding method as follows:

```
List<SearchResultItem> list = SearchBook("truth", "name",
  10, 1, out totalResults);
```

4. To make this work, you can get the full source code from the code bundle provided with this book, which is written in a web form. Bind it to a content page and preview it. You can search, sort, and set the page size with pagination, as shown in the following image:

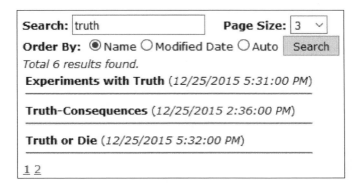

How it works...

By default, Sitecore indexes all its system fields such as **Name**, **Display Name**, **Created**, **Updated**, and so on. Fields to be indexed or not to be indexed are configured in the `Sitecore.ContentSearch.Lucene.DefaultIndexConfiguration.config` file.

You can include fields inside the `<fieldNames = hint="raw:AddfieldByFieldName" />` node, field types inside the `<fieldTypes hint="raw:AddfieldByFieldTypeName" />` node, or templates inside the `<include hint="list:IncludeTemplate">` node, and similarly, you can maintain a list of exclusions as well. For example, indexing the title field requires you to do the following settings in this configuration file:

```
<field fieldName="title" storageType="YES" indexType="TOKENIZED"
    vectorType="NO" boost="1f" ... />
```

Sitecore creates individual indexes for each database, for example, `sitecore_master_index`, `sitecore_core_index` and `sitecore_web_index`, which you can find in the `Data\indexes` folder outside the web root.

 Use **Luke - Lucene Index Toolbox** (download it from `https://github.com/DmitryKey/luke`) to read and write indexes offline. Read this blog to use this tool, `http://goo.gl/cBS3sy`.

Sitecore has the `Sitecore.ContentSearch.ContentManager` class that can provide us with a unified API to the Lucene or Solr index, based on the configurations set. So the same piece of code will work for either Lucene or Solr index files. In step 1, we created the following LINQ to search results from content items and filtered them by name and template:

```
var query = context.GetQueryable<SearchResultItem>()
   .Where(p => p.Path.StartsWith("/sitecore/Content/home"))
   .Where(p => p.TemplateName == "book")
   .Where(p => p.Name.Contains(str));
```

The result we got here is nothing but a collection of documents or the `SearchResultItem` object, which is the Sitecore's out-of-box document mapper class. It has different properties mapped with Sitecore fields, so using them, we can read preconfigured system fields. We used `Path`, `TemplateName`, `Name`, and `Updated` fields in this recipe. You can also index your custom fields and have the custom document mapper class, which you will learn in the next recipe.

Here, we got the total number of searched results using the `query.Count()` method and sorted the results with the `Name` field using the `query.OrderBy(p => p.Name)` code. To get documents for the respective page number (to achieve pagination), we extended the query using `query.Page(pageNo - 1, pageSize)`.

There's more...

You can also perform multi-field sorting using `OrderBy(t => t.Name).ThenBy(i => i.Updated)` and can even change the sort direction using the `query.orderByDescending(t => t.Name).ThenByDescending(I => i.Updated)` method.

As an alternative for the `query.Page()` method for the pagination, we can also use the `query.Skip(skipRecords).Take(pageSize)` method.

In this recipe, we achieved search results with the use of LINQ. We can also achieve dynamic LINQ using `PredicateBuilder`. You can find a code block for it from the code bundle provided with this book. You can read more at `http://goo.gl/nVRpbT`.

 If you want to migrate your Sitecore instance to Solr, refer to the steps mentioned at `https://goo.gl/qQQnTB`.

You can also highlight your searched terms in the results by wrapping the search term with the `<strong/>` element. Currently, it's not supported in Sitecore ContentSearch APIs, but you can use **Lucene.Net** APIs to achieve it, which you can find at `https://goo.gl/Yqu3bu`.

Creating a computed index field for categorization

Sitecore by default stores index fields with their raw values, but sometimes we need to store calculated information in the searched index. Here, a custom computed index field can be very useful.

Consider a case where we have a large collection of books, where end users can find books based on predefined categories, which are stored in a `Multilist` field that contains a list of item IDs. So, there is no use of indexing such a field with raw values. Here, you will learn how to create a custom computed index field. Here, for the `Multilist` field, we will store the names of selected items instead of their item IDs, which will be useful in filtering books by their category.

Getting ready

The `book` template contains fields such as `Title`, `Author`, `Price`, and `Image`. It also has a `Multilist` field, **Categories**. The following image shows you that the selected book is assigned two categories, **Biography** and **History**. So, when we search books by category, for example, `History`, we will get a result of all the books that fall into the `History` category:

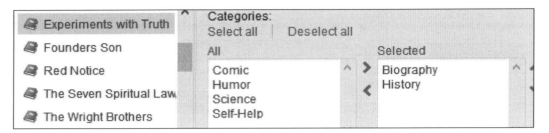

How to do it...

We'll create a computed index field, `bookcategories`, to store categories of books:

1. In the `SitecoreCookbook` project, create a `BookCategory` class in the `Search` folder, which implements `Sitecore.ContentSearch.ComputedFields.IComputedIndexField`. Implement two string properties named `FieldName` and `ReturnType`, which are required by this interface. This class will be used to index the computed field:

```
public class BookCategory : IComputedIndexField
{
  public string FieldName { get; set; }
  public string ReturnType { get; set; }
}
```

2. Similarly, it requires you to implement the `ComputeFieldValue()` method as follows. Here, we listed the names of all the categories for the books in a `List<string>` collection. It is the computed value for the computed field, stored in an index:

```
public object ComputeFieldValue(IIndexable indexable)
{
  Item item = indexable as SitecoreIndexableItem;
  if (item != null && item.TemplateName == "Book") {
    MultilistField categories = item.Fields["Categories"];
    List<string> list = new List<string>();
    foreach (ID id in categories.TargetIDs) {
      Item category = item.Database.GetItem(id);
      if(category!=null)
```

```
        list.Add(category.DisplayName);
    }
    return list;
}
return null;
}
```

3. Now, we'll create a document mapper class to make Linq-to-Sitecore queries and read the index field values. In the `SitecoreCookbook` project, create the `Book` class in the `Search` folder and inherit it from the `SearchResultItem` class. Create different properties to read book fields such as `Title`, `Author`, and `Categories` with `Sitecore.ContentSearch.IndexFieldAttribute` (`IndexField`) for each property with the name of the index field, as mentioned in the following code:

```
[IndexField("title")]
public string Title {get;set;}


[IndexField("author")]
public string Author {get;set;}


[IndexField("bookcategories")]
public IEnumerable<string> Categories{get;set;}
```

4. Now we will add the preceding computed fields to a configuration file. In the `Sitecore.ContentSearch.Lucene.DefaultIndexConfiguration.config` file or in a custom patch configuration file, register the computed `bookcategories` field. Add it to the `<configuration/sitecore/contentSearch/indexConfigurations/defaultLuceneIndexConfiguration>` node as follows:

```
<fields hint="raw:AddComputedIndexField">
  <field fieldName="bookcategories">
    SitecoreCookbook.Search.BookCategory, SitecoreCookbook
  </field>
</fields>
```

5. Specify this computed field along with all the other required fields such as `title` and `author` as follows:

```
<fieldMap type="Sitecore.ContentSearch.FieldMap,
  Sitecore.ContentSearch">
  <fieldNames hint="raw:AddFieldByFieldName">
    <field fieldName="author" storageType="YES" ... />
    <field fieldName="title" storageType="YES" ... />
    <field fieldName="bookcategories" storageType="YES" ...
      />
  </fieldNames>
</fieldMap>
```

6. Now, build the index so that we can read the indexed fields using the following code. Write the following code in a convenient place—sublayout or any other rendering—to find books. This will search a list of books having `History` as the category:

```
string category = "history";
string index = string.Format("sitecore_{0}_index",
  Sitecore.Context.Database.Name);
using (var searchContext = ContentSearchManager.GetIndex(
  index).CreateSearchContext())
{
  var searchQuery = searchContext.GetQueryable<Book>()
  .Where(item => item.Categories.Contains(category));
  List<Book> books = searchQuery.ToList();
}
```

7. You can also store the image URL assigned to the book, item URL of the book, and so on by storing them in computed fields, same as the `bookcategories` field. Once you create these fields, you will be able to achieve the following output. You can find the full source code for the recipe in a web form from the code bundle provided with this book, which will give you the following output:

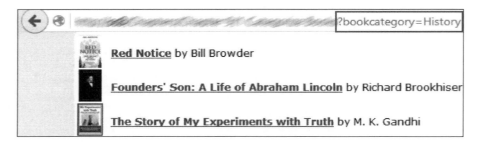

How it works...

In steps 1 and 2, we created a `bookcategory` computed field in the `BookCategory` class. While indexing for the database, the `ComputeFieldValue()` method of this class will get executed for each item. This method accepts an argument that implements the `Sitecore.ContentSearch.IIndexable` interface, which specifies the data to index. Using `indexable as SitecoreIndexableItem`, we can get the current item getting indexed. This method returns `object` that represents calculated information (computed value) for the item field, which will be stored in the index file.

> While creating your own computed or virtual field, don't return `String.Empty` unless it is important that your index should contain an empty string.

Here, we stored selected categories' names instead of item IDs in the computed index field so that we can easily find categories by name.

In step 3, we created `Book` properties with the `IndexField` attribute. Here, `Title` and `Author` properties will read the value from `title` and `author` index fields. The `Categories` property will read the value from the `bookcategories` computed index field, which will read our custom-generated list of name categories.

The `bookcategories` field requires a computed value, so we configured it in step 4, in the `AddComputedIndexField` section. So, while indexing, Sitecore will identify where to compute this field value from.

Sitecore allows you to map a field name in Sitecore to the index and store it in the appropriate way. You can map the fields in the `<fieldMap/fieldNames>` section, which has different attributes such as `storageType`, `indexType`, `vectoryType`, and so on. You will also learn more about these attributes later in this chapter.

> To get field values in index results, index field should be mapped in the configuration file, the mapped index field should have the `storageType` attribute set to YES, and the index field name should not contain whitespaces. Replace whitespaces with an underscore or just remove them from the field name.

Refining search results by tagging based facets

The out-of-the-box feature of tagging can be used to provide relevance to content or items so that users can search content easily and quickly. Tagging can be used to prepare a tag cloud and, based on this, users can filter results directly. In the previous recipe, we used the same kind of concept with the custom `Categories` field.

In this recipe, you will learn how to use tagging to create facets. When a user searches any keyword, we will find all the related tags from the search results so that users can filter results based on these tags.

Getting ready

For this recipe, we will use the `Book` template that we created in the previous recipe.

How to do it...

We will first create multiple tags and assign them to relevant books:

1. Create multiple unique tags related to books under `/sitecore/system/Settings/Buckets/TagRepository`. This is a bucketed folder so you might not be able to get a list of items directly.

2. Create multiple books and assign relevant tags in the **Tagging** section, the **Semantics** field (available as **Standard Fields**). You can search a tag from the repository and assign it to multiple books through the **Add tag** search operation from the Content Editor:

3. We'll create a document mapper class to read **Book** fields. In the `SitecoreCookbook` project, create the `Book` class (if not created in the previous recipe) in the `Search` folder, inherit it from `SearchResultItem`, and add properties such as `Title`, `Author`, and `Tags`, with the `title`, `author`, and `__semantics` index fields with string data type in the same way as we did in the previous recipe. You can also read the item URL and image URL assigned to the book if required:

```
public class Book
{
    [IndexField("title")]
    public string Title { get; set; }

    [IndexField("author")]
    public string Author { get; set; }

    [IndexField("__semantics")]
    public IEnumerable<string> Categories { get; set; }
}
```

4. In the `Search` folder, create a `Facet` entity class with the `Id` and `Name` properties. They will be used to store the tag's item ID and name. Create a constructor as follows:

```
public class Facet
{
  public string Id { get; set; }
  public string Name { get; set; }

  public Facet(string id, string name) {
    this.Id = id;
    this.Name = name;
  }
}
```

5. Create the `FacetedSearchForBooks()` method, which expects a search text and array of selected facets as parameters. You can invoke this method from any convenient place from your rendering.

```
public void FacetedSearchForBooks(string searchText,
  string[] facets)
{
  var bookResult = new List<Book>();
  var facetResult = new List<Facet>();

  string index = string.Format("sitecore_{0}_index",
    Sitecore.Context.Database.Name);
  using (var searchContext = ContentSearchManager.GetIndex(
    index).CreateSearchContext())
  {
    var results = ApplyTextAndFacetedSearch(searchText,
      facets, searchContext);
    foreach (SearchHit<Book> result in results.Hits) {
      bookResult.Add((Book)result.Document);
    }
    facetResult = GetFacets(results);
  }
}
```

6. Create the `ApplyTextAndFacetedSearch()` method to find results based on the searched text and selected facets (tags):

```
private static SearchResults<Book>
  ApplyTextAndFacetedSearch(string searchText, string[]
  facets, IProviderSearchContext searchContext)
{
  var query = searchContext.GetQueryable<Book>()
    .Where(item => item.TemplateName == "book")
```

```
      .Where(item => item.Title.Contains(searchText));

  if (facets != null) {
    foreach (string facet in facets)
      query = query.Where(item =>
        item.Tags.Contains(facet));
  }

  var results = query.FacetOn(facet =>
    facet.Tags).GetResults();
  return results;
}
```

7. Create the GetFacets() method to list all the facets (tags) found from the search results:

```
private static List<Facet> GetFacets(SearchResults<Book>
  results)
{
  var facets = new List<Facet>();
  foreach (var facetCategories in
    results.Facets.Categories) {
    foreach (var facet in facetCategories.Values) {
      string id = facet.Name;
      Item facetItem =
        Sitecore.Context.Database.GetItem(new ID(id));
      if (facetItem != null) {
        facets.Add(new Facet(id, facetItem.Name));
      }
    }
  }
  facets = facets.OrderBy(f => f.Name).ToList();
  return facets;
}
```

8. So, now you have faceted search results in bookResult and facets found in these results in facetResult, which you can bind to relevant data objects to render them.

9. You can get the full source code from the code bundle provided with this book, which is written in a web form. Bind it to a content page and preview it. Here, we search with a search text, truth. So, using the results, we listed all the books that contain the truth word in the **Title** field on the right-hand side of the following image, and listed all the tags (facets) assigned to resulted books on the left-hand side:

Search keyword: truth   [Search]

Tags

☐ ethics   **You searched for: truth**

☐ history   **Truth (Consequences)** by *Aleatha Romig*

☐ leader

☐ morality   **Truth or Die** by *James Patterson*

☐ science   **The Story of My Experiments with Truth** by *M. K. Gandhi*

☐ truth

10. Now, in the preceding results, select the **truth** and **leader** facets. It will refine the search results based on the facets selected, as shown in the following image:

Search keyword: truth   [Search]

Tags

☐ ethics   **You searched for: truth**

☐ history   **The Story of My Experiments with Truth** by *M. K. Gandhi*

☑ leader

☑ truth

How it works...

Sitecore contains all tags under the `TagRepository` folder, and so Sitecore contains a common list of tags that can be used for different functionalities across the Sitecore instance. We can create multiple tag repositories in the current `TagRepository` to categorize different tags for different templates or for a multisite environment. You can read more at `https://goo.gl/fKZRVl`.

In step 5, we created the `FacetedSearchForBooks()` method, which expects searched text and selected facets that will filter results based on these input parameters and return results as well as facets found in it. From your rendering, invoke this method on every postback.

In step 6, we applied `FacetOn` and `IQueryable` with the `Tags` property using `query.FacetOn(facet => facet.Tags)`. It means that Sitecore will instruct the query to apply faceting to the selected fields, the `Tags` property or the `__semantics` field. When we executed a search using the `GetResults()` method, we will get results as a `SearchResults<Book>` object.

In step 7, we retrieved a list of facets from the faceted search results that we got in step 6. We can get facets using either `results.Facets.Categories` or `query.GetFacets().Categories`, which is a collection of facets.

There's more...

You can also implement range-based faceting in Sitecore; for this, refer to
`http://goo.gl/FocOib`.

Achieving the autocomplete feature with a wildcard

The autocomplete feature in a search box will predict the words that users want to search for. For example, a user wants to buy Apple iPhone 6S from `http://www.amazon.com/`. So, when the user starts typing `Apple`, before the user finishes typing the first three characters, different products of apple get listed in autosuggest. This speeds up human-computer interactions.

In this recipe, you will learn how to use different index fields with an **n-gram analyzer** to achieve the autocomplete feature. Sitecore provides an out-of-the-box n-gram analyzer, but we will create our own analyzer based on Lucene to make it better and faster. After learning this recipe, you will also be able to use Sitecore's out-of-the-box analyzers and create your custom analyzers too.

Getting ready

For this recipe, we need two templates, `Company` to create a list of companies and `Product` with the `Title` field to mention the product name and `Company` field of the **Droptree** type to select the company. Create multiple product items. We will merge the company name and product title to achieve autocomplete.

How to do it...

We will first create a custom n-gram analyzer. The analyzer converts tokens to lowercase and breaks them up into unigrams, bigrams, trigrams, and so on.

1. In the `SitecoreCookbook` project, create an `NGramAnalyzer` class in the `Search` folder. Reference `Lucene.Net.dll` and `Lucene.Net.Contrib.Analyzers.dll` assemblies to the project.

2. Inherit this class from `Lucene.Net.Analysis.Analyzer`. Override its `TokenStream()` method to break field values into tokens and convert them to lowercase:

```
public class NGramAnalyzer : Analyzer
{
  public override TokenStream TokenStream(string fieldName,
    System.IO.TextReader reader)
  {
```

```
    TokenStream ts = new StandardAnalyzer(
      Lucene.Net.Util.Version.LUCENE_30
      ).ReusableTokenStream(fieldName, reader);
    ts = new LowerCaseFilter(ts);
    int shinglesSize = 3;
    ts = new ShingleFilter(ts, shinglesSize);
    return ts;
  }
}
```

3. As you learned in the previous recipe, create a computed `ProductName` index field, which will store the value in concatenation with the company name and product name. Map the `ProductName` field as a computed field to a patch configuration.

4. Now, we need to assign this analyzer to the field we created. However, it's not possible to assign the analyzer to a computed field. So, we will map this computed `productname` field to the `<fieldNames hint="raw:AddFieldByFieldName">` node as well and assign the n-gram analyzer that we created in step 2 as follows:

```
<fieldNames hint="raw:AddFieldByFieldName">
  <field fieldName="productname" storageType="YES"
    indexType="TOKENIZED" vectorType="NO" boost="1f"
    type="System.String" settingType="...">
  <Analyzer type="SitecoreCookbook.Search.NGramAnalyzer,
  SitecoreCookbook" />
  </field>
</fieldNames>
```

5. Rebuild the index. So, the `productname` field will have values such as `apple iphone 5S`, `apple iphone 6`, `apple iphone 6s`, and others.

6. Create a custom handler, `Autocomplete.ashx`, in the appropriate folder. Implement the `IsReusable` property and the `ProcessRequest()` method for the `IHttpHandler` interface as follows. As an alternate, you can also create a controller:

```
public bool IsReusable {
  get { return true; }
}

public void ProcessRequest(HttpContext context)
{
  string fieldName = "productname";
  string searchText =
    HttpContext.Current.Request["searchText"];

  context.Response.ContentType = "application/json";
  string result = GetResults(fieldName, searchText);
  context.Response.Write(result);
}
```

7. Create the `GetResults()` method to get autosuggest phrases as follows:

```
public static string GetResults(string fieldName, string
  searchTerm)
{
  string index = string.Format("sitecore_{0}_index",
    Sitecore.Context.Database.Name);
  IndexReader ir = ((
    LuceneIndex)ContentSearchManager.GetIndex(
    index)).CreateReader(LuceneIndexAccess.ReadOnly);
  WildcardTermEnum wte = new WildcardTermEnum(ir, new
    Term(fieldName, searchTerm.Trim() + '*'));

  List<string> results = new List<string>();
  while (wte.Next()) {
    results.Add(wte.Term.Text);
  }
  return (new JavaScriptSerializer()).Serialize(results);
}
```

8. Preview this handler using the `http://sitecorecookbook/Cookbook/Autocomplete.ashx?searchText=apple` URL; you will find its result as follows:

9. Now, use this handler on your page to fetch suggested phrases. Get the source code from the code bundle provided with this book; you will get an output as follows:

Autocomplete:	iph
	IPHONE 5S
	IPHONE 6
	IPHONE 6S

How it works...

An analyzer builds `TokenStreams`, which analyzes the text while the field is getting indexed. It thus represents a policy to extract index terms from the text. Sitecore has many out-of-the-box analyzers, such as **LowerCaseKeywordAnalyzer**, which is used to convert text values in lowercase using `LowerCaseFilter` of Lucene. Such analyzers are mapped to index fields in the `<fieldNames/field>` section in the configuration file, as we did in step 4.

Sitecore has an out-of-the-box n-gram analyzer that can be found at `https://goo.gl/F69UN5`. In this approach, all documents are filtered using the `.Contains(searchText)` API and then results for autosuggest are collected by reading relevant fields. This approach is slower in performance in comparison with our approach.

In this recipe, we created a custom n-gram analyzer using `ShingleFilter` in steps 1 and 2. `ShingleFilter` expects two parameters; the first is `TokenStream` and second is the maximum size of the shingle. Here, we have set the number of shingles to three, so it will tokenize the field values and index the phrases of up to three words.

In step 7, we used `IndexReader` to find wildcard terms from the index file. The `WildcardTermEnum` class enumerates all terms that match the specified wildcard filter term. You can also apply different wildcard patterns to find results.

 Autosuggest is possible for a single field, multiple fields of an item, or multiple fields of different template items as well as by concatenating their values.

There's more...

In the same way, you can create your custom analyzers such as `SynonymAnalyzer`. So, if someone searches `home for rent`, they will also get results for `house for rent`, `apartment for rent`, and so on. For this, you can create a dictionary with keywords and its synonyms and add it to the index.

Influencing search results with boosting

In information retrieval, a document's relevance to a search is measured by how similar it is to the query. Sometimes, we need to boost or prioritize some search to get them elevated to show their importance by increasing their score based on their popularity, ratings, or page rank. Sitecore or Lucene provide different types of boosting mechanisms, in both static and dynamic ways.

In this recipe, we will cover both static and dynamic boosting using item-level, field-level, rules-based, and query-time boosting. For example, we need to implement the search functionality for a mobile phone selling website, where we need to show the results of product details and related blogs. Here, in search results, we need to give more importance to product items than blog items. Similarly, give more importance to results where the search keyword is found in the **Title** field than in the **Description** field. We also need to give a high boost to any selected product or all products of a particular company. You will learn all such kinds of boosting in this recipe.

Getting ready

We have already created multiple products and companies using `Product` and `Company` templates in the previous recipe. Create another `Blog` template and create a few blogs for those products with some explanatory values.

How to do it...

First of all, we will implement a search query without boosting and get results:

1. In the `SitecoreCookbook` project, create a document mapper class `Product` in the `Search` folder with `productname` and `description` fields. Here, the `productname` field is a concatenation of **Company** and **Title** fields, which is what we did in the *Achieving the autocomplete feature with a wildcard* recipe by creating a computed field.

2. Create the `SearchResults()` method to search results using query-based boosting as follows:

```
private void SearchResults(string query)
{
  string index = string.Format("sitecore_{0}_index",
    Sitecore.Context.Database.Name);
  using (var searchContext = ContentSearchManager.GetIndex(
    index).CreateSearchContext())
  {
    var filter = PredicateBuilder.True<Product>();

    var template = PredicateBuilder.False<Product>()
      .Or(i => i.TemplateName.Equals("product"))
      .Or(i => i.TemplateName.Equals("blog").Boost(20f));
    filter = filter.And(template);

    var fields = PredicateBuilder.False<Product>()
      .Or(i => i.ProductName.Contains(query))
      .Or(i => i.Description.Contains(query));
    filter = filter.And(fields);

    var searchResults =
      searchContext.GetQueryable<Product>()
      .Where(filter).GetResults()
      .OrderByDescending(i => i.Score);

    foreach (var item in searchResults)
    {
```

```
phResults.Controls.Add(new LiteralControl("<b>" +
    item.Score.ToString("00.00") + "</b>  <a href='#'
    >" + item.Document.ProductName + "</a><hr/>"));
        }
    }
}
```

3. In the preceding code, we boosted search results for items having the `Blog` template using the `.Boost()` extension method. Now, preview the page, search with a keyword, and get results. You can also compare its result after removing the `.Boost()` method from the same code.

4. You will find that after applying boosting, the score for blog items will increase compared to the score without boosting. The following image shows both results, without boosting and with boosting. You can find the score for each search result in *bold* letters. Here, we boosted `Blog` items by `20f`, so they got elevated compared to product items, as shown in the following image (Here, in boosted results, the first two results are blogs and others are products.):

Without Boosting	With Boosting
phone　　　　　Search	phone　　　　　Search
20.00 Apple iPhone 5S	**08.18** iPhone 7 release date, news and ru
14.77 Apple iPhone 6	**07.77** Fix the Phone 6S poor battery life
14.77 Apple iPhone 6S	**07.02** iPhone 6S Vs Galaxy S6
12.79 iPhone 7 release date, news and rt	**06.94** Apple iPhone 5S
11.64 Fix the Phone 6S poor battery life	**05.10** Apple iPhone 6
10.06 Samsung Note 4	**05.10** Apple iPhone 6S
10.06 Samsung Galaxy S5	**03.51** Samsung Note 4

5. So, we implemented query-time boosting. Now, we will implement rule-based boosting using **Rule Engine**. From the **Content Editor**, select `/sitecore/system/ Settings/Rules/Indexing & Search/Global Rules`. Create a **Boosting Rule**, `Featured Product`. As shown in the following image, apply a rule to it that if the **Company** field is equal to `Samsung`, then boost it by `30`. Here, **Company** is a Droptree field, so we entered the item ID of the `Samsung` item:

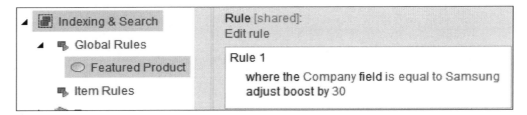

6. Now, search the same query with the same code; you will find that products of the `Samsung` company are boosted in results.

7. Now, let's see item-based boosting. We want to boost `iPhone 6S` with the topmost priority. So, we will boost it by `35`. For this, select the iPhone 6S item from the Content Editor. Under the **Indexing** section, set the **Boost value** field to `35`, as shown in the following image. Now, see the search results; you will find that `iPhone 6S` will get more scores:

How it works...

The Search API by default considers the descending sort order of `Score`, but we intentionally used `.OrderByDescending(i => i.Score)`, just to get a clear idea.

If we do not use boosting for our search results, Lucene will consider `1.0` as the default boost value. A boost value greater than `1.0` will elevate results to the top and less than `1.0` will demote results. Its value must be greater than zero. Boost expects `float` values.

The score of an item also depends on the number of children that it has. This means that an item having more children will increase the item score, which is the default behavior in Sitecore.

In step 5, we applied rule-based boosting globally. It's also possible to create a common boosting rule and apply it to different items or templates. You can create such boosting rules in `/sitecore/system/Settings/Rules/Indexing and Search/Item Rules` and then assign this rule to the item from the **Indexing** section in the **Boosting rules** field.

To apply field-level or fieldtype-level boosting, you can set the boost value of the boost attribute for the field mappings done in the `Sitecore.ContentSearch.Lucene.DefaultIndexConfiguration.config` file.

Hunting MoreLikeThis results

We might not get relevant results with keywords all the time, so we need to find similar results based on a document; something like what Google provides, as shown in the following image:

MoreLikeThis is a component to find documents that are most similar to a document. It does this using terms from the original document to find similar documents in the index. In this recipe, you will learn different approaches to using this component.

Getting ready

For this recipe, we will use the same product and their blog items and both will have `Title` and `Description` fields, on which we will perform a MoreLikeThis search.

How to do it...

First of all, we will implement a search query without boosting and get results:

1. We will use the `Product` document mapper class with `productname` (or `title`) and `description` fields that we created in the previous recipe.

2. Write code to search and list results based on a search keyword so that we will get the following results. Here, to each result is a Sitecore item. So, clicking on the **Similar** link for an item, pass Item Id of the item. Now, we will find related (MoreLikeThis) results for this item:

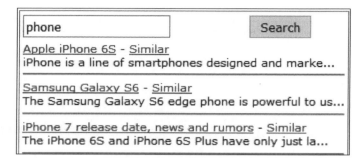

3. Now we will start collecting prerequisites for using the MoreLikeThis query. To find similar results, we need four things—IndexSearcher, a MoreLikeThis query, documentId for which we need to find similar results, and a number of top hits to match. The following code will help collect them. Make sure to reference the Sitecore.ContentSearch.LuceneProvider.dll assembly to the project:

```
string indexName = string.Format("sitecore_{0}_index",
  Sitecore.Context.Database.Name);
var index = (
  LuceneIndex)ContentSearchManager.GetIndex(indexName);

var reader =
  index.CreateReader(LuceneIndexAccess.ReadOnly);
var moreLikeThis = new MoreLikeThis(reader);
CreateMLTQuery(moreLikeThis);

string itemId = Request["relatedto"];
var searcher = (IndexSearcher)
  index.CreateSearcher(LuceneIndexAccess.ReadOnly);
int docId = GetDocumentId(itemId, searcher);

int minimumNumberShouldMatch = 5;
```

4. Create the CreateMLTQuery() method used in the preceding code to build the MoreLikeThis query:

```
private void CreateMLTQuery(MoreLikeThis query)
{
  query.Analyzer = new
    StandardAnalyzer(Lucene.Net.Util.Version.LUCENE_30);
```

```
query.MinTermFreq = 1;
query.MinDocFreq = 1;
query.MaxQueryTerms = 5;
query.SetFieldNames(new string[] { "title", "description"
  });
query.SetStopWords(StopAnalyzer.ENGLISH_STOP_WORDS_SET);
}
```

5. Create the `GetDocumentId()` method to get the document ID for the item:

```
private static int GetDocumentId(string itemId,
  IndexSearcher searcher)
{
  Lucene.Net.Util.Version version =
    Lucene.Net.Util.Version.LUCENE_30;
  StandardAnalyzer analyzer = new
    StandardAnalyzer(version);
  QueryParser parser = new QueryParser(version, "_group",
    analyzer);
  Query result = parser.Parse(itemId);
  ScoreDoc[] singleDoc = searcher.Search(result,
    1).ScoreDocs;
  if (singleDoc.Length > 0)
    return singleDoc[0].Doc;
  return 0;
}
```

6. Now, using the preceding values, we will find similar results. Create a `ShowSimilarResults()` method to get a list of similar results as follows and pass all the preceding values to it. Here, we used a custom document mapper class, `SearchResult`, with three properties: `Title`, `Description`, and `ID` (use the `_group` index field to get the item ID). You can get this mapper class from the code bundle provided with this book:

```
private List<SearchResult> ShowSimilarResults(IndexSearcher
  searcher, MoreLikeThis mlt, int docId, int topHits)
{
  BooleanQuery boolQuery = (BooleanQuery)mlt.Like(docId);
  ScoreDoc[] scoreDocs = searcher.Search(boolQuery,
    topHits).ScoreDocs;

  List<SearchResult> results = new List<SearchResult>();
  foreach (var scoreDoc in scoreDocs) {
    Document doc = searcher.Doc(scoreDoc.Doc);
    SearchResult result = new
      SearchResult(doc.Get("title"),
      doc.Get("description"), doc.Get("_group"));
```

```
        results.Add(result);
    }
    return results;
}
```

7. Bind the `List<SearchResult>` collection of results to the repeater component to show similar results. You can also get the source code from the code bundle provided with this book to find similar results.

How it works...

Sitecore provides you with a wrapper to work with Lucene's MoreLikeThis component and finds similar documents based on a list of keywords or document. The preceding code explains how we achieved similar results based on the selected document.

As we have seen in step 3, to use the MoreLikeThis component, we need `IndexReader`, a MoreLikeThis query, and `document id` to find similar results.

The MoreLikeThis query expects some parameters, which we collected from the `CreateMLTQuery()` method in step 4, listed as follows:

Query parameter	Explanation
MinTermFreq	Ignore terms with less than this frequency in the source document
MinDocFreq	Ignore words that do not occur in at least this many documents
MaxQueryTerms	Return a query with no more than this many terms
MaxDocFreq	Ignore words that occur in more than this many documents
SetFieldNames	Field names in which you can search the terms
SetStopWords	List of words not to check

Each Sitecore item stored in the index has a unique document ID. So, in the `GetDocumentId()` method in step 5, we found the document ID for the selected item. Now, we created a `BooleanQuery` using the `mlt.Like(documentId)` method and, based on this query, we searched the results that we are looking for in step 6.

There's more...

We could also have found similar results with search phrases using the `MoreLikeThisQuery` class as follows. Here, we searched similar documents, which contain `iphone`, `apple`, and `samsung` keywords in the `title` and `description` fields:

```
MoreLikeThisQuery query = new MoreLikeThisQuery("iphone apple
    samsung", new string[] { "title", "description" }, new
    StandardAnalyzer(Lucene.Net.Util.Version.LUCENE_30));
query.MinDocFreq = 1;
query.MinTermFrequency = 1;
ScoreDoc[] scoreDocs = searcher.Search(query, TopHits).ScoreDocs;
```

In step 4, we set stop words, which is a list of words that are not to be checked while finding similar results. You can also create a custom list of words instead of the predefined list.

You can get this additional custom code in the `ShowSimilarResultsUsingMLTQuery()` method and `StopWords` property from the web form file in the code bundle provided with this book.

Correcting a search with did you mean

Did you mean is a search engine function that scans for potential spelling or grammatical errors in user queries and recommends alternative keywords. This feature is designed to assist users in refining their search results.

In this recipe, you will learn how we can create a basic spellcheck version of this feature. Here, we will create our own spellcheck dictionary based on our content itself. When a user types an incorrect spelling or word, we will check its correctness from this dictionary itself and suggest best-suited words.

Getting ready

For this recipe, we need items having `Title` and `Description` fields and a document mapper class that we created and used in the previous recipes. Here, we will create a spellcheck dictionary based on the `Description` field.

How to do it...

First of all, we will map the field that we will use to find suggested words with the n-gram analyzer in the same way that we implemented in the *Achieving the autocomplete feature with a wildcard* recipe:

1. Map the `Description` field in a patch configuration with `storageType` as `YES`. Also, set `NGramAnalyzer` for this field to get similar phrases or words. You can also use our custom n-gram analyzer that we created in the *Achieving the autocomplete feature with a wildcard* recipe of this chapter. We can map the field and configure with the analyzer as follows. Make sure that you rebuild the index after the configuration:

```
<field fieldName="description" storageType="YES" ... >
  <Analyzer type="SitecoreCookbook.Search.NGramAnalyzer,
    SitecoreCookbook" />
</field>
```

2. We will now create a new dictionary index file based on our existing index file. In your sublayout or any other appropriate rendering, create the `IndexSpellCheckDictionary()` method to create a spellcheck dictionary index file as follows. The dbIndexName parameter is the name of the index (that is, `sitecore_master_index` or `sitecore_web_index`), where we will create a new dictionary index with the description field:

```
public void IndexSpellCheckDictionary(string dbIndexName,
  string spellIndex)
{
  LuceneIndex index = (
    LuceneIndex)ContentSearchManager.GetIndex(dbIndexName);
  IndexReader reader = index.CreateReader(
    LuceneIndexAccess.ReadOnly);

  FSDirectory dir = FSDirectory.Open(spellIndex);
  var spell = new
    SpellChecker.Net.Search.Spell.SpellChecker(dir);

  string fieldName = "description";
  LuceneDictionary dictionary = new
    LuceneDictionary(reader, fieldName);
  spell.IndexDictionary(dictionary, 10, 32);
}
```

3. Create the `GetSuggestedWords()` method to find similar words for the terms or phrase passed from the spellcheck index:

```
public string[] GetSuggestedWords(string spellIndex, string
  phrase, int maxCount)
{
  FSDirectory dir = FSDirectory.Open(spellIndex);
  var spell = new
    SpellChecker.Net.Search.Spell.SpellChecker(dir);

  spell.SetAccuracy(0.6f);
  spell.setStringDistance(new LevenshteinDistance());

  return spell.SuggestSimilar(phrase, maxCount);
}
```

4. You can use the preceding methods to fetch similar words as follows:

```
string spellIndex = Settings.IndexFolder +
  "/custom_spellcheck_index";
IndexSpellCheckDictionary("sitecore_master_index",
  spellIndex);
string[] suggestions = GetSuggestedWords(spellIndex,
  phrase, 3);
```

5. Bind the the preceding sublayout or rendering to a content page and preview it by passing a phrase; you will get similar words, found in the index file. You can also find the whole code of this recipe as a sublayout from the code bundle provided with this book and preview it. Here, we searched two different words or a phrase and we got results, as shown in the following image:

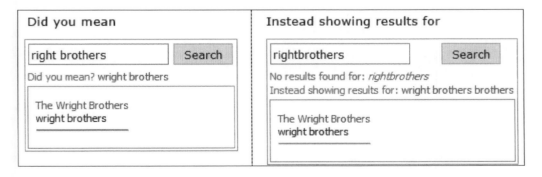

How it works...

We used an n-gram analyzer for the `Description` field so that we can get similar words or a phrase. Without an n-gram analyzer, this recipe will work for only one word.

Lucene provides you with a facility to create custom index files based on an already built index file. First of all, we created `IndexReader` of the `sitecore_master_index` file and a new index dictionary with the `Description` field using the following code:

```
LuceneDictionary dictionary = new LuceneDictionary(reader,
    fieldName);
spell.IndexDictionary(dictionary, 10, 32);
```

The last two parameters of the `IndexDictionary()` method, which are `mergeFactor` and `maxMB`, are optional, and you can set their values as per your need to improve indexing performance and speed or you can read out-of-the-box settings provided by Sitecore in `ContentSearch.MaxMergeMB` and `ContentSearch.IndexMergeFactor` in the `Sitecore.ContentSearch.Lucene.DefaultIndexConfiguration.config` file.

In step 2, we collected maximum three similar words or phrases for the requested phrase using Lucene's out-of-the-box **Levenshtein** distance algorithm and at least `0.6f` accuracy. The value of accuracy can be set between `0` and `1` and the default value is `0.5f`.

There's more...

Here, we created a spellcheck index dictionary on the fly for each search in the `IndexSpellCheckDictionary()` method to give a better explanation of this recipe. This may give a performance overhead to the application. You can build the index file at a regular time interval to prevent it getting created every time.

Managing millions of items using an item bucket

Item buckets is a system that lets you store millions of content items in one container so that an item bucket can contain any number of subitems. Sitecore provides you with a rich and scalable UI for bucketed items so that content owners can manage items very easily.

In this recipe, you will learn creating item buckets and searching items from a bucket from the Content Editor.

How to do it...

We will first choose an item that contains a huge number of subitems and maintaining them is getting very difficult for content owners:

1. From the Content Editor, select the /sitecore/Content/Home/Products/ Phones item. From the ribbon, click on the **Bucket** button in the **Buckets** section from the **Configure** tab.

2. We now have the Phones item converted to an item bucket, and a new **Search** pane appears on the right-hand side pane, as shown in the following image:

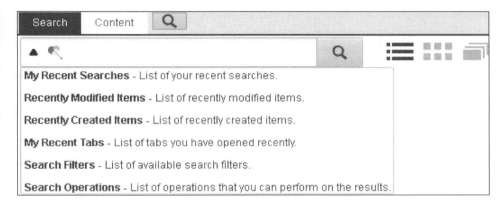

3. Click on the drop-down arrow to open more search options. It will show different search filters to search items in the bucket and also give a list of operations to perform on the searched items. This helps content owners to find their items very easily rather than navigating to the content tree.

4. However, when we have millions of items in the item bucket, then expanding it from the content tree will heavily slow down the client browser as well as the Sitecore server. To get rid of this, Sitecore allows us to hide all subitems by making them bucketable. The Phones item bucket contains items of the Product template. So, let's make this template bucketable. Select standard values of this template. In the **Item Buckets** section, tick the Bucketable checkbox field. Now, all items of the Product template are bucketable.

5. This change requires the item bucket to be synced. For this, select the Phones item. From the ribbon, click on the **Sync** button in the **Buckets** section from the **Configure** tab. Now, by expanding the Phones item, you will find that all the products got hidden, as shown in the following image:

So, now content owners will not have to worry about searching any product from the huge list and no worries for application or user interface performance as well on expanding the item.

How it works...

Sitecore indexes the item buckets in the same way as other items are indexed. So, you can use content search APIs to search items in it, which you learned in the previous recipes.

When an item bucket is created or synched, items in it are automatically organized in different folders according to their creation date time. To check the folder structure of bucketed items, tick the Buckets checkbox in the **View** tab from the ribbon. This will show all the bucketed items in the content tree, as shown in the following image:

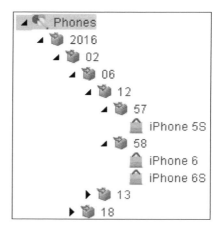

The preceding image shows that the iPhone 6S item was created on February 06, 2016, time—12:58 hours. This means that bucketed items get stored in the folder structure in the *yyyy/MM/dd/HH/mm* format. You can also change the folder structure by changing the bucketing strategy. For this, navigate to the /sitecore/system/Settings/Buckets/ Item Buckets Settings item. In the **Rules for Resolving the Bucket Folder Path** field, you can apply your custom rule for a custom format of the folder structure. You can read more about this at http://goo.gl/ux7RXo. You can also define your own custom strategy with custom code. Refer to http://goo.gl/OoODif to learn about its implementation.

While working with item buckets, content owners might need to run the same search query for the same item bucket regularly. To get rid of this, Sitecore provides you with the ability to save the search query so that just by clicking on an item bucket, the search runs the saved search query automatically. Learn more about saving a search query at https://goo.gl/bn1jcn.

10
Experience Personalization and Analytics Using xDB

In this chapter, you will learn the following recipes:

- ▶ Personalizing experience based on goals and Engagement Values
- ▶ Personalizing content by predicting a visitor's profile
- ▶ Storing visitor information in xDB contacts
- ▶ Extending xDB by creating a custom contact facet
- ▶ Creating a custom rule and condition for personalization
- ▶ Automating the engagement plan
- ▶ Finding nearby places using the Geolocation service
- ▶ Aggregating xDB data to generate custom reports
- ▶ Extending analytics reports using custom dimensions
- ▶ Creating section-specific analytics reports using custom dimensions

Introduction

Sitecore contains a state-of-the-art **Analysis, Insights, Decisions, and Automation (AIDA)** framework, which is the heart for marketing programs. It provides comprehensive analytics data and reports, insights from every website interaction with nice rules, and behavior-based personalization and marketing automation. Sitecore collects all visitor interactions in a real-time, big data repository, **Experience Database** (**xDB**) to increase availability, scalability, and performance of the website.

This chapter focuses on rule-based and behavioral personalization based on goals and profiles and marketing automation with engagement plans. This chapter also gives nice examples of how you can use and extend xDB, generate different types of analytics reports, and create custom conditions and actions for further personalization customizations. Recipes in this chapter require that you have enabled the Sitecore **Experience Platform** (**XP**) and won't work on experience management (CMS only). To enable Sitecore xDB, you must install MongoDB and configure it in Sitecore. You can learn it from `https://goo.gl/PPhT7I`.

Personalizing experience based on goals and Engagement Values

It's always important to show your visitors what they are looking for rather than just showing what we want to show. For this, you first need to determine what your visitors are doing and how they are engaging your website. This behavior can be tracked by goals, also called a conversion, such as signing up on the website, submitting contact information, visiting the newly launched products, and so on.

Let's consider a practical case. If a user has visited any of our featured products and also downloaded its brochure, then it clearly shows that the user is interested in the product. So, on the next page visit, we will show a **Subscribe to newsletter** popup. In this recipe, you will learn how to achieve this personalization.

Getting ready

For this recipe, create a product details page with a hyperlink to download the product brochure. Create one rendering to subscribe for a newsletter.

How to do it...

Let's first create goals and configure their **Engagement Values** (points):

1. Open the Content Editor. Navigate to `/sitecore/system/Marketing Control Panel/Goals`. In it, create different goals such as `Visited Featured Product` and `Downloaded Brochure`. Based on the importance of both these goals, assign the **Points** field value to 2 and 3 accordingly:

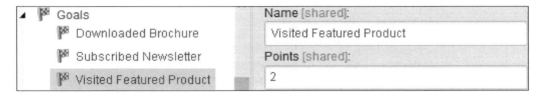

 It's good practice to use smaller numbers as Engagement Values, starting from 1 and marginally increasing the value based on importance.

2. From the ribbon, click on the **Deploy** button in the **Workflow** group from the **Review** menu to push both the goals in the final state of the goal workflow.

3. Now we will associate both goals with appropriate Sitecore items. From the Content Editor, select a featured product item. From the ribbon, click on the **Goals** button in the **Attributes** group from the **Analyze** menu. This will open the **Goals** dialog, where you will find these goals. Select the **Visited Featured Product** checkbox from the list of goals.

4. Similarly, select a product brochure media item and assign the **Downloaded Brochure** goal to it.

5. Now, whenever the featured product page is visited, Sitecore will trigger the **Visited Featured Product** goal and add 2 Engagement Values to the visitor's engagement profile, and similarly, add 3 Engagement Values on downloading the brochure media file. These engagement details can be found in the Experience Editor in Explore mode, as shown in the following image:

6. Now, when a visitor has achieved both the preceding goals, then we have to show a popup on the next interaction to encourage the visitor to subscribe to a newsletter. Select the featured product page, open **Presentation Details**, and then open the **Device Editor** dialog. Add the Signup Newsletter rendering and click on **Personalize**:

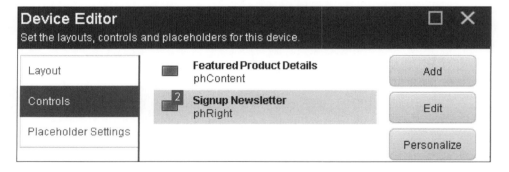

7. This will open the **Personalize the component** dialog, which will show a **Default** condition. Click on the **Hide Component** checkbox.

8. Create a new condition and name it `Show newsletter Subscription`. Click on the **Edit** button to write a condition for personalization. This will open another dialog of **Rule Set Editor** and apply rules, as shown in the following image:

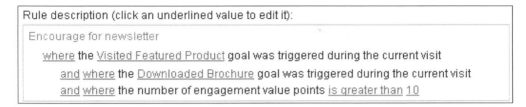

9. Now, the **Personalization** window should look like the following image, which shows that the **Signup Newsletter** will be hidden on the page by default, but once the condition gets satisfied, the rendering will be visible to the visitor:

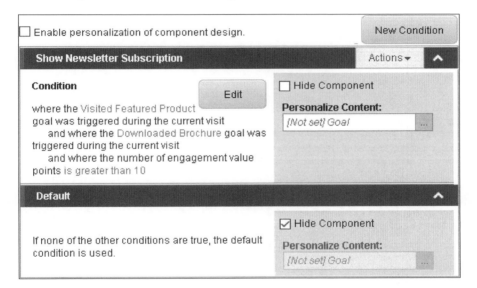

How it works...

When the goal gets triggered, it gets recorded to the xDB (MongoDB) in the `Interactions` collection in the `Pages/PageEvents` keys. To see xDB data, you can download the **Robomongo** tool from `https://robomongo.org/`.

 When you create a goal or any `Marketing Control Panel` item, it is subject to a workflow. So, it should be deployed once to a clear workflow.

There's more...

We can also trigger goals programmatically using the following code. Make sure to reference the `Sitecore.Analytics` assembly to the project:

```
Tracker.Current.CurrentPage.Register(goalName, "Text");
```

Another way to trigger a goal is by registering them using `PageEventsData`:

```
public void TrigerGoal(string eventName, Guid pageId, string
  dataKey, string data, string text)
{
  if (Sitecore.Analytics.Tracker.IsActive) {
    Tracker.Current.CurrentPage.Register(new
      Sitecore.Analytics.Data.PageEventData(eventName) {
      ItemId = pageId,
      Data = data,
      DataKey = dataKey,
      Text = text
    });
  }
}
```

> Goals are useful not only in measuring successes, but also in tracking error pages that visitors face, which can be helpful in enhancing user experience.

Personalizing content by predicting a visitor's profile

Predictive personalization is defined as the ability to predict visitor behavior, needs, or wants (and tailor offers and communications) very precisely. Once you predict your customer, it becomes very easy to personalize content for that user, which helps increase conversion rate, improve customer satisfaction, and better advertisement.

For example, a car manufacturer sells a variety of cars, for example, hatchback, sedan, SUV, and others, in different price ranges. Now, the website contains lots of information about all cars, such as news, articles, reviews, complaints, and so on. Based on website content browsing, we will predict a visitor's profile and personalize content based on it, for example, after the duration of a visit, if the visitor falls into the hybrid car segment, we can show suggested hybrid cars, or if a visitor looks confused by visiting multiple cars repetitively, we can show a form by filling in which car salesperson can contact the visitor.

Getting ready

This recipe assumes that you have already created car-related information, news, reviews, complaints, and other pages.

How to do it...

First, we will create a profile (that is, category) based on the car type and profile keys (attributes):

1. Create a `Car Type` profile in `/sitecore/system/Marketing Control Panel/ Profiles/`. In this profile, create different profile keys, for example, `Economical`, `Family`, `Transport`, and so on, as shown in the following image. Set the **Max Value** field to 5 in each profile key:

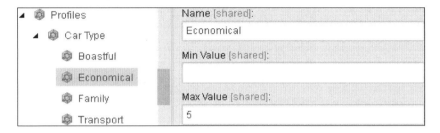

2. Now, we will create **Profile Cards** that are a set of profile keys with a predefined value for each. Create different Profile Cards, for example, `Comfort Car`, `Hatchback`, `Hybrid`, and so on under the `Profile Cards` folder in the `Profile` that we created in the preceding step. In each Profile Card, assign values to relevant profile keys. As we have set the maximum value of profile keys to 5, you can set values from 0 to 5 to each profile key, which will get reflected in a radar diagram, as shown on the right-hand side. Assign an image to individual cards to identify them quickly while tagging them on content pages:

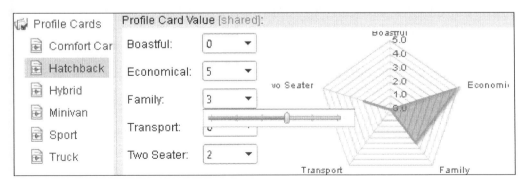

3. You can use the following **Profile** and **Profile Key** score table to assign Profile Card values:

Profile Cards	Car Type (Profile)					
	Comfort Car	Hatchback	Hybrid	Minivan	Sport	Truck
Boastful	5	0	0	3	4	0
Economical	0	5	3	2	0	0
Family	3	4	2	5	0	0
Transport	0	0	0	0	0	5
Two Seater	0	2	0	0	5	4

4. Create pattern cards for the car type categories profile against which the visitor's profile will be matched in real time to decide in what car category the visitor fits. To each pattern card, assign the same values to each profile key that we set for Profile Cards:

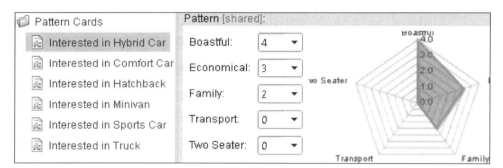

5. Now, assign one or more relevant Profile Cards to different content items. For example, Toyota Camry falls under the Hybrid category. Select its content page, and click on the Profile icon, which is found on the right-hand side of the Field Editor page, to assign a Profile Card to it. This will open the **Profile Cards** dialog. Click on the **Edit** button for the **Car Type** profile and select the **Hybrid Profile Card**. You can also customize Profile Card values by clicking on the **Customize** button found in the top-right corner of the dialog. Once you apply the Profile Card, you will find that the selected Profile Card icon will get reflected just beside the Profile icon in the Field Editor:

6. Similarly, apply different Profile Cards to different content pages, such as news, articles, reviews, and other pages so that on visiting them, assigned Profile Cards or pattern values will be assigned to the visiting customer's contact or profile.

7. Publish all these items and visit different content pages on the website; you will find that a **Car Type** profile pattern will be assigned to your profile. The pattern of car type will get changed based on what kind of content or pages you are visiting, which you can find from the Experience Editor in Explore mode.

8. Now we will personalize the content for a visitor based on the predicted profile pattern. If a user has spent more than five minutes on the website and has a pattern assigned to it, we will show suggested cars based on the pattern card. Personalize a rendering based on the following condition to show suggested cars:

Rule description (click an underlined value to edit it):

Condition Name
    where the duration of the visit is greater than 300
        and where the current visit matches the Interested in Hybrid Car pattern card in the Car Type profile

How it works...

A profile has a **Type** field that can have values such as `Percentage`, `Average`, and `Sum`, which can be used to track how visitor behavior points are accrued. Its default value is percentage, which is the most widely used method.

Similarly, the `Profile Cards` folder has an **Authoring Selection** field, which can have values such as `Single`, `Multiple`, and `Multiple with Percentages`. A `Single` authoring selection will stick to assigning only one persona or Profile Card to a content page, as we did in step 5. A `Multiple` authoring selection will allow you to select multiple Profile Cards, and `Multiple with Percentages` will allow multiple Profile Cards where you can mention how many percentages of points each Profile Card will share.

Sitecore matches the visits' profiling information with pattern cards. For this, it uses the Euclidean principle to determine the closest pattern of the current visit.

Sitecore 8 comes with an advantage of having persisting profiles, but in some cases, there is no means of finding patterns based on past behavior. Sitecore 8.1 introduces the concept of *Profile Decay*, a way to gradually reduce the relevance of scores accumulated in the past. You can find this field in **Profile** items and its default value as 0, which means that it's disabled by default.

To get a more accurate prediction and personalization, you can find multiple patterns of visitors. In our case, we can predict stage of visitors for buying car, for example, Engager, Evaluator, Enthusiast, Supporter, and so on.

There's more...

Sometimes, you may get a requirement to predict a profile explicitly, for example, when a user searches for a keyword such as `luxury car`, you can say that the user is surely falling into the **Comfort Car** category. So, you can assign a key value of **Comfort Car** Profile Card that is a multiple of a number. The example is nicely explained at `http://goo.gl/YNRtUo`.

Storing visitor information in xDB contacts

All visitors are stored in xDB, including anonymous visitors. It allow us to store information such as personal details, e-mail addresses, addresses, phone numbers, and so on in the `Contact` entity in xDB.

In this recipe, you will learn how to store user profile information in xDB contacts at the time of user signup using out-of-the-box **System** and **Standard** contact facets.

Getting ready

This recipe assumes that you have created a sign-up sublayout or rendering, which collects details such as username (e-mail address), password, phone number, full address, birthdate, and so on.

How to do it...

We will first prepare a helper method from where we can store user information in xDB:

1. In the `SitecoreCookbook` project, create a `ContactHelper` class in the `Helper` subfolder in the `Analytics` folder. Create a `SaveContact()` method as follows. For this, you first need to reference the `Sitecore.Analytics.Model` assembly to the project:

   ```
   public static void SaveContact(string userName, string
   ```

```
firstName, string lastName, DateTime birthDate, string
emailAddress)
{
    Tracker.Current.Session.Identify(userName);
    Contact contact = Tracker.Current.Contact;

    IContactPersonalInfo personal =
        contact.GetFacet<IContactPersonalInfo>("Personal");
    personal.FirstName = firstName;
    personal.Surname = lastName;
    personal.BirthDate = birthDate;

    IContactEmailAddresses email =
        contact.GetFacet<IContactEmailAddresses>("Emails");
    email.Entries.Create("personal").SmtpAddress =
        emailAddress;
}
```

2. Now, from your sublayout or another rendering, invoke this method from your sign-up form by passing the required user information. Once a user fills in the information and submits the form, the contact will get reflected in the Contact collection of xDB as follows:

✓ ▣ (12) LUUID("bc8547ce-aaee-... { 9 fields }		Object
▦ _id	LUUID("bc8547ce-aaee-b244-9967-62b8...	Legacy UUID
✓ ▣ Identifiers	{ 3 fields }	Object
# AuthenticationLevel	2	Int32
# IdentificationLevel	2	Int32
▥ Identifier	extranet\contact@patelyogesh.in	String
▥ Lease	null	Null
> ▣ System	{ 2 fields }	Object
✓ ▣ Personal	{ 3 fields }	Object
▥ FirstName	Yogesh	String
▥ Surname	Patel	String
▤ Birthdate	1983-05-27 18:17:03.039Z	Date
> ▣ Addresses	{ 2 fields }	Object
✓ ▣ Emails	{ 2 fields }	Object
▥ Preferred	personal	String
✓ ▣ Entries	{ 2 fields }	Object
> ▣ personal	{ 1 fields }	Object
> ▣ work	{ 1 fields }	Object

Remember that facets are written to xDB only when your session ends. You can try calling the `Session.Abandon()` method to force Sitecore to write facet details to xDB.

How it works...

The `Contact` data model allows you to store data in facets. There are three types of facets available for the `Contact` entity in xDB—`System`, `Standard`, and `Custom`:

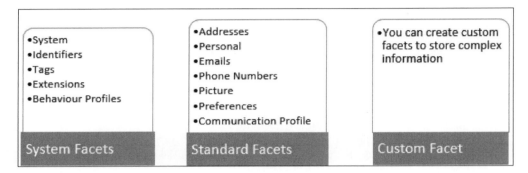

Here, we used `Standard` facets that can be found in the `\App_Config\Include\Sitecore.Analytics.Model.config` file in the `<sitecore/model/entities/contact/facets>` section, as shown in the following screenshot:

```
<facets>
  <facet name="Personal"
         contract="Sitecore.Analytics.Model.Entities.IContactPersonalInfo,
                   Sitecore.Analytics.Model" />
  <facet name="Addresses" contract="..." />
  <facet name="Emails" contract="..." />
</facets>
```

The `contract` attribute of the `Personal` facet indicates that it can be used to read or store personal facet information using the `Sitecore.Analytics.Model.Entities.IContactPersonalInfo` interface. We can read it using the `GetFacet<>()` method of `Contact` as follows:

```
IContactPersonalInfo personal =
  contact.GetFacet<IContactPersonalInfo>("Personal");
personal.FirstName = firstName;
```

Similarly, we can use different facets such as `Addresses`, `E-mails`, and `Phone Numbers`, which can contain different entries. The following code snippet shows you how to use them:

```
IContactAddresses address =
  contact.GetFacet<IContactAddresses>("Addresses");
IAddress homeAddress = address.Entries.Create("home_address");
homeAddress.StreetLine1 = homeAdd1;

IAddress officeAddress = address.Entries.Create("office_address");
officeAddress.StreetLine1 = officeAdd1;

address.Preferred = "home_address";
```

The facets can have multiple entries; we can specify any entry as a preferred one using the `Preferred` property. Get the full source code from the code bundle provided with this book to use different facets on signup.

There's more...

Information that cannot be stored using out-of-the-box `Standard` facets can be stored in `Contact` using `System` facets such as `Tags` and `Extensions`. Both of them allow you to store a collection of simple name/value string pairs:

```
contact.Extensions.SimpleValues["Full Name"] = "Pavel Nezhencev";
contact.Tags.Add("Full Name", "Yogesh Patel");
```

To store custom complex information in the `Contact`, you can create `Custom` facets, which you will learn in the next recipe.

Apart from all these facets, we used one more facet, `Identifiers`, which is used to identify the visitor using the e-mail-address or username and relate it with a contact. Read more on identifying contacts at `https://goo.gl/fCaZFN`.

> While doing signup or sign in or storing custom information to a contact, you should use the `Tracker.Current.Session.Identify()` method so that an anonymous visitor's activity before signing in will get merged into the named `Contact` created using an identifier.

Extending xDB by creating a custom contact facet

In xDB, you can store custom contact information using `System` facets such as `Tags` and `Extensions`. However, to store complex information such as dictionaries or collections, you can extend the `Contact` with your custom facet. In this recipe, you will learn how to store shopping cart information to the `Contacts` collection in xDB.

Getting ready

For this recipe, you should create product pages with an **Add to cart** button on it.

How to do it...

We will first create a `Contract` to define the structure of elements of the facet:

1. In the `SitecoreCookbook` project, create an `IShoppingCartRecord` interface in the `Model` subfolder in the `Analytics` folder that extends the `IElement` and `IValidatable` interfaces as follows:

    ```
    public interface IShoppingCartRecord : IElement,
      IValidatable
    {
      Guid ProductItemId { get; set; }
      int Quantity { get; set; }
    }
    ```

2. To create a facet, create another `IContactShoppingCart` interface extending the `IFacet` interface in the same folder as follows. Define the `Entries` property to store a collection of different cart items and the `LastUpdatedOn` property to store the time when the last product was added to the cart:

    ```
    public interface IContactShoppingCart : IFacet, IElement,
      IValidatable
    {
      IElementDictionary<IShoppingCartRecord> Entries { get; }
      DateTime LastUpdatedOn { get; set; }
    }
    ```

3. Now we will implement the `Contract` created. In the project, create a
   `ShoppingCartRecord` class in the `Generated` subfolder in the `Analytics` folder
   that extends the `System.Analytics.Model.Framework.Element` class and the
   `IShoppingCartRecord` interface. Create a default constructor as follows to register
   the element attributes:

```
[Serializable]
public class ShoppingCartRecord : Element,
  IShoppingCartRecord
{
  public ShoppingCartRecord()
  {
    base.EnsureAttribute<Guid>("Product Item Id");
    base.EnsureAttribute<int>("Quantity");
  }
}
```

4. In the same class, implement properties of the interface to register them with the
   `IShoppingCartRecord` model:

```
public Guid ProductItemId {
  get { return base.GetAttribute<Guid>("Product Item Id");}
  set { base.SetAttribute<Guid>("Product Item Id", value);}
}

public int Quantity {
  get { return base.GetAttribute<int>("Quantity"); }
  set { base.SetAttribute<int>("Quantity", value); }
}
```

5. In the `Generated` folder, create another `ContactShoppingCart` class that
   extends the `Sitecore.Analytics.Model.Framework.Facet` class and
   `IContactShoppingCart` interface. Create a default constructor as follows to
   register the facet's attributes and dictionaries:

```
[Serializable]
public class ContactShoppingCart : Facet,
  IContactShoppingCart, IFacet, IElement, IValidatable
{
  public ContactShoppingCart()
  {
    base.EnsureAttribute<DateTime>("Last Updated On");
    base.EnsureDictionary<IShoppingCartRecord>("Entries");
  }
}
```

6. In the same class, implement properties of the interface to register them with the `IContactShoppingCart` model:

```
public DateTime LastUpdatedOn {
  get { return base.GetAttribute<DateTime>("Last Updated
    On"); }
  set { base.SetAttribute<DateTime>("Last Updated On",
    value); }
}


public IElementDictionary<IShoppingCartRecord> Entries {
  get { return
    base.GetDictionary<IShoppingCartRecord>("Entries");}
}
```

7. Now it's time to configure this facet to Sitecore. In the `\App_Config\Include\` `Cookbook\` folder, create a `SitecoreCookbook.CustomFacet.config` file and register the model and its implementation elements in the `<configuration/` `sitecore/model/elements>` section as follows:

```
<element interface="SitecoreCookbook.Analytics.Model.
  IContactShoppingCart, SitecoreCookbook" implementation=
  "SitecoreCookbook.Analytics.Generated.
  ContactShoppingCart, SitecoreCookbook" />


<element interface="SitecoreCookbook.Analytics.Model.
  IShoppingCartRecord, SitecoreCookbook" implementation=
  "SitecoreCookbook.Analytics.Generated.ShoppingCartRecord,
  SitecoreCookbook" />
```

8. In the same patch configuration file, register the facet named `Shopping Cart` in the `<configuration/sitecore/model/entities/contact/facets>` section:

```
<facet name="Shopping Cart"
  contract="SitecoreCookbook.Analytics.Model.
  IContactShoppingCart, SitecoreCookbook" />
```

9. Now we will use this facet to store shopping cart details in the `Contacts` collection. In the project, create a `ShoppingCartHelper` class and `AddToCart()` method in the `Helper` subfolder in the `Analytics` folder as follows:

```
public static void AddToCart(Guid productItemId, string
  productName, int quantity)
{
  Contact contact = Tracker.Current.Contact;
  var shoppingCart = contact.GetFacet<
    IContactShoppingCart>("Shopping Cart");
  shoppingCart.LastUpdatedOn = DateTime.Now;

  IShoppingCartRecord cartRecord;
```

```
if (!shoppingCart.Entries.Contains(productName))
  cartRecord = shoppingCart.Entries.Create(productName);
else
  cartRecord = shoppingCart.Entries[productName];

cartRecord.ProductItemId = productItemId;
cartRecord.Quantity = quantity;
}
```

10. You can add multiple products to the cart. Cart details will get reflected in the
    Contacts collection in xDB as follows:

⌄ 🔲 Shopping Cart	{ 2 fields }	Object
📅 Last Updated On	2016-01-24 10:56:23.132Z	Date
⌄ 🔲 Entries	{ 2 fields }	Object
⌄ 🔲 Mobile Cover	{ 3 fields }	Object
🔢 Product Item Id	LUUID("3459605d-6605-2443-b602-909972509eaf")	Legacy UUID
# Quantity	1	Int32
⌄ 🔲 Mobile Charger	{ 3 fields }	Object
🔢 Product Item Id	LUUID("43877103-446a-1149-afc9-0bc568506098")	Legacy UUID
# Quantity	2	Int32

How it works...

A facet can contain three characteristics: Elements, Attributes, and Dictionaries. An
element can contain multiple attributes or dictionaries. So, we implemented both contracts
with the IElement interface; IShoppingCartRecord contains cart item details such as
product and quantity and IContactShoppingCart contains multiple cart records.

If you want to create a custom facet with single attribute fields only, then it requires only a
single contract and implementation.

> Make sure that the contract implementation classes are marked with the
> [Serializable] attribute to ensure that instances of this class can
> be stored in a shared session (shared across simultaneous sessions).
>
> xDB is used to store analytics information that can be useful later to
> optimize user experience. So, it's not advisable to use it to store any
> secured information.

Creating a custom rule and condition for personalization

Sitecore provides a couple of out-of-the-box conditions and relevant actions based on elements, for example, conditional renderings, date, context, GeoIP, visitor, and others so that most of the requirements for personalization rules can get fulfilled.

Here, to create a custom condition, let's consider an example. A marketing team wants to show a promotional offer on the *continue to payment* page to customers who have added any of the featured products to the cart. So, in this recipe, you will learn creating a custom condition to check whether the selected featured products exist in the cart or not.

Getting ready

This recipe assumes that you have already implemented the previous recipe to store shopping cart details in the custom `Contacts` facet.

How to do it...

First, we will create the condition class to check the shopping cart:

1. In the `SitecoreCookbook` project, create an `IsProductInCart` class in the `Rules` subfolder in the `Analytics` folder, extend it from the `WhenCondition<T>` abstract class, and override its `Execute()` method as follows:

```
public class IsProductInCart<T> : WhenCondition<T> where
  T : RuleContext
{
  public string ProductId { get; set; }

  protected override bool Execute(T ruleContext)
  {
    if (Tracker.IsActive) {
      Contact contact = Tracker.Current.Contact;
      var shoppingCart = contact.GetFacet<
        IContactShoppingCart>("Shopping Cart");
      foreach (var entry in shoppingCart.Entries.Keys) {
        var cartItem = shoppingCart.Entries[entry];
        return (cartItem.ProductItemId == new
          Guid(this.ProductId));
      }
    }
    return false;
  }
}
```

2. Now we will create a new `Rule` element in Sitecore and map this condition in an action. In the Content Editor, create a new `Shopping Cart` element in the `/sitecore/system/Settings/Rules/Definitions/Elements` item, which will create a few `Tags` and `Visibility` items in it automatically.

3. Create a `Has Product` condition in the `Shopping Cart` item. Add the following condition formula to the **Text** field and the preceding class details to the **Type** field, as shown in the following image:

4. Select the `Shopping Cart/Tags/Default` item. In the **Tags** field, select the **Conditional Renderings** rule from the listed tags so that this condition will be visible only while applying personalization conditional rendering.

5. Now apply personalization on the continue to payment page to show promotional offers on it. The condition for personalization will look like the following image, where clicking on the **specific** link will open a dialog that will allow you to choose a product from the specified products item path:

> Rule description (click an underlined value to edit it):
>
> Show me
>
>   where the specific product is added to shopping cart

6. Check the continue to payment page before and after adding the featured product to the shopping cart and see how the promotional offer is visible!

How it works...

The condition formula that we applied plays a very important role here. `[ProductId, Tree, root=/sitecore/Content/Home/Products, specific]` says that when you click on the **specific** text, it will open a dialog showing a tree with the mentioned path as a root item. When the personalization condition is executed, the selected item gets assigned to the `ProductId` property of the condition class we created. That's it, you can now play with its value to apply your condition!

In previous chapters, we used different out-of-the-box rule conditions and actions for different purposes. In this recipe, we created a custom condition. In the next recipe, we will create a custom action to automate the engagement plan. **Rules engine** is the heart of Sitecore architecture, which can be used to manipulate insert options dynamically, handle system events, personalization, and so on. You can learn more about it at `https://goo.gl/2Zbsv3`.

There's more...

Until now, you learned how to show a hidden rendering using personalization. It's also possible to replace renderings once the personalization condition gets satisfied. For this, from **Presentation Details** in the **Device Editor** dialog, select a rendering that you want to replace. Now, from the **Personalization** dialog, tick the **Enable personalization of component design** checkbox and select a rendering to replace it from **Personalize Component**.

Automating the engagement plan

An **engagement plan** is a predefined plan that lets you control how your website interacts with visitors. You use engagement plans to nurture relationships with your visitors by adapting personalized communication based on which state the visitors are in.

For example, a marketing team needs to automate an engagement plan that when any user downloads the product brochure, visitors should be added to an engagement plan automatically. If this user has not subscribed to a newsletter and has some engagement value points, send them an e-mail to encourage them to subscribe for the newsletter. In this recipe, we will achieve two things—automating visitor enrollment in the engagement plan on downloading a brochure and sending an e-mail to them if they don't subscribe to the newsletter.

Getting ready

For this recipe, create and deploy a goal, `Subscribed Newsletter`. We will also use the `Downloaded Brochure` and `Visited Featured Products` goals that we already created in the previous recipe. This recipe also assumes that the visitors are already registered with the website using an e-mail address where we will send e-mails.

How to do it...

We will first create an engagement plan:

1. From the Content Editor, select the `/sitecore/system/Marketing Control Panel/Engagement Plans` item. Create an engagement plan item, `Newsletter Evaluation Plan`.

2. Click on the **Engagement Plan** tab in the **Field Editor** section. Click on the Design icon, which will open a **Designer** dialog to design the engagement plan. In this dialog, click on the **State** button in the **New Items** section, as shown in the following image:

3. This will create a State icon in the design pane; select this State and click on the **Edit** button shown at the top or double-click on it. This will open the **State Details** dialog; set the **Display Name** field as Downloaded Brochure and set an appropriate description for it:

4. Click on the **Trigger** button on State, as shown in the preceding image, which will open a **State Evaluation Triggers** dialog. Here, select some goals or page events such as **Downloaded Brochure**, **Visited Featured Product**, and so on so that when a visitor achieves any of these selected goals or page events, Sitecore automatically evaluates further actions.

5. Now we will create a condition. Click on one of the diamond shapes around the state, which will create a condition shape, as shown in the following image:

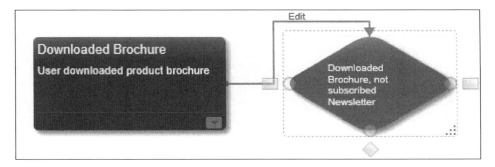

6. Click on the **Edit** button of the condition to set its field values, as shown in the preceding image. Set appropriate **Display Name** and **Description** fields. Set the **Evaluate** field as **Always Evaluate** and apply a rule to check whether the user has downloaded a brochure, not subscribed to the newsletter, and has at least 10 engagement value points. The rule for the condition will look as follows:

Rule - for this condition to be true, one of the following rules must be true: [unversioned, shared]:
Edit rule

Rule 1

where the Downloaded Brochure goal was triggered during the current visit
and except where the Subscribed Newsletter goal was triggered during the current visit
and where the number of engagement value points is greater than 10

7. Now we will create another state. Visitors that satisfy the preceding condition will be moved to this state. Click on the Condition icon from the **Design** pane; click on any of the rectangle shapes around the condition, which will create a state, as shown in the following image:

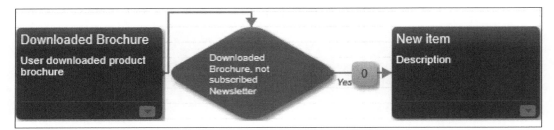

8. Set this state's **Display Name** as Sent email for Newsletter and an appropriate description.

9. Now, we will create an action to perform when the visitor moves to this state. Click on the arrow stating from condition to state showing 0 (number of actions), as shown in the preceding image. This will show a popup, as shown in the following image. Select the **Send E-Mail Message** option:

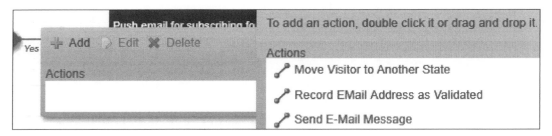

10. Double-click this selected action, which will open a dialog to send an e-mail. Fill in the appropriate details and save it.

11. Deploy the `Newsletter Evaluation Plan` engagement plan item to finish its workflow. This will enable the engagement plan to be used.

12. Now, when a visitor downloads a brochure, he should be enrolled in the `Downloaded Brochure` state of the engagement plan that we created. We will achieve this by creating a custom `RuleAction`. In the `SitecoreCookbook` project, create an `EnrollInAutomationState` action class in the `Rules` subfolder in the `Analytics` folder as follows. Also, reference the `Sitecore.Analytics` and `Sitecore.Analytics.Automation` assemblies to the project:

```
public class EnrollInAutomationState<T> : RuleAction<T>
  where T : RuleContext
{
  public string StateId { get; set; }
  public override void Apply([NotNull] T ruleContext)
  {
    var state = Context.Database.GetItem(new ID(StateId));
    if (state != null && state.Template.Key == "engagement plan
state") {
      var a = AutomationStateManager.Create(
        Tracker.Current.Contact);
      a.EnrollInEngagementPlan(state.ParentID, state.ID);
    }
  }
}
```

13. From the Content Editor, create an `EnrollInAutomationState` action item in `/sitecore/system/Settings/Rules/Definitions/Elements/Engagement Automation/` and map the preceding action class, as shown in the following image:

Text:

Enroll the user in the [stateid,tree,root=/sitecore/system/Marketing Control Panel/ Engagement Plans,specific] Automation State

Type [shared]:

SitecoreCookbook.Analytics.Rules.EnrollInAutomationState,SitecoreCookbook

14. Select the `Downloaded Brochure` goal. Apply the created action to its **Rule** field, as shown the following image, to enroll the user in the `Downloaded Brochure` state of engagement plan:

```
Rule - the rule is evaluated when the page event is triggered [unversioned, shared]
Edit rule

Rule 1

    where true (actions always execute)
    Enroll the user in the Downloaded Brochure Automation State
```

To test this engagement plan, register a user in the site and download the brochure (or trigger the `Downloaded Brochure` goal); you will get an e-mail for the newsletter. If you have subscribed to the newsletter before downloading the brochure, you should not get an e-mail as it will not satisfy our specified condition.

How it works...

In the case we considered, when a user does registration or logs in to the website, the visitor won't be assigned to any state of engagement plan. When a visitor downloads the brochure, the `Downloaded Brochure` goal will get triggered so that the visitor will be enrolled in the `Downloaded Brochure` state of this engagement plan automatically, based on our custom action created in steps 12 to 14. You can enroll a visitor in the engagement plan using campaign, (**Web Forms for Marketers** (**WFFM**), or APIs.

Now, whenever a visitor triggers any of the goals or page events mentioned in step 4 to evaluate further conditions from the `Downloaded Brochure` state, the condition will get evaluated every time. When this condition gets satisfied, Sitecore will execute the `Send E-mail` action and move the visitor to the `Sent email for Newsletter` state.

For better explanation, we considered a simpler example of an engagement plan with two states only. You can have any number of engagement states and conditions. The engagement plan is a very broad topic; you can learn more about it at `https://goo.gl/fh5Fn3`, which covers creating and monitoring engagement plans.

Finding nearby places using the Geolocation service

Sitecore provides Geolocation-based services out of the box, which can help marketers create a personalized experience. It can also help empower consumers in finding trending products in their region or the nearest service stations.

In this recipe, we will take an example of an electronics product company, which wants to provide the nearest service station details to its visitor.

Getting ready

For this recipe, you should have configured the Sitecore Geolocation service, which you can do in a few steps shown at `https://goo.gl/c9OQWj`. Also, create some service providers' items with `Title`, `Address`, `City`, `Latitude`, and `Longitude` fields.

How to do it...

We will first find the latitude and longitude of the visitor and search for nearby restaurants:

1. In the `SitecoreCookbook` project, create a `PlacesHelper` class and a `GetNearbyPlaces()` action method in the `Helper` subfolder in the `Analytics` folder as follows:

```
public static List<Item> GetNearbyPlaces()
{
  var geoData = Tracker.Current.Interaction.GeoData;
  if (geoData.Latitude == null)
    return null;
  double latitude = (double)geoData.Latitude;
  double longitude = (double)geoData.Longitude;

  var orderedDistances = FindNearbyPlaces(latitude,
    longitude);
  var places = new List<Item>();
  foreach (var iterator in orderedDistances) {
    places.Add(iterator.Key);
  }
  return places;
}
```

 Sitecore can find your geolocation details only when your page request is traversed through the Internet. So, for local testing purposes, you can hardcode some real values to latitude and longitude variables, for example, 40.69 and 73.95.

2. Create a `FindNearbyPlaces()` method to find five service stations nearest to the visitor. In this method, we use the `FindDistance()` method to find the distance between two places, which you can get from the code bundle provided with this book:

```
private static IEnumerable<KeyValuePair<Item, double>>
  FindNearbyPlaces(double latitude, double longitude)
{
  Item locations = Context.Database.GetItem(
    "/sitecore/Content/Home/ServiceStations");
```

```
var places = new Dictionary<Item, double>();
foreach (Item place in locations.Children) {
  double placeLat = double.Parse(place["Latitude"]);
  double placeLong = double.Parse(place["Longitude"]);

  double distance = FindDistance(placeLat, placeLong,
    latitude, longitude);
  places.Add(place, distance);
}
return places.OrderBy(p => p.Value).Take(5);
}
```

3. Now, invoke the `GetNearbyPlaces()` method from your rendering or sublayout to view nearby places. Using the code in the code bundle provided with this book, you will find nearby places, as shown in the following image. For this, specify valid latitude and longitude values to places created in Sitecore:

Service Stations near you:

- ABC Services (1.112 km)
  157 9th Avenue, New York
- XYZ Service Center (2.378 km)
  25 9th Avenue, New York
- PQR Service Station (2.529 km)
  9th Main, 19th Street, Downtown Brooklyn, New York

How it works...

Sitecore collects Geolocation details on every interaction of the visitor, which is collected based on the IP address of the visitor's device and stored in the `Interactions` collection of xDB. `Sitecore.Analytics.Tracker.Current.Interactions.GeoData` can provide you with all these details:

GeoData	{ 12 fields }	Object
AreaCode	N/A	String
BusinessName	AT&T U-verse	String
City	Spring	String
Country	US	String
Dns	N/A	String
Isp	AT&T U-verse	String
Latitude	30.037800	Double
Longitude	-95.532600	Double
MetroCode	618	String
PostalCode	77379	String
Region	TX	String

It also provides the ISP network or business network of the visitors. Geolocation details such as the country, area, city, business name, and so on of visitors can become very beneficial for marketers to engage them, like who, from where, and what they were looking for.

There's more...

If you want to test Sitecore's Geolocation service locally without hardcoding latitude and longitude, you can add any IP address in the X-Forwarded-For request header from your bnhju87browser. For this, you can download the **Modify Headers** add-on for Firefox or Chrome and set values, as shown in the following image:

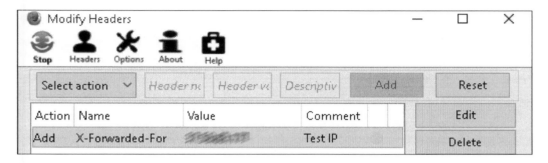

By default, the Sitecore Geolocation service does not understand this header. To make it work, open the \App_Config\Include\Sitecore.Analytics.Tracking.config file, specify the X-Forwarded-For value to the Analytics.ForwardedRequestHttpHeader setting as follows:

```
<setting name="Analytics.ForwardedRequestHttpHeader"
  value="X-Forwarded-For" />
```

When your content delivery server is serving behind a CDN, reverse proxy, or load balancer, you must enable this setting as the end user's IP will be received by the web server through the X-Forwarded-For header only. The header can contain multiple IP addresses separated by a comma and the first IP address will be the visitor's.

Sitecore has launched the **Device Detection** service for Sitecore 8.1 and above, which identifies the digital device that your visitors are using along with highly accurate information such as the device type, screen size, memory, and so on. This service can also be very useful in device-based personalization.

Aggregating xDB data to generate custom reports

The Sitecore analytics framework allows developers to extend and create custom reports as per their business need using the available xDB data, just like in the **Experience Analytics** dashboard.

Segments and dimensions are useful in identifying how and which data to aggregate from xDB. In this recipe, you will learn aggregating data based on visitors' browsers, which can be used to generate different reports.

How to do it...

First, we will create dimension and segment definition items:

1. Open the Content Editor, and select the `/sitecore/system/Marketing Control Panel/Experience Analytics/Dimensions/Visits` item. Create a new `By Browser Version` dimension item. This will automatically create a segment type child item, `All`. Rename it `All visits by Browser Version`. Deploy this segment and publish both the items:

2. On deploying the segment item, it will get added to the **Segments** table of the **Reporting** database, as shown in the following image. Find the segment created and update its **DeployDate** field to any older date so that xDB can process data. Here, **SegmentId** is the item ID of the segment item:

```
UPDATE Segments
  SET DeployDate = DATEADD(day, -1, getdate())
  WHERE SegmentId='{CC9A9375-49D4-4501-86A1-55B5F8EF2966}
```

The updated segment can be seen in the following image:

3. Now we will create a `Dimension` class, which will actually process xDB data. In the `SitecoreCookbook` project, create a new `ByBrowserVersion` class in the `Dimensions` subfolder in the `Analytics` folder. Make sure to reference the `Sitecore.Analytics.Aggregation.dll`, `Sitecore.Analytics.Model.dll`, and `Sitecore.ExperienceAnalytics.dll` assemblies to the project. Inherit this class from the `VisitDimensionBase` class and create a constructor as follows:

```
public class ByBrowserVersion: VisitDimensionBase
{
  public ByBrowserVersion(Guid dimensionId) :
    base(dimensionId) {}
}
```

4. Implement an abstract method, `HasDimensionKey()`, to tell the reporting service whether the interaction has a valid browser version or not so that it can process data accordingly. This method should have the `public` access modifier for Sitecore 8.1 and `protected` for earlier versions:

```
public override bool HasDimensionKey(
  IVisitAggregationContext context)
{
  BrowserData browser = context.Visit.Browser;
  return (!string.IsNullOrEmpty(browser.BrowserMajorName)
    && !string.IsNullOrEmpty(browser.BrowserVersion));
}
```

5. Implement another abstract `GetKey()` method to provide a key for the report. Here, we decided `<Browser Name>-<Browser Version>` as the key. This method should have the `public` access modifier for Sitecore 8.1 and `protected` for earlier versions:

```
public override string GetKey(IVisitAggregationContext
  context)
{
  BrowserData browser = context.Visit.Browser;
  return browser.BrowserMajorName + "-" +
    browser.BrowserVersion;
}
```

6. Now we will map this dimension class to the dimension that we created in step 1. In the `\App_Config\Include\Cookbook` folder, create a patch configuration file, `SitecoreCookbook.BrowserDimensions.config`, to store our custom dimension as follows. Here, the `id` attribute of the `dimension` node is the item ID of the dimension item that we created in step 1:

```
<sitecore>
  <experienceAnalytics>
    <aggregation>
```

```
<dimensions>
    <dimension id=
        "{B8AC1D5A-1282-4D42-AA4D-36A684247296}"
        type="SitecoreCookbook.Analytics.Dimensions.
        ByBrowserVersion, SitecoreCookbook" />
    </dimensions>
    </aggregation>
    </experienceAnalytics>
    </sitecore>
```

7. Build your project and make some visits to the website from different browsers.

8. Sitecore aggregates xDB data at regular intervals, so after a few minutes, you will find that these visits are recorded in the **ReportDataView** view in the **Reporting** database, as shown in the following image, which you can identify based on the **SegmentID** using the following query:

```
SELECT * FROM ReportDataView
    WHERE SegmentId='{CC9A9375-49D4-4501-86A1-55B5F8EF2966}
```

	SegmentId	Date	DimensionKey	Visits	Value	Conversions	PageViews
1	CC9A9375-49D4-4...	2016-01-25 ...	Firefox-43.0	1	2	1	3
2	CC9A9375-49D4-4...	2016-01-25 ...	IE-7.0	1	4	2	4
3	CC9A9375-49D4-4...	2016-01-25 ...	Chrome-47.0	3	10	5	16

How it works...

In **Experience Analytics**, dimensions and segments are used to create charts for reports. They define the data available in the reports.

Dimensions determine how visits are analyzed. Here, we specified **DimensionKey** for each visit based on the browser name and version number. Based on this, the dimension will analyze visits, which is taken care of by the `VisitDimensionBase` class itself.

 Once you have deployed a segment and data collection has begun, you should not change the segment as this could cause inconsistencies in your collected data.

Segments control which visits are analyzed, which means that they provide the filter facility. You can apply filters to the segments, which can be created in `/sitecore/system/Marketing Control Panel/Experience Analytics/Filters`, where you just have to apply rules. In this example, we didn't apply any filter, which means that it analyzed all the visits.

Interaction details of xDB will be aggregated only if they are created after the **DeployDate** set for the dimension (`interaction.SaveDateTime > segment.DeployDate`). That's the reason why we set the **DeployDate** to the previous date in step 2, so we can get reports from the previous date after regenerating the report.

> Read more at `http://goo.gl/hvhT8S` to regenerate or refresh analytics reports.

There's more...

To generate a report for business networks visiting your website, that is, *Who is looking for you?*, you can use `BusinessName` as the **DimensionKey**, as shown the following code. Similarly, to create a report of referring sites, you can use `context.Visit.ReferringSite` as **DimensionKey**:

```
public override string GetKey(IVisitAggregationContext context)
{
   return context.Visit.GeoData.BusinessName;
}
```

> Any attribute or facet of `Contact` or interaction (visits) from xDB can be used to create such reports based on marketers' requirements. It's just a matter of implementing the appropriate **DimensionKey**.

Extending analytics reports using custom dimensions

In this recipe, you will learn how to create reports on the **Experience Analytics** dashboard. Based on the previous recipe, we will create two different reports to show browser visits and page views using different Experience Analytics chart controls.

Getting ready

For this recipe, make sure that you have already aggregated data in the `Reporting` database, which you learned in the previous recipe.

How to do it...

Now, it's time to create a reporting page on the **Experience Analytics** dashboard:

1. Open **Sitecore Rocks**, expand the `core` database, duplicate the `/sitecore/client/Applications/ExperienceAnalytics/Dashboard/Audience/Overview` item with subitems, rename it `Browsers`, and remove all the children of `Browsers/PageSettings`. We copied the `Overview` item to copy its layout renderings.

2. In the `PageSettings` item, create a `Daily Browser Visits` item using the `ExperienceAnalyticsLineChart Parameters` template. Apply an appropriate `Title` and set the following field values:

Field	Value
Metrics	Visits
Segments	All visits by browser version (segment from the master DB)
KeysCount	3 or 4 (based on how many browsers you want to show)

3. In the `PageSettings` item, create a `Browser Page views` item using the `ExperienceAnalyticsBarChart Parameters` template. Apply an appropriate `Title` and set the following field values:

Field	Value
Metric	Page views
Segments	All visits by browser version (segment from the master DB)
KeysSortByMetric	Page views
KeySortDirection	Descending
KeysCount	3 or 4 (based on how many browsers you want to show)

4. Open the **Design Layout** of the `Browsers` item. Remove all chart renderings from the bottom of the layout. Add two new renderings, `ExperienceAnalyticsLineChart` and `ExperienceAnalyticsBarChart`, as shown in the following image, and set their **DataSource** to the previously created items—`Daily Browser Visits` and `Browser Page views`—accordingly:

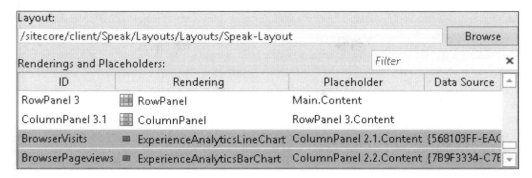

5. Open the **Experience Analytics** dashboard. In the **Audience** section, click on
    Browsers. Browser-based reports will be shown as in the following image. The
    chart shown on the left side shows daily visits using different browsers, whereas the
    right-hand side chart shows the overall browser page views from different browsers:

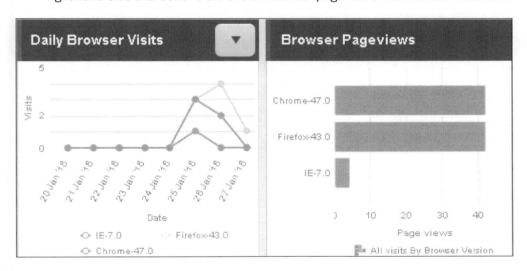

How it works...

Sitecore has provided us with different controls such as list view, line chart, bar chart, area
chart, and so on to display aggregated Experience Analytics data. These controls can be found
in `/sitecore/client/Applications/ExperienceAnalytics/Common/Layouts/`
`Renderings` in the `core` database.

Each of these controls contains a parameter template as a child item, which contains different
parameters required for that control. For example, the `ExperienceAnalyticsLineChart`
control contains an `ExperienceAnalyticsLineChart Parameters` template, using
which we created the `Daily Browser Visits` item in step 2.

Experience Analytics controls support different metrics such as **Visits**, **Page views**, **Values**, **Conversions**, **Time on site**, and others, but currently, these charting controls support having only one metric and segment.

When the report is requested, it first reads the rendering parameters item. Then, based on its selected segment and metric, it tries to load data from the `Reporting` database. If any filter is applied to the segment, the report will auto-filter data before being shown. You can also limit the number of keys getting displayed and sort values based on keys in different orders, which is what we configured in step 3.

There's more...

Sitecore aggregates only interaction and contact details, which are preconfigured. It's also possible to aggregate custom facet data with custom metrics. Read more on this at `http://goo.gl/5VwK7i`.

To create your custom Experience Analytics controls, refer to `http://goo.gl/pwlruW`.

Creating section-specific analytics reports using custom dimensions

In previous recipes, you learned how to create simple dimensions, where every interaction in a visit had a common key to aggregate browser details. In this recipe, you will learn how to create dimensions where interactions in each visit can have different keys. We will consider an example of creating a detailed report based on website sections, where a visitor can visit pages from different sections of the website in a visit.

How to do it...

First, we will create dimension and segment definition items:

1. Create a new segment and dimension in the `/sitecore/system/Marketing Control Panel/Experience Analytics/Dimensions/Pages` item, as shown in the following image. Now deploy this segment:

2. Now we will create a `Dimension` class, which will actually process xDB data. In the `SitecoreCookbook` project, create a new `ByWebsiteSection` class in the `Dimensions` folder in the `Analytics` folder and inherit it from the `DimensionBase` class and create a constructor as follows:

```
public ByWebsiteSection(Guid dimensionId) :
  base(dimensionId) { }
```

3. Implement its abstract `GetData()` method to get a collection of `DimensionData` that contains `DimensionKey` and `MetricsValue`:

```
public override IEnumerable<DimensionData>
  GetData(IVisitAggregationContext context)
{
  SegmentMetricsValue metrics =
    this.CalculateCommonMetrics(context, 0);
  ConcurrentDictionary<string, int> keyCount =
    this.GetDimensionKeys(context);
  foreach (string index in
    (IEnumerable<string>)keyCount.Keys) {
    int count = keyCount[index];
    SegmentMetricsValue metricsValue = metrics.Clone();
    metricsValue.Count = count;
    yield return new DimensionData() {
      DimensionKey = index,
      MetricsValue = metricsValue
    };
  }
}
```

4. Create a `GetDimensionKeys()` method to collect different keys and metrics values by iterating all the pages of visits and finding section names as keys:

```
public ConcurrentDictionary<string, int>
  GetDimensionKeys(IVisitAggregationContext context)
{
  ConcurrentDictionary<string, int> concurrentDictionary =
    new ConcurrentDictionary<string, int>();
  foreach (PageData page in context.Visit.Pages) {
    string[] urlSegments = page.Url.ToString().Split(new
      char[] { '/' },
      StringSplitOptions.RemoveEmptyEntries);
    if (urlSegments.Length > 0 &&
      urlSegments[0].IndexOf("?") < 0) {
      string dimKey = urlSegments[0];
      concurrentDictionary.AddOrUpdate(dimKey, 1,
        (Func<string, int, int>)((key, oldValue) =>
        oldValue + 1));
```

```
        }
    }
    return concurrentDictionary;
}
```

5. Now we will map this `Dimension` class to Sitecore. Map this dimension class to the dimension item that we created in step 1 in the patch configuration file, the same as we did in the previous recipe, and build your project.

6. Make some visits to the website for different sections from different browsers. Once the data is aggregated for this dimension, you can find this data in the `ReportDataView` table of the `Reporting` view.

7. Now create a report from Sitecore Rocks, in the same way as the previous recipe. In the `core` database, duplicate the `/sitecore/client/Applications/ExperienceAnalytics/Dashboard/Behavior/Pages/Entry` pages item and rename it `Section Pages`. Delete all its children from the `Section Page/PageSettings` item. Create two items with `ExperienceAnalyticsAreaChart Parameters` and `ExperienceAnalyticsListControl Parameters` templates and set an appropriate **Title**, **Key details**, and so on. Additionally, assign the segment that we created in the preceding step in the **Segments** field.

8. Now open the **Layout Designer** for the `Section Pages` item. Remove all Experience Analytics renderings from it and add two renderings, `ExperienceAnalyticsAreaChart` and `ExperienceAnalyticsListControl`, and set their **DataSource** to the items that we created in the preceding step accordingly:

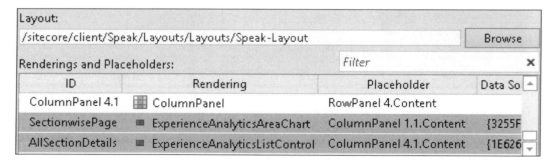

9. View the reports from Experience Analytics reports in the **Behavior | Pages | Section Page**. You will find both reports as shown in the following image:

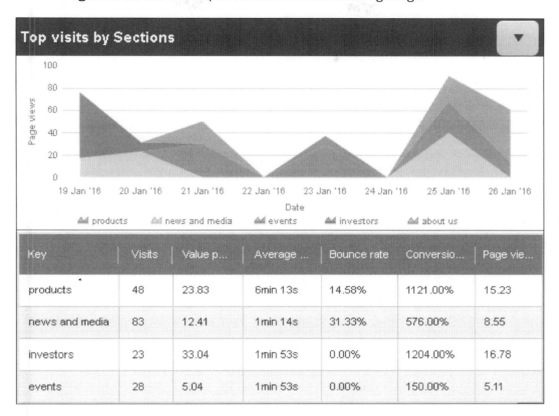

How it works...

Sitecore provides you with different dimension base classes such as `PageEventDimensionBase`, `VisitDimensionBase`, `ChannelDimensionBase`, `GeoDimensionBase`, and others, which are used to achieve different types of dimensions. All these classes are inherited from the `DimensionBase` class, which we used in this recipe in order to get a clearer picture of it.

As our requirement can contain multiple keys in a single interaction, we looped through each interaction to extract the section name as a key from the URL and added them to a `ConcurrentDictionary` object for further processing in finding the metrics.

Now, you will surely be able to create different types of reports using different segments.

11

Securing, Scaling, Optimizing, and Troubleshooting

In this chapter, we will cover some interesting tasks that you can use to troubleshoot, secure, scale, and optimize a Sitecore solution. You will learn the following recipes:

- ▶ Profiling and tracing content pages to find out the slowest operations
- ▶ Transferring items from one database to another
- ▶ Making security-hardened environments
- ▶ Adding multiple publishing targets for scalability or preproduction
- ▶ Creating clustered instances for scalability and performance
- ▶ Getting high availability of Sitecore instances
- ▶ Improving the performance of Sitecore instances

Introduction

On referring to all the previous chapters, you will be able to develop your website as per requirements. However, will this be enough? The answer is no. The site will surely demand to be more proficient with the help of more security, scalability, and performance tuning, which will always be a never-ending demand for any site.

This chapter will cover many unavoidable tasks that make your site secure. You will also see performance tuning techniques and tactics that you can apply to a Sitecore solution, ASP.NET, and IIS. Being fallible, an application or web server will have limitations to get an optimized performance all the time with high uptime. So, in such cases, the scalability of your Sitecore instance comes into the picture. We will cover scaling the Sitecore web servers and databases efficiently to get high uptime during application or hardware crash and even during deployments as well.

Profiling and tracing content pages to find out the slowest operations

Tracking the performance of Sitecore pages can be crucial in diagnosing website performance issues. It's really important to troubleshoot the slowest renderings, sublayouts, custom pipelines, or processors to improve website performance.

In this recipe, you will learn the profiling of your renderings or sublayouts and tracing events that occur in building the Sitecore page within the content authoring environment. You will also learn how to trace custom actions as well.

Getting ready

For this recipe, you need a working content page with a few renderings or sublayouts used in it.

How to do it...

1. Open the Experience Editor and navigate to any content page of your site. From the ribbon, select the **Other** button in the **Mode** group from the **Home** tab. Click on **Debug** from the menu, as shown in the following image:

2. You will find two extra sections loaded below the content page, **Sitecore Profile** and **Sitecore Trace**. You can enable or disable profiling or tracing from the ribbon itself by clicking on the **Activate** button of the **Profile** and **Trace** groups.

3. First, we will see how to check profile details. **Sitecore Profile** tries to find out the worst performing components or components that are reading a large number of items, as shown in the following image. It's a very high-level summary of performance of your page:

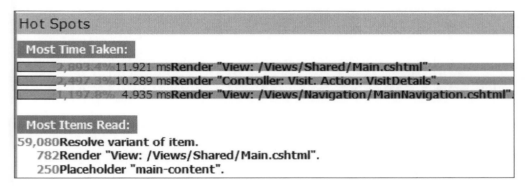

4. Based on these filtered components, you can try to reduce the loading time of renderings and optimize them to read a minimum number of items. You can also gain performance of the website by tuning item and data caches based on the number of **Items Read** and the **Data Cache Misses** report:

Time	Action	Total	Own	Items Read	Data Cache Misses	Data Cache Hits	Physical Reads
	3.5% Resolve device.	0.092 ms	0.092 ms	0	0	0	0
	12.3% Resolve current item.	0.325 ms	0.325 ms	37	0	40	0
	84.3% Resolve layout for "Products".	2.233 ms	2.233 ms	2	4	4	21
	NaN% Resolve variant of item.	NaN ms	NaN ms	97,251	22,149	225,463	282,723
	117,521.1% Render "View: /Views /Cookbook/MVC.cshtml".	4,616.615 ms	3,114.308 ms	39	0	51	24
	4.0% Placeholder "phHeader".	0.106 ms	0.106 ms	0	0	0	0

5. You can also apply caching (HTML cache) to renderings or sublayouts that are taking more time, which you learned in the *Improving site performance by caching renderings* recipe in *Chapter 2, Extending Presentation Components*. Doing so will reduce physical reads of items and improve performance drastically.

6. Now we will see how to check trace details. Trace contains a very low-level summary of your page, which includes statistics of different actions, pipelines, or renderings that get involved in page generation, as shown in the following image:

Sitecore Trace

TypeAction	Elapsed since last entry	Elapsed since start
Current site is "website".	0.04 ms	0.04 ms
Language changed to "en" as the query string of the current request contains language (sc_lang).	2.83 ms	217.29 ms
Current item is "/sitecore/content/home/".	291.19 ms	508.47 ms
Current layout is "Main".	96.93 ms	605.40 ms
Begin - Pipeline: mvc.requestBegin	0.55 ms	606.07 ms
End - Pipeline: mvc.requestBegin (time: 1342.25 ms)	1,342.88 ms	1,948.95 ms

7. Sitecore does not provide tracing at the method level or code block level. We will now see how we can achieve this. In the code block that you want to trace, add the following lines of code to start and end the profiling. Here, we added profiling to the `ListAllProducts()` action method of a controller:

```
public ViewResult ListAllProducts()
{
  Sitecore.Diagnostics.Profiler.StartOperation("Listing
    products");
  // Code to list products
  Sitecore.Diagnostics.Profiler.EndOperation();
  return View(products);
}
```

8. You can find the preceding applied tracing information in the tracing section as follows:

0.2%	Render "Controller: SitecoreCookbook.MVC.ProductController, SitecoreCookbook. Action: ListAllProducts".	164.533 ms	12.214 ms	0	6	17
2.0%	Listing products	102.675 ms	102.675 ms	0	0	0
1.0%	Filtering products	49.644 ms	49.644 ms	0	0	0

There's more...

We used the `Profiler` class to measure performance. Sitecore also provides a `Tracer` class that is useful to notify errors and show information that we mostly write in logs. Debugging pages in this way would be better and quicker than checking logs. You can use the `Sitecore.Diagnostics.Tracer.Error()` method for this. Any error trace will look like the following image in the **Sitecore Trace** section:

Error	**Custom Error Message.System.DivideByZeroException:**	4.90 ms 4,106.13
	Attempted to divide by zero. at	ms
	SitecoreCookbook.MVC.ProductController.ListAllProducts()	
	in ▨▨▨▨▨▨▨▨▨▨▨▨▨▨▨▨▨▨	
	▨▨**\SitecoreCookbook\MVC\ProductController.cs:line 21**	
	Product Listing	

Transferring items from one database to another

In the real world, developers or content authors may face situations such as accidently deleting or changing an item from the master database and wanting to copy the item from the web database back to the master database. We have many other options such as serialization and packaging, but these only work for databases with the same name.

In this case, that is, recovering data from one database to another, you can use this out-of-the-box mechanism of transferring items.

Getting ready

A user must have administrator rights in Sitecore to transfer items from one database to another.

How to do it...

We will first open the **Move an Item to Another Database** tool:

1. Log in to Sitecore with an administrator account, and open **Desktop**.

2. From the bottom right corner, select the source database from where you want to copy the item, that is, select the `web` database as we want to transfer the item from `web` to `master`.

3. From the Start menu, select **Control Panel**.

4. In the **Database** category from the **Control Panel**, click on **Move an Item to Another Database**; this will open a new dialog as follows:

5. In this dialog, select the item that you want to transfer to another database. Here, we select /sitecore/Content/Home/About Us/Getting Started and click on **Next**. This will open another wizard as follows:

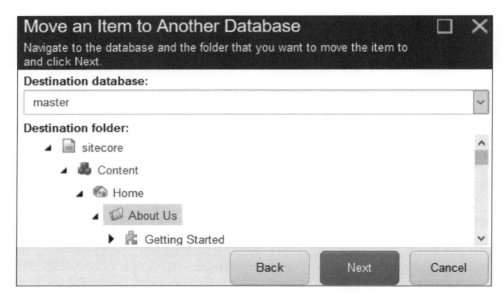

6. Here, select the database from the **Destination database** drop-down to where you want to transfer the item and select the **Destination folder** where you want to transfer the source item. In our case, we select the master database and parent item as the destination folder, /sitecore/Content/Home/About Us, and click on **Next**. This will open another wizard, as shown in the following image:

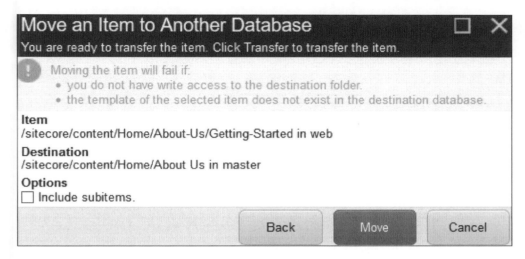

Move an Item to Another Database

You are ready to transfer the item. Click Transfer to transfer the item.

Moving the item will fail if:
- you do not have write access to the destination folder.
- the template of the selected item does not exist in the destination database.

Item
/sitecore/content/Home/About-Us/Getting-Started in web

Destination
/sitecore/content/Home/About Us in master

Options
☐ Include subitems.

Back   Move   Cancel

7. You will find what action this tool is going to take. Select **Include subitems** if you want to transfer the item with its subitems. If you don't select it, it will copy that item only and remove all the children from the destination folder. Click on **Move**. You will find that the transfer process will get started.

8. Now go back to the master database and check whether the item that you are looking for is there.

How it works...

Remember that if you transfer an item without subitems, then it will transfer that item only but delete its existing subitems from the destination database. Transferring items performs database operations, so it does not clear or update any cache immediately, which is what packaging and serialization do.

There's more...

There are a few tools available in the market such as **Razl** (http://www.razl.net/), to compare and merge your Sitecore databases.

Serialization and packaging would be the best options if you want to revert or update items to the same database or from one solution to another solution on the same database. They are also useful features for item backup and restore. Read more on serialization at `https://goo.gl/2AqwxH`.

Making security-hardened environments

It is extremely important to make your Sitecore installation configured properly in order to protect it against attacks from malicious forces. In this recipe, you will learn security hardening using some settings and coding.

How to do it...

We will first perform security hardening recommendations on the Sitecore application:

1. Create a new admin user and delete the default admin user. Also, try to create as few admin users as possible.

2. From IIS, navigate to the following folders. From their properties, disable their anonymous access. You can even secure admin folders using Windows authentication.

   - `/App_Config`
   - `/sitecore/admin`
   - `/sitecore/debug`
   - `/sitecore/shell/WebService`

3. From IIS, deny the execute permission on the `/upload` folder (`mediaFolder`) so that any executable file uploaded to the server in this folder won't get executed on downloading it.

4. Install and configure the **Upload Filter Tool** (`https://sdn.sitecore.net/upload/sitecore6/security_hardening_guide_upload_filter_tool.zip`) from the **Sitecore Developer Network** so that we can control malicious file uploads such as `.exe`, `.msi`, `.bat`, and other files. We can also enhance this tool by preventing file uploads with extensions, MIME types, and magic numbers to provide better security, which you learned in the *Restricting malicious files being uploaded to the media library* recipe in *Chapter 6, Working with Media*.

5. Turn off autocomplete and store the username in a cookie from the Sitecore login forms by setting `Login.DisableAutoComplete` and `Login.DisableRememberMe` settings to `true` in the `Sitecore.config` file. If possible, force users to redirect to HTTPS instead of HTTP for the login page.

6. You can override the login form by implementing captcha. So, after a given number of failed attempts of a user's login, you can show a captcha. After validating the captcha, the user can log in. This will help prevent brute force attacks or we can disable that user for a period of time.

7. Disable XML controls on delivery servers so that it can prevent an XSS attack. For this, set the `disableXmlControls` attribute to `true` while configuring sites under the `<sites>` section.

8. Sitecore allows us to scale images on the fly using different query string parameters, which can lead to malicious requests with different scaling options. To restrict scaling for server-generated requests only, you must enable hash-based request protection, which was introduced from Sitecore 7.2 and is enabled by default. To enable it, you can set the `Media.RequestProtection.SharedSecret` setting to a random string in the `\App_Config\Include\Sitecore.Media.RequestProtection.config` file.

9. Disable the client RSS feed by removing the **sitecore_feed** handler from `Sitecore.config`. For this, locate the `<httpHandlers>` or `<handlers>` section based on your IIS application pool and remove the following line:

```
<add verb="*" path="sitecore_feed.ashx"
  type="Sitecore.Shell.Feeds.FeedRequestHandler,
  Sitecore.Kernel"/>
```

Even after doing this, client RSS feeds will still be accessible.

10. Sitecore uses **PhantomJS** to generate screenshots of pages, which is an EXE file that is shipped with Sitecore in the `$(dataFolder)\tools\phantomjs` folder. Give Sitecore the least privileges so that PhantomJS can access files and folders that Sitecore needs access to. Additionally, you can remove this EXE file from content delivery servers as it may not be useful there.

11. We will now see how we can secure a web application from IIS or ASP.NET configuration settings. Use the **Request Filtering** (URL scan for IIS 7.0 and older) module to prevent many security-related threats. You can read more on how to enable and configure it at `http://goo.gl/j9sdB6`.

12. ASP.NET maintains a state using **ViewState**, which is encoded by default. This can be decoded and be readable easily, and this leads to **Cross-Site Scripting** (**XSS**) and **Cross-Site Request Forgery** (**CSRF**) attacks. Read more about it at `http://goo.gl/bLZ2mr`. To make ViewState tamperproof, set the `viewStateEncryptionMode` attribute as `Always` and the `enableViewStateMac` attribute as `true` in the `Web.config` file in the `<pages>` section:

```
<pages enableViewStateMac="true"
  viewStateEncryptionMode="Always">
```

13. Generate an encrypted machine key using the machine key generator, or select **Site** and click on the **Machine Key** button from IIS, apply encryption and decryption methods, and save. Read more about it at `https://goo.gl/ijsd4Z`. This will update the `<machineKey>` node in the `Web.config` file. Read more about it at `https://goo.gl/JE1vLz`.

14. Use `HttpOnly` cookies to prevent XSS attacks. Read more at `https://goo.gl/TrICTz`. From the `Web.config` file, in the `<system.web/httpCookies>` node, set `httpOnlyCookies` to `true`. When your site is served using HTTPS, set `requireSSL` to `true`:

```
<httpCookies httpOnlyCookies="true" requireSSL="true" />
```

15. Keep the session timeout as low as possible in order to destroy the session during the time of least activity. You can set the timeout attribute in the `<sessionState>` node in the `Web.config` file. The default value is `20` and should be the maximum as well. You can reduce its value if required.

16. Remove header information from responses sent by the website/IIS as follows:

    ❑ Remove the `X-Aspnet-Version` header using the following code in `Web.config`:

    ```
    <system.web>
      <httpRuntime enableVersionHeader="false" />
    </system.web>
    ```

    ❑ Remove the `X-Powered-By` header using the following code in `Web.config`:

    ```
    <system.webServer>
      <httpProtocol>
        <customHeaders>
          <remove name="X-Powered-By" />
        </customHeaders>
      </httpProtocol>
    </system.webServer>
    ```

    ❑ Remove the `X-AspNetMvc-Version` header by writing the following code in `Global.asax.cs`:

    ```
    protected void Application_Start(object sender, EventArgs e)
    {
      MvcHandler.DisableMvcResponseHeader = true;
    }
    ```

As an alternate, you can also remove headers from the `Global.asax.cs` file using `Response.Headers.Remove(header)`.

There's more...

There's no end to securing your web environment. It first requires study to understand security vulnerabilities of Windows, ASP.NET framework, Sitecore, and your custom code. You can learn more best practices of security from the following links:

```
https://goo.gl/fzI9IZ
```

```
https://goo.gl/OopywV
```

Security is a vast topic and not all the things can be covered from the development point of view. There are many providers available in the world providing security as a service such as **Incapsula** (`https://www.incapsula.com/`), **Alert Logic** (`https://www.alertlogic.com/`), and others. We can consume their services to protect our network, servers, and applications from security threats.

Adding multiple publishing targets for scalability or preproduction

Having multiple publishing targets becomes very important for geographic traffic distribution and redundancy. This provides better scalability, performance, and high uptime during deployments.

In this recipe, you will learn how to configure multiple publishing targets to serve live sites from multiple databases. You will also learn configuring preproduction (preview) publishing targets to evaluate a site by publishing items before they reach their final state of workflow before actually going live.

Getting ready

This recipe assumes that you already have a working environment with a single publishing target database.

How to do it...

First, we will add one publishing target to the Sitecore environment:

1. Take a backup of the existing web (publishing target) database and restore it to a different database server in a different geographic location. If you have the Sitecore environment in working mode, then you can freeze publishing until we finish creating a new publishing target so that we can keep both databases in sync.

2. Now we will configure this database in our Sitecore application. On each CM server, add a connection string for this newly created database to the `ConnectionStrings.config` file, that is, `web-2` or `preprod`:

```
<add name="web-2" connectionString="user
    id=sa;password=sa;Data Source=server-2;Database=Web-2" />
```

3. In the `Sitecore.config` file, search for the `<databases>` node. Find the existing node for the web database, `<database id="web" >`, and make a duplicate copy of it under the `<databases>` node itself. You can configure different cache sizes based on the web servers in the `<cacheSizes>` section:

```
<database id="web-2" singleInstance="true"
    type="Sitecore.Data.Database, Sitecore.Kernel">
...
</database>
```

4. Now it's time to register this configured database as a publishing target in Sitecore. Open the Content Editor with the `master` database and navigate to the `/sitecore/system/Publishing targets` item. In this, create a new publishing target, `Internet-2`, and set the **Target Database** name as the connection string name, **web-2**:

5. Set up one or more CD servers connecting this **web-2** database as its content delivery (`web`) database. So, now your new publishing target database is ready for the publishing, and you will find it reflected on the publish form as follows:

6. We will now create a `Preview` publishing target for preproduction publishing. On each CM, repeat the first three steps to set up a new publishing target for previewing purposes and name it `Preview`.

7. Open the Content Editor with the `master` database and navigate to the `/sitecore/system/Publishing targets` item. In this, create a new publishing target, `Preview`, and set the target database name as the connection string name, **Preview**. Tick the **Preview publishing target** checkbox:

8. To allow items in a workflow state to be published to a preview publishing target, navigate to `/sitecore/System/Workflows` and select the workflow state that you want to assign to a preview publishing target. In the **Preview publishing targets** field, select the publishing target:

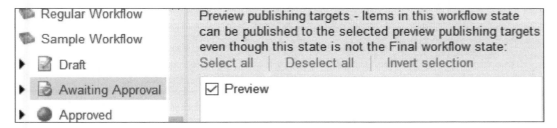

9. So, the item in this workflow state (in this case, in the **Awaiting Approval** state) with the preview publishing target assigned (in step 8) will appear with a notification. By publishing this item, it will get published to the preview publishing target only and not on the live publishing target.

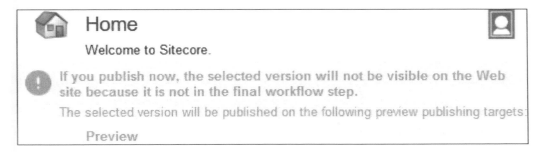

How it works...

While working with multiple publishing target databases, the potential architecture will look like the following image:

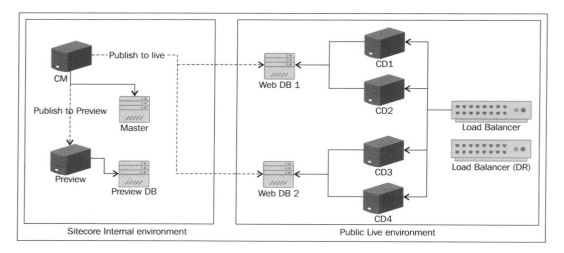

It is always advisable to have multiple publishing targets and related web servers in different availability zones to gain the maximum benefit of geographic traffic distribution and disaster recovery. The preview database and web server should be prepared in the same content authoring environment for security purposes.

From Sitecore 7.2, a new feature of the preview publishing target was introduced; using this, users can still publish items before the actual workflow gets finished so that non-Sitecore reviewers can review the site in the preview environment.

 When you publish to a preview publishing target, any publishing restrictions set on the items are still valid.

Creating clustered instances for scalability and performance

To improve the scalability and performance of Sitecore environments, we have to run multiple Sitecore instances in a cluster. In this recipe, you will learn a few configurations that are needed to be done before using multiple Sitecore instances in one or more environments such as **content management** (**CM**) and **content delivery** (**CD**).

How to do it...

1. Keep the `master`, `core`, and `web` databases on a single database server or the same network as all of the web servers should be shared for all Sitecore instances. You can configure databases from the `\App_Config\Include\ConnectionStrings.config` file.

2. Store media item blobs in database; for this, you must disable file-based media. By default, it's disabled.

   ```
   <setting name="Media.UploadAsFiles" value="false" />
   ```

3. If you have multiple CM instances, make one of the CM instances as the publishing instance. After doing this, if you initiate publishing from any CM instance, the actual publishing will be done from that publishing instance only. For this, you should specify the publishing instance name in `ScalabilitySettings.config` of all the CM instances. The default value is (empty), which means that publishing will be done locally on each CM instance:

   ```
   <setting name="Publishing.PublishingInstance">
     <patch:attribute name="value"><PI Name></patch:attribute>
   </setting>
   ```

4. Here, the `PI Name` will be `<Machine Name>-<Site Name>`. You can also check the instance name from the log file:

   ```
   5774 12:00:00 INFO Instance Name: CM-SITECORE-PUBLISHING
   ```

5. In the `Web.config` file, you may have set `machineKey` to make the ViewState tamperproof. Make `validationKey` and `decryptionKey` attributes of the `/configuration/system.web/machineKey` element into a non-autogenerated value and ensure that the values are identical for all the instances within the environment and the **IsolateApps** modifier is not present in either value:

   ```
   <machineKey validation="SHA1" decryption="AES" validationKey="15E
   88AA72C264C8FE65AA2A7DF17DDF1B78155CCBD72B55DC4ABA293BCC1F217081
   DF7E9880F0233217936245E4725400E11E58AF0E802DF054AE3549BF8E329" dec
   ryptionKey="2B5A04D3F11A07D76C87B7F4ACFF6C19557B73A50CE77D8E3A5617
   3AC3F0FD33" />
   ```

6. Install **Distributed File System** (**DFS**) with mesh topology for all the security configuration folders, `\App_Config\Security`, which contain a domain list. So, creating a domain on one instance will get reflected to other instances as well. If you have an architecture where you need to create and publish sublayouts online, you must synchronize these as well using DFS. You can also sync media files if you want to achieve file-based media.

7. While working with multiple CM or CD instances, you should use the `InProc` session state mode and load balancers managed by sticky sessions for server affinity. This will help persist user sessions and related caches by assigning a dedicated instance throughout the session. As an alternative, you can also use the session state server to maintain sessions across multiple Sitecore instances but this may affect performance.

8. If you have enabled media protection for media requests using hash, you must keep the same value in the `Media.RequestProtection.SharedSecret` setting on every server, which you can find in the `\App_Config\Include\Sitecore.Media.RequestProtection.config` file.

There's more...

To create a clustered environment for xDB, you can refer to the following document from Sitecore itself:

`https://goo.gl/krp5Bk`

Getting high availability of Sitecore instances

It is always a very difficult task to get your web environment up and running all the time as various factors may play into it, such as application crash, database or hardware down, deployments, and so on. We have to accept that both software and hardware are fallible to some extent, so 100% uptime is not possible in the real world.

In this recipe, you will learn Availability Engineering by applying some tactics on Sitecore, ASP.NET, IIS, and the infrastructure side with the help of redundancy and failover techniques. After implementing them, your application will probably have at least fewer failures and quick recovery technology to minimize (or even eliminate) downtime.

How to do it...

We will first cover some action points to be applied to the web application:

1. Open the `Web.config` file. In the `configuration/system.web/compilation` node, set the `numRecompilesBeforeAppRestart` attribute to `100` or as per your need. Its default value is `15`, which means that after 15 compilations of sublayouts or views, the application pool will get recycled. Increasing its value will delay its restart:

```
<compilation numRecompilesBeforeAppRestart="100"
  targetFramework="4.5">
```

2. In `Web.config`, comment the `SitecoreConfigWatcher` module in `configuration/system.webServer/modules`. The Sitecore application gets restarted when we modify any Sitecore configuration file in the `\App_Config\` folder. By commenting or disabling `SitecoreConfigwatcher`, you can stop recycling your application on configuration changes.

3. In the `Global.asax.cs` file, write code in the `Application_End()` event to send an e-mail with the application restart reason so that we can fix these issues in the future. You can find the code at `http://goo.gl/BdeR6T`. It is also important to prevent some actions causing application pool recycling restarts; you can get this list from `http://goo.gl/wfhva0`.

4. Now, we will cover some action points to be applied to the site's application pool from IIS. In the **IIS Manager**, select the website application pool. In the **Edit Application Pool** section from the right-hand side pane, click on the **Advanced Settings** link. This will open a dialog. For the **Idle Time-out** property, set its value to 0. The default is 20 minutes, which means that after 20 minutes of inactivity, it will kill the application pool and a new process will be created on the next incoming request. Setting it to 0 will never recycle the application when it's idle:

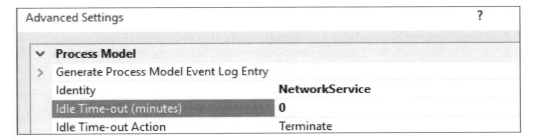

5. As per the default settings of the application pool, it will get recycled every 1,740 minutes (29 hours) after it's created. Disable this periodic recycling by setting the value of the **Regular Time Interval (minutes)** property to 0, as shown in the following image:

Recycling	
Disable Overlapped Recycle	False
Disable Recycling for Configuration Changes	**True**
Generate Recycle Event Log Entry	
Private Memory Limit (KB)	0
Regular Time Interval (minutes)	**0**
Request Limit	0
Specific Times	**TimeSpan[] Array**
[0]	00:00:00

6. While changing `Web.config` settings, the application gets restarted. You can disable this behavior by turning on `DisallowRotationOnConfigChange`. For this, set the value of the **Disable Recycling for Configuration Changes** property to `True`.

7. If you are facing memory leaks in the application, then—until it does not get fixed—it's advisable to schedule the recycling of the application pool periodically on different servers at different times by setting a value to the **Specific Times** property.

8. Use IIS **Application Initialization** to keep ASP.NET apps alive for IIS 7 and above. Read more about this at `http://goo.gl/lgHJXT`.

There's more...

You will agree that infrastructure architecture will play a big role in getting high availability.

Scaling the application server under a load balancer is the easiest option that we can choose. This will be helpful in avoiding downtime due to application or web server failure. Even deployments can be smoother without downtime.

 Load balancers should consider each web server healthy/unhealthy by checking the health of each web server (the capacity of serving HTTP requests) instead of just relying on HTTP request (port 80 or any other) accessibility or round-robin algorithm to avoid gateway timeouts.

Scaling databases is as important as scaling application servers. You can create multiple clusters of Sitecore databases and web servers by providing multiple publishing targets. In cases where a database crashes or even the whole cluster crashes, your site will still get served from another cluster. However, always remember to create different clusters in different availability zones (geographical locations). At the time of deployments, you can take both clusters offline for deployments one by one to gain the maximum uptime.

Sitecore startup is the heaviest process in the whole application cycle. Sometimes, due to an increased number of requests or heavier traffic, its startup might get delayed a lot; in such cases, it's always advisable to block all external requests to that web server using a local firewall to take it online faster.

You can also use IIS **Application Request Routing** (**ARR**) 3 to increase web application scalability and reliability through rule-based routing, client and hostname affinity, load balancing of HTTP server requests, and distributed disk caching. This would be a good option to reduce resources and cost as well. Read more about it at `http://goo.gl/u1ajMv`.

Improving the performance of Sitecore instances

Performance tuning is always a tricky task, especially in web-based applications as it depends on a lot of parameters such as a server, browser, database, web server, application configuration, resource management, and so on, and sometimes by changing one or more parameters, you can improve the performance drastically.

In this recipe, you will learn different parameters with which you can get an optimized performance of your Sitecore application.

How to do it...

We will first try to achieve performance optimization from the Sitecore application itself:

1. Ensure that you have cached your presentation components to gain maximum benefits of HTML cache in the CD server, which you learned in *Chapter 2, Extending Presentation Components*. This will improve page performance drastically as this will reduce connections between the database and web server as well as hitting item or data cache. Also, initially set the HTML cache size, that is, 100 MB, and later on increase it based on your observations of its usage. You can do these settings for your sites in the `<sitecore/sites/>` section of the `Sitecore.config` file:

    ```
    <site name="website" cacheHtml="true" htmlCacheSize="100MB" … />
    ```

2. You can also use Sitecore custom cache to cache external or non-Sitecore content, which you learned in the *Storing external content using a custom cache* recipe in *Chapter 5, Making Content Management More Efficient*. If you are using a 64-bit environment, you can disable cache size limits so that Sitecore will not control your memory. Open `Sitecore.config` and set `Caching.DisableCacheSizeLimits` to `true` as follows:

    ```
    <setting name="Caching.DisableCacheSizeLimits" value="true"/>
    ```

     This will surely improve application performance but you need to monitor memory at regular intervals as this change can cause out of memory errors. If so, you can set it back to false.

3. Disable performance counters using the `Counters.Enabled` setting from the `Sitecore.config` file as they can add overhead to the performance:

    ```
    <setting name="Counters.Enabled" value="false"/>
    ```

You should enable them only while troubleshooting performance issues so that you can access Sitecore-related performance counters from the Windows **Performance Monitor** (**Perfmon**) tool.

4. Disable unwanted background jobs or scheduling agents from the `<sitecore/scheduling>` section of the `Sitecore.config` file.

5. Disable **Web-based Distributed Authoring and Versioning** (**WebDAV**) by removing the references in `<log4net />`, `<system.webServer />`, `<httpHandlers />` from the `Web.config` file.

6. Disable the memory monitor by removing the hook from the `<sitecore/hooks/>` section of the `Sitecore.config` file.

7. Set `AccessResultCache` as low as possible to gain improvement for CD environments. If you are not using it on CD environments, just disable it by setting it to `0` from the `Sitecore.config` file:

```
<setting name="Caching.AccessResultCacheSize" value="0"/>
```

8. Include the path to static media files (images, CSS files, and JavaScript files) in the `IgnoreURLPrefixes` settings to prevent Sitecore from intercepting the requests so that ASP.NET will process these requests without Sitecore. Update this setting in the `Sitecore.config` file as follows:

```
<setting name="IgnoreUrlPrefixes"
    value="/javascripts|/stylesheets|/images|…" />
```

9. Tune Sitecore caches (data, item, and HTML caches) regularly based on observations of item usage, cache hits and misses, occupied cache sizes, number of web requests, and hardware resources, that is, memory usage. The more items you have in data and items caches, the more benefits you will get. You can set cache settings from `Sitecore.config` for each database. Initially, you can continue with the following cache sizes; later on, increase them as per your observations:

```
<cacheSizes hint="setting">
    <data>200MB</data>
    <items>200MB</items>
    <paths>10MB</paths>
    <itempaths>10MB</itempaths>
    <standardValues>10MB</standardValues>
</cacheSizes>
```

10. Make sure that you are caching media files to the browser using the following setting from the `Sitecore.config` file:

```
<setting name="MediaResponse.Cacheability" value="Public"/>
```

11. Make sure that you are caching and compressing the responses of Sitecore items such as style sheet, JavaScript, and any other media files.

12. Reduce the number of HTTP requests by merging and minifying all static scripts into a single script and similarly for style sheets as well using .NET bundling. For dynamic resources served from Sitecore items, you can use **YUI Compressor** (`http://yui.github.io/yuicompressor/`).

13. Combine multiple static background images into a common image and use these with **CSS sprites** to reduce the number of image requests.

14. On a web page, add style sheets at the top and scripts at the bottom to get better user experience of the page load.

15. Disable trace and debug from the `Web.config` file as follows:

```
<trace enabled="false">
<compilation debug="false">
```

16. If you are not using `SessionState` and `ViewState` in your pages or application, disable it or make it `ReadOnly`:

```
<@%Page EnableSessionState="false"%>
<@%Page EnableSessionState ="ReadOnly"%>
```

17. Make sure that you disable `ViewState` for pages where it's not required:

```
<%@ Page EnableViewState="false" %>
```

18. Now we will learn some parameters from the IIS side to optimize the performance. In application pool's **Advanced Settings**, ensure that **Maximum Worker Processes** is set to `1`:

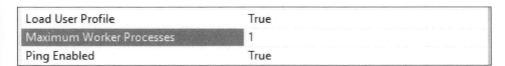

19. The **Enable HTTP keep-alive** option will improve the web server performance by keeping a client/server connection open across multiple requests to the server so that the client can make multiple requests for a web page and the server can return a response more quickly. For this, select **Site**. From **Featured View**, select **HTTP Response Headers** and select **Set Common Headers** from the right-hand side pane. Now, tick the **Enable HTTP keep-alive** checkbox, as shown in the following image:

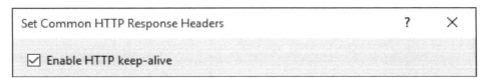

20. To enable **Enable static content compression** and **Enable dynamic content compression** options, select **Site**. From **Featured View**, select **Compression** under the **IIS** section. Now, you can enable compression, as shown in the following image:

 Compression

Use this feature to configure settings for compression of responses. This can improve the perceived performance of a website greatly and reduce bandwidth-related charges.

☑ Enable dynamic content compression

☑ Enable static content compression

21. Sitecore by default does not support content caching to the browser, but if it's suitable for your website, you can surely cache content pages to the browser using **304 if-modified-since** and **Last-Modified** headers. You can write your custom code to achieve this. After doing this, your content will get cached in the browser and your page request can invalidate it based on the page's modified date. Learn about the 304 not modified filter from `https://goo.gl/7f796G`, which considers an example of the RSS feed.

There's more...

You learned different parameters that can improve the Sitecore website or web server performance using some Sitecore, ASP.NET, and IIS configurations. You can read best practices to improve the website performance at `https://goo.gl/jyhgI0`.

Database tuning

Apart from them, there are a few database maintenance plans, which you must follow to get maximum benefits from Sitecore databases.

1. Ensure that the **Auto Close** property is set to `False`. Doing this, if a new connection to the database comes, SQL does not allocate new resources but serves from resources allocated for an older connection created within a short period of time. Otherwise, it will create new resources for all the connections that may impact the performance.

2. Ensure that the **Auto Shrink** property is set to `False` to avoid costly dynamic resizing.

3. Ensure that **Recovery Model** is set to `Simple` to avoid the high overhead of transaction logs.

4. Enable Sitecore database cleanup agents, that is, **CleanupHistory**, **CleanupPublishQueue**, and **CleanupEventQueue**, in the `</sitecore/scheduling>` section of the `Sitecore.config` file and set its interval to 3-5 hours.

CDN

In the case of high-traffic websites, it is an industry practice to use a CDN to serve certain kinds of assets (images, documents, CSS, and JavaScript files) in order to boost the performance. We can use CDN for fairly static assets that do not require Sitecore security.

A

Getting Started with Sitecore

This appendix contains information that will help you with the Sitecore installation and create a project for your Sitecore solution using Microsoft Visual Studio.

Installing Sitecore

To start developing with Sitecore **Experience Platform** (**XP**), we will consider the simplest and most convenient approach of installing Sitecore using its setup program. You can find different Sitecore versions to download at `https://goo.gl/kelRnC`, where you can choose the required Sitecore Experience Platform version and download the **Sitecore web application installer**, which provides you with an easy EXE-based Sitecore setup. For further help on the installation, you can download the Sitecore installation guide from `https://goo.gl/b4cnAQ`, which describes the prerequisites and hardware and software requirements for a Sitecore XP host and client computers. It also provides a step-by-step guide on installing Sitecore with different options.

Before installing Sitecore, ensure that your browsers, IIS, .NET Framework, and SQL server meet Sitecore's recommended requirements. You can check this compatibility table at `https://goo.gl/4kkCHe`. Also, you must determine some configuration values for system components, as shown in the following table:

Component	Description	Example Value
Installation path	A directory where Sitecore will be installed with Sitecore subdirectories and files	`C:\inetpub\wwwroot\SitecoreCookbook`
Website name	The name of the IIS website to host the Sitecore solution	`SitecoreCookbook`

Component	Description	Example Value
Hostname	A hostname to route Sitecore requests, which will be bound to the IIS website and have an entry in the host's file	`sitecorecookbook` or `sitecorecookbook.net`
Database prefix	A prefix to name Sitecore databases, helpful in differential multiple versions of Sitecore on the machine	`SitecoreCookbook`
License	A valid license file to run Sitecore XP	`license.XML`

Once the setup is complete, launch Sitecore using the hostname that we used, that is, `http://sitecorecookbook/`. After the Sitecore installation, you will find three directories in the installation path: `Website`, `Data`, and `Databases`. Here, `Website` is the web root of the Sitecore application. You can read more about the *Sitecore System Components* installed by the web application installer at `https://goo.gl/0JKatR`.

Creating a Visual Studio project

This section describes how to create a Visual Studio project and solution for an installed Sitecore application. There are two different approaches of working with a Sitecore project—inside the web root and outside the web root—and developers can choose either of these approaches based on their requirements. Both the approaches come with their own pros and cons. Sitecore recommends working outside of your web root directory, but for beginners or for the ease of learning the recipes in this book, you can create a project inside the web root directory.

Creating a project in the web root

A solution inside the web root is easier to set up and more straightforward, and you will find development changes almost immediately. However, using this approach, you have to maintain your own solution files along with thousands of Sitecore files, so there won't be a clear separation between them, which would make managing a solution very difficult in the long term.

Perform the following steps to create a **Web Application** project for a new Sitecore installation in Visual Studio 2013:

1. From Visual Studio, navigate to **File | New | Project**, which will open a **New Project** dialog, as shown in the following image:

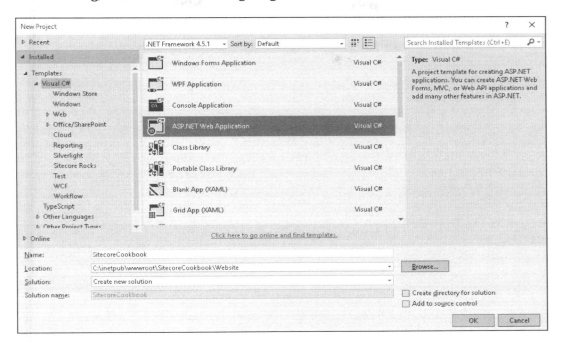

2. Select **.NET Framework 4.5** or any appropriate framework, as shown in the preceding image.

3. Select the **ASP.NET Web Application** project template.

4. Name the project SitecoreCookbook.

5. Enter the web root path in the **Location** field. For example, if you have installed Sitecore inside the C:\inetpub\wwwroot\SitecoreCookbook directory, then create the project inside the C:\inetpub\wwwroot\SitecoreCookbook\Website directory.

6. Make sure that you uncheck the **Create directory for solution** checkbox, and then click on the **OK** button.

7. It will open another dialog to select project templates. Select the **Empty** template and check the **MVC** checkbox, as shown in the following image, and click on **OK**:

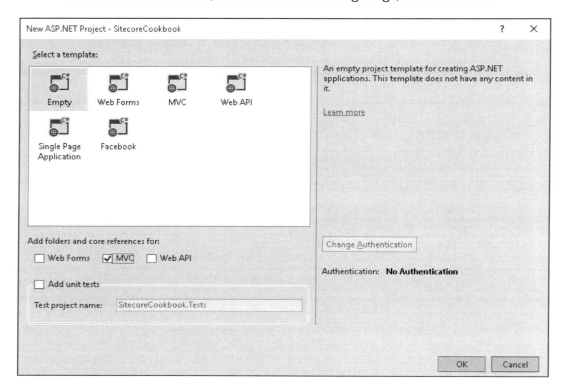

8. Once the project has been created, close the solution.

9. We will now move this SitecoreCookbook project to the web root directory (to work inside the web root). Navigate to the project directory, for example, C:\ inetpub\wwwroot\SitecoreCookbook\Website\SitecoreCookbook. Move the /Properties subdirectory, the SitecoreCookbook.csproj file, and the SitecoreCookbook.csproj.user file to the parent directory, C:\inetpub\ wwwroot\SitecoreCookbook\Website.

10. Delete the SitecoreCookbook subdirectory.

11. Now we will configure this Sitecore web application project. Open the SitecoreCookbook.csproj project file in the \Website directory.

12. Expand the \Web.config file, and delete Web.Debug.config and Web.Release. config. Similarly, delete all the other missing files from the project.

13. Add references to Sitecore assemblies (.dll files) such as Sitecore.Kernel, Sitecore.Client, Sitecore.Analytics, and so on from the \Website\Bin directory, based on your requirements.

14. Set these assemblies' **Copy Local** property to `False`; otherwise, on building the solution, it will delete Sitecore assemblies from the `bin` folder.

15. From **Solution Explorer**, click on the **Show All Files** button, which will show that all subdirectories and files exist inside the web root. Select the `/layouts` directory or any other required subdirectories or files and include them in the project and exclude any unwanted subdirectories and files from the project.

 Debugging your application while having the **Show All Files** button enabled will either slow down or fail the Sitecore application.

So, your changes in the project will get reflected immediately in the Sitecore application. For changes in class files, you need to build the project in order to get it reflected in the application.

Creating a project outside the web root

A solution outside the web root can make a clear separation between Sitecore files and solution files so that you get a clear understanding of the ownership of files and a clear development solution. Having minimum files in the solution will result in easier source controlling, backing up, and restoring of the solution files. Initially, this setup looks complex to manage and time-consuming to publish changes, but it's beneficial in the long term.

Perform the following steps to create a web application project for a new Sitecore installation in Visual Studio 2013:

1. Outside the Sitecore web root, create an ASP.NET web application project named `SitecoreCookbook`, for example, at the `D:\SitecoreProjects\SitecoreCookbook` location. You can follow the same steps mentioned in the *Creating a project in the web root* section.

2. Add references to Sitecore assemblies (`.dll` files) such as `Sitecore.Kernel`, `Sitecore.Client`, `Sitecore.Analytics`, and so on from the `\Website\Bin` directory as needed.

3. Set these assemblies' **Copy Local** property to `False`.

4. So, we have a clean solution separated from the Sitecore application. Now, you can configure **Visual Studio Publish** or **Web Deploy Publish** to save, build, and copy files from this solution to the web root. Right-click on the `SitecoreCookbook` project and click on **Publish**. Create a new publish profile in the **Connection** tab, as shown in the following image. Select any **Publish method** type based on your architecture:

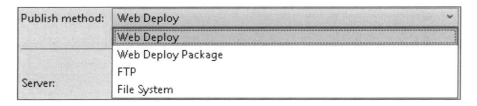

 Here, publishing means deploying Sitecore application, which is different from the Sitecore item publish.

5. Configure the publishing; you need the destination website details based on your selected **Publish method** type:

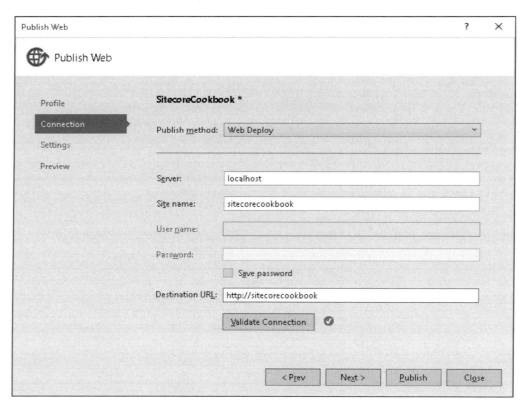

6. Clicking on **Next** will show you the **Settings** tab, and you can choose what you want to do on publishing:

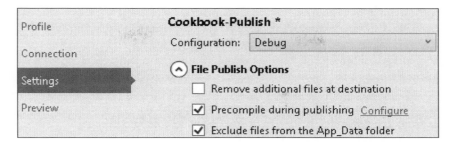

7. From the **Preview** tab, uncheck directories or files that are not required in the web root, for example, controllers, models, and so on, and click on **Publish**. This will build the project and copy all the configured files to the destination web root directory.

8. So, now whenever you make any changes in the project, you must publish them in order to get them reflected in your web root or Sitecore application. So, your Sitecore project and web root will look like the following image:

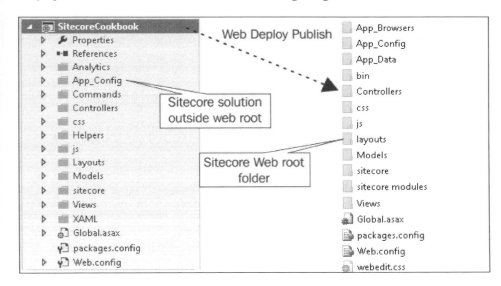

While working on bigger Sitecore projects, you might need to create a modular architecture. **Habitat** is an ASP.NET MVC-based Sitecore solution example built on a modular architecture, which you can find at `https://goo.gl/naC1hP`.

Debugging a Sitecore application

You might find yourself in a situation where you need to debug your custom code that is placed in a solution outside the web root, but it's getting executed inside the web root. To do this, open your solution in Visual Studio as an administrator. From the **Debug** menu, click on the **Attach to Process** menu item. This will open the **Attach to Process** dialog; check the **Show processes from all the users** checkbox, find **w3wp.exe** running with appropriate **User Name**, for example, **NETWORK SERVICE** or **APPLICATION POOL IDENTITY**, whatever you set from **IIS Manager**, as shown in the following image, and click on the **Attach** button. Set breakpoints from Visual Studio, where you want to debug your code:

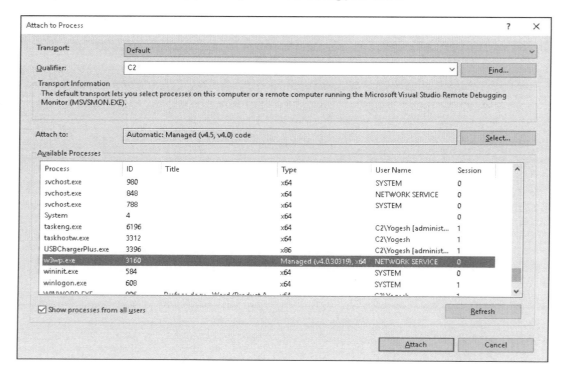

While developing with Sitecore, you will need different tools and online resources. You will learn more about them in the next appendix.

B

Tools and Resources for Sitecore Developers

This appendix contains information on tools and resources available for Sitecore developers to install Sitecore and maximize their productivity and expertise with it.

Useful tools for Sitecore developers

This section describes different tools available for Sitecore developers, useful from installation to deployment.

Sitecore Instance Manager

Sitecore Instance Manager (**SIM**) is an open source tool to manage your Sitecore instances locally. It's the best-suited tool to manage Sitecore instances while working on multiple Sitecore projects. It provides the following features:

- ▶ Installing, locating, backing up, restoring, reinstalling, or deleting Sitecore products
- ▶ Installing Sitecore modules and packages and exporting and importing Sitecore websites
- ▶ Opening websites in the browser, opening Visual Studio projects, checking log files, stopping/starting application pools, and editing the host file
- ▶ Providing an API and plugin engine so that you can extend it for any of your needs

You can download it from `https://goo.gl/VG71PV`.

Sitecore Rocks

Sitecore Rocks is a Visual Studio plugin and also available as a standalone application. It is aimed to be useful for developers for developing purposes in local environments. It helps content editing in all Sitecore databases, administrating different tasks, and so on without logging into the Sitecore client. You just need to configure your Sitecore instance once, which requires a data provider – **Hard Rock Web Service** (which it will install automatically), host, credentials, and location details.

It also provides different Visual Studio templates to create the Sitecore Rocks plugin and server components. It also helps developers in creating classes for commands, processors, rules, renderers, and so on from their predefined templates.

You can install this plugin from Visual Studio extensions or download it from `http://goo.gl/pk2rzW`.

Reflecting on Sitecore

There are many decompiling tools available to decompile or dissemble Sitecore and other .NET assemblies, such as **Red Gate Reflector**, **ILSpy**, **dotPeek**, and others. Dissembling becomes very useful to get the source code compiled into assembly files. Sitecore provides a vast architecture. Being an advanced developer, customizing or extending user interfaces or backend architecture needs a clear understanding of Sitecore APIs; for this, decompilers can be the best friend of developers. You can read more about reflecting on Sitecore at `https://goo.gl/L9ZHKM`.

Source control for Sitecore databases

Team Development for Sitecore (**TDS**) reduces your deployment time by allowing you to leverage a continuous integration or automated deployment strategy. It allows you to leverage source control, which means that all of the constant changes made during a usual project merge seamlessly. It also allows you to create an environment in which you can easily and quickly move code from your local environment all the way through your development workflow. It secures your changes among your team and throughout time by making sure that your work is properly controlled and maintained in source control. You can read more at `https://www.teamdevelopmentforsitecore.com/`.

Unicorn is an open source utility, designed to simplify the deployment of Sitecore items across environments automatically. It's a robust tool for developers working on dedicated Sitecore databases who want to version-control their item changes for backup, moving to other databases, deployments, and so on. You can read more about this at `https://github.com/kamsar/Unicorn`.

The Sitecore database comparer tool

Razl allows developers to have a complete side-by-side comparison between two Sitecore databases. You can compare Sitecore databases quickly, easily, and in an organized fashion. Razl allows you to find that one missing template, move it to the correct database, and not have to spend hours looking for what's wrong. You can read more at `http://www.razl.net/`.

Glass.Mapper

Glass.Mapper is a fully featured **object-relational mapping** (**ORM**) framework that's useful to improve your Sitecore development. It provides easier ways to read and write to fields, create parent-child and link relationships, search in Sitecore, perform ad hoc queries, map to and from standard and customized .NET types directly, map to both your custom interfaces and classes, and much more. It supports both MVC and Web Forms. It helps you stay away from repetitive code, but it comes with a limitation: it can affect performance if compared to native Sitecore APIs. You can read more at `http://www.glass.lu/`.

Continuous integration and deployment

Automated build and automated deployment play a vital role while working on multiple projects and giving quick deliveries. Apart from TDS, you have plenty of software available in the market; you can choose the best based on your project requirements:

- Version control: Git, **Apache Subversion** (**SVN**), and **Team Foundation Server** (**TFS**)
- Build server: TeamCity, Octopus Deploy, Jenkins, Bamboo, and **CruiseControl.NET** (**CCNet**)
- Deployment server: TeamCity, Octopus Deploy, and Jenkins

Other products and modules

Apart from Sitecore **Experience Platform** (**XP**), there are many products and modules provided by Sitecore to integrate Sitecore with third-party applications or automating marketers' jobs, which become very useful in winning customers. You can download these products and modules from `https://dev.sitecore.net/Downloads`.

Useful resources for Sitecore developers

Sitecore provides you with a rich documentation on Sitecore XP. Apart from this, developers can maximize their productivity and expertise by learning from online resources available such as blogs, forums, and so on and participate in the Sitecore community to learn and share knowledge. This section provides information on such resources available for Sitecore.

Sitecore documentation for developers

Sitecore provides you with an official documentation site, `https://doc.sitecore.net/`, which has rich documentation for developers who are willing to get a basic framework overview of Sitecore XP and other products. You can also keep yourself up to date with changes or new additions to different versions of Sitecore for Sitecore XP 8 or later.

There is one more Sitecore community-driven collection of developer resources, `https://sitecore-community.github.io/docs/`, which includes blogs, videos, references, and articles.

A knowledge base for developers

`https://kb.sitecore.net/` is a hub to gain technical information through articles about Sitecore:

- Learn about and track known issues
- Learn how to solve tasks to accomplish a user's goal
- Security bulletin to get up to date with the latest updates
- Learn about current policies, guidelines, and practices of interacting with Sitecore support

The Sitecore marketplace

The Sitecore marketplace (`https://marketplace.sitecore.net/`) is a collection of hundreds of modules developed and contributed by Sitecore developers. Any contributed module first gets tested by Sitecore and later added to this place. These modules are available for download along with source code, which can be easily plugged into the Sitecore solution. However, it's always advisable to test any module before using it in your live environment. Sitecore has started a **better shared source** initiative; you can read more about it at `https://goo.gl/4pWqXc`.

Technical blogs

Sitecore has a vast community of developers; you will find a lot of material to learn Sitecore architecture, best practices, real-world problems and solutions, development tricks, and a lot more. For any help on Sitecore, Google will be your best friend; you will find hundreds of blogs and thousands of posts from Sitecore MVPs and Sitecore-certified developers. To refine your search results, you can use customized search engine, `http://sitecoresearch.patelyogesh.in/`, which will give results from Sitecore technical blogs and Sitecore MVP blogs only. You can also subscribe for RSS feed to find the latest posts from Sitecore blogs, `http://feeds.sitecore.net/Feed/LatestPosts`.

Social media

Sitecore developers and MVPs are very active in social media communities: **Twitter, LinkedIn,** and **Facebook**. Just join the groups related to Sitecore developers and benefit from the online Sitecore community, which is another medium for the sharing of ideas, knowledge, challenges, and other discussions.

You can also join a Slack for the Sitecore community, `http://sitecorechat.slack.com`, which is a free platform for group discussions, file sharing, and, more than that, real-time chatting with hundreds of peers to get or give help on Sitecore.

Community for Sitecore professionals

Community for Sitecore professionals (`http://community.sitecore.net`) is the best place for Sitecore professionals such as developers, digital strategists, and business users around the globe to connect and engage with one another to learn, share, and discuss Sitecore XP with blogs and forums.

Sitecore Support

Most of your questions will be answered by the technical blogs or the Sitecore community itself. If they are not, the Sitecore Support Portal for developers (`http://support.sitecore.net`) is the final stop for you, where you will get all the answers. This portal is accessible only for Sitecore-certified developers. You can get solutions to your problems, raise bugs and get faster solutions, raise feature requests, and so on. You can read more about the Sitecore support program at `http://goo.gl/EVd60Q`.

Sitecore MVP

Each year, professionals from all over the world are recognized by Sitecore as **Most Valuable Professionals** (**MVP**). A Sitecore MVP is an individual Sitecore expert or community leader who actively participates in online and offline communities to share their knowledge and expertise with other Sitecore partners and customers.

Becoming a Sitecore MVP gives you a lot of benefits; you can read more at `http://goo.gl/1SQc45`. To become a Sitecore MVP, you should first understand the process of becoming an MVP (`https://goo.gl/tg0auf`).

Index

M

machineKey Element
URL 284
malicious files
restricting, to media library 150-152
ManagedPoolThread 116
media cache
reference link 154
Media Editor 80
media files
protecting, under disclaimer 155-158
serving, from content delivery
network (CDN) 163-166
serving, from external storage 163-166
media library
aliases, reference link 128
folder, downloading 153, 154
malicious files, restricting 150-152
method rendering
reference link 19
MIME type 150
Model-View-Controller (MVC) 2
MoreLikeThis results
about 227
searching 227-231
Most Valuable Professionals (MVP) 311
multilingual content pages
managing 39-42
multiple publishing targets
adding, for preproduction 285-288
adding, for scalability 285-288
multiple sites
working with 96-99
Multiple Sites Manager module 99
multisite environment
dictionary domains, using for
multilingual sites 124-126
HTML cache, clearing based on published
items 184-187
site-specific URL pattern,
achieving for 108-111

N

Nearby you places
finding, Geolocation service used 260-263

n-gram analyzer 220

O

object-relational mapping (ORM)
framework 309
optimized responsive images
URL 163
Output Cache 44

P

Performance Monitor (Perfmon) tool 294
performance optimization
CDN 297
database tuning 296
of Sitecore instances 293-296
reference link 296
PhantomJS 283
pipelines
customizing, to achieve custom
404 page 99-103
patch configuration 104
placeholders
rendering controls, restricting 25-28
rendering controls, swapping on 25-28
used, for placing renderings
dynamically 19-22
placeholder settings
data template specific placeholder
settings 24
global placeholder settings 24
used, for empowering Experience
Editor 22-25
predictive personalization 242-245
product details
binding, SPEAK used 73-77
products
filtering, SPEAK used 71-73
listing, Sheer UI application with XAML control
used 61-65
listing, with SPEAK application 66-70
searching, SPEAK used 71-73
sorting, with SPEAK application 66-70
proxy items
reference link 130
publish completion e-mail
sending, publishing events used 178, 179

published items
HTML cache, clearing 184-187
Publisher 172
publishing events
used, for sending publish completion
e-mail 178, 179
publishItem pipeline
customizing, for avoiding duplicate names on
live site 188-190

Q

Quick Action Bar field 85

R

Razl
URL 281
Red Gate Reflector 308
rendering behavior
altering, component properties used 30-33
rendering controls
restricting, on placeholders 25-28
swapping, on placeholders 25-28
RenderingModel
used, for creating sidebar menu 8-11
renderings
placing, dynamically with placeholders 19-22
reference link 21, 28
Request cache 102
Request Filtering module
about 283
URL 283
responsive images
rendering 159-163
Reviewer 172
Rich Text Editor (RTE)
about 133
custom tool, adding for generating
tokens 137-141
dynamic content, placing 133-136
URL 141
Robomongo tool
URL 241
RowPanel rendering 74
RSS feeds
generating, for syndicated items 42-44

rules engine
URL 256

S

scheduling agent
used, for deleting older item
versions 118-120
search
correcting, with did you mean 231-234
Search editor 80
search results
influencing, with boosting 223-227
refining, by tagging based facets 215-219
section-specific analytics reports
custom dimensions used 270-273
security
disabling, for Sitecore 200-202
reference link 285
security-hardened environments
creating 282-285
serialization
URL 282
Sheer UI application
creating, XAML control used 61-65
sidebar menu
creating, RenderingModel used 8-11
creating, view rendering used 8-11
single sign-on
achieving, by virtual user creation 197-200
Sitecore
about 96
application, debugging 306
compatibility table, URL 299
installation guide, URL 299
installing 299, 300
preventing, from security
application 200-202
URL 7
URL, for downloading 299
Sitecore Client Authoring 205
Sitecore ContentSearch LINQ API 208
Sitecore Developer Network 282
Sitecore developers resources
about 309
knowledge base, for developers 310
Sitecore documentation 310